toeckl, Jay, SFO.
t. Francis and Brother
uck /
2013]

SAINT FRANCIS AND BROTHER DUCK

Written and Illustrated by
JAY STOECKL, SFO

PARACLETE PRESS
BREWSTER, MASSACHUSETTS

This book is dedicated
to my nephew
and all the young people who have experienced despair.
May they all find new hope.

2013 First Printing

Saint Francis and Brother Duck

Copyright © 2013 by James Raymond Stoeckl

ISBN 978-1-61261-159-4

Scripture texts in this work are taken from the
New American Bible. The Old Testament of the New
American Bible © 1970 by the Confraternity of
Christian Doctrine (CCD), Washington, D.C. (Books
1 Samuel to 2 Maccabees © 1969); Revised New
Testament of the New American Bible Copyright
© 1986 CCD; Revised Psalms of the New American
Bible Copyright © 1991 CCD. All Rights Reserved. No
part of the New American Bible may be reproduced
in any form without permission in writing from the
copyright owner.

The Paraclete Press name and logo (dove on cross)
are trademarks of Paraclete Press, Inc.

Library of Congress Cataloging-in-Publication Data
Stoeckl, Jay, SFO.
  St. Francis and Brother Duck / Jay Stoeckl, SFO.
    pages cm
  ISBN 978-1-61261-159-4 (trade pbk.)
  1. Francis, of Assisi, Saint, 1182-1226--Juvenile
literature. 2. Christian saints--Italy--Assisi--
Biography--Juvenile literature. 3. Nature--Religious
aspects--Juvenile literature. I. Title. II. Title: Saint
Francis and Brother Duck.
  BX4700.F69S865 2012
  271'.302--dc23   2012043927

10 9 8 7 6 5 4 3 2 1

All rights reserved. No portion of this book may be
reproduced, stored in an electronic retrieval system,
or transmitted in any form or by any means --
electronic, mechanical, photocopy, recording, or
any other -- except for brief quotations in printed
reviews, without the prior permission of the publisher.

ACKNOWLEDGMENTS

I wish to especially thank my wife,
Jennifer, for all her work and
support in this book -- my color
artist, my editor, and my best friend
throughout. Thanks also to my
mother, Geraldine Stoeckl-Conklin,
and my brothers, Bob and John,
for their willing and expert advice;
Mickey Adelhardt and all my friends
and family who never let me give up
on my dream throughout the years;
my friends and neighbors on Faith
Lane, especially Geri, Debra, Ken,
Tango, and Donna for lending their
creative hands and good humor
whenever requested; and Fr. Doug
Hunt and Fr. Jim Koenigsfeld, for
their prayers and blessings. And,
finally, thanks for the support of Jon
Sweeney and Bob Edmonson, editors
extraordinaire of Paraclete Press,
who have been essential in guiding
me through this process.

Published by Paraclete Press
Brewster, Massachusetts
www.paracletepress.com
Printed in the United States of America

CHAPTER 1
HOW FRANCIS BECAME A TRUE KNIGHT

Lord, you have probed me and you know me;
You know when I sit and when I stand;
You understand my thoughts from afar.
—*PSALM 139:1-2*

ASSISI, ITALY -- OCTOBER 3, 1226.

Lord, today is a day of great mourning.

My most beloved companion is dying this day upon a stone chapel floor while I, Brother Duck, wander alone.

He was everything -- inspirational preacher, healer, visionary, and saint.

I am none of these things.

Though I was with him through so much of his life, I still don't understand the ways of this man, Giovanni Francesco Bernardone...

...Francis of Assisi.

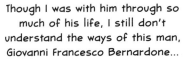

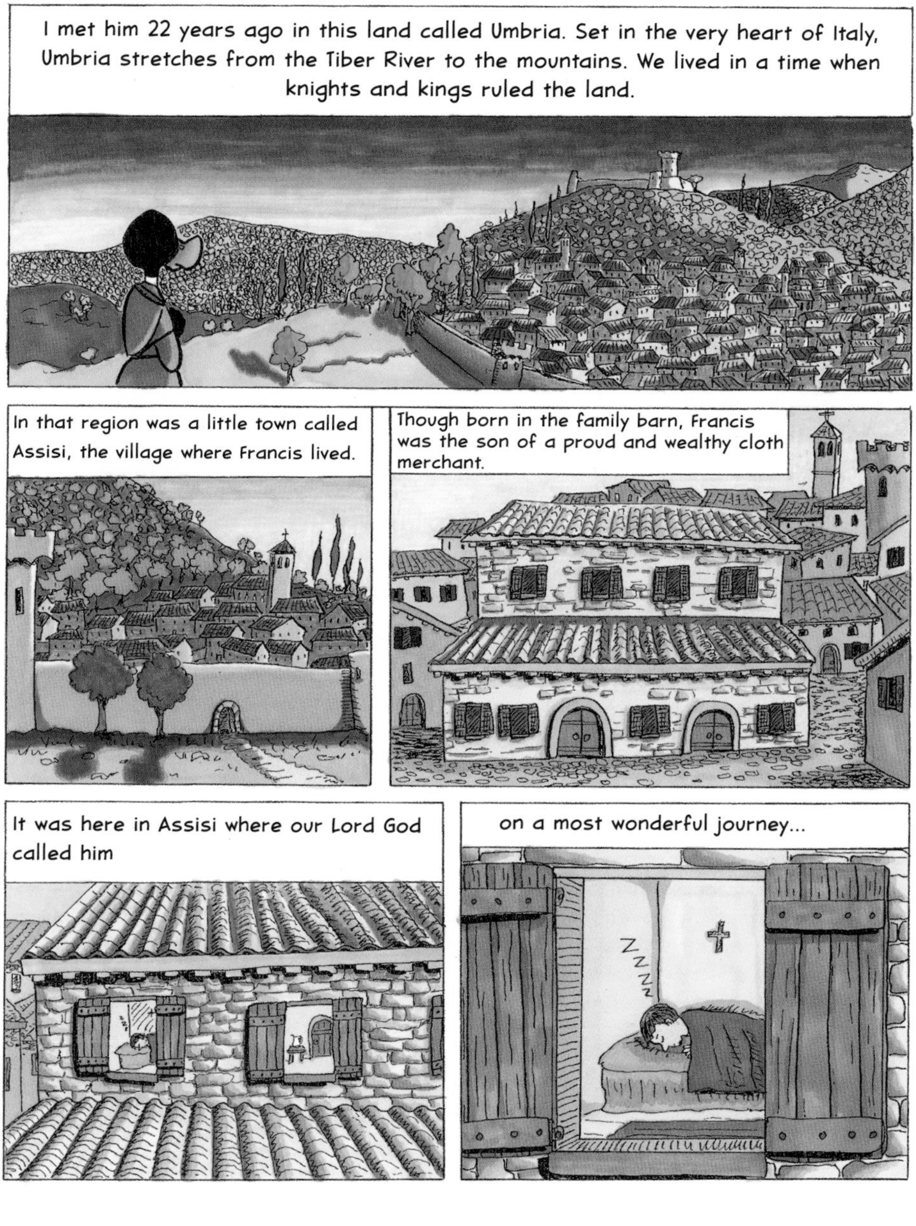
I met him 22 years ago in this land called Umbria. Set in the very heart of Italy, Umbria stretches from the Tiber River to the mountains. We lived in a time when knights and kings ruled the land.
In that region was a little town called Assisi, the village where Francis lived.
Though born in the family barn, Francis was the son of a proud and wealthy cloth merchant.
It was here in Assisi where our Lord God called him
on a most wonderful journey...
ZZZ

IT ALL BEGAN WITH A DREAM...

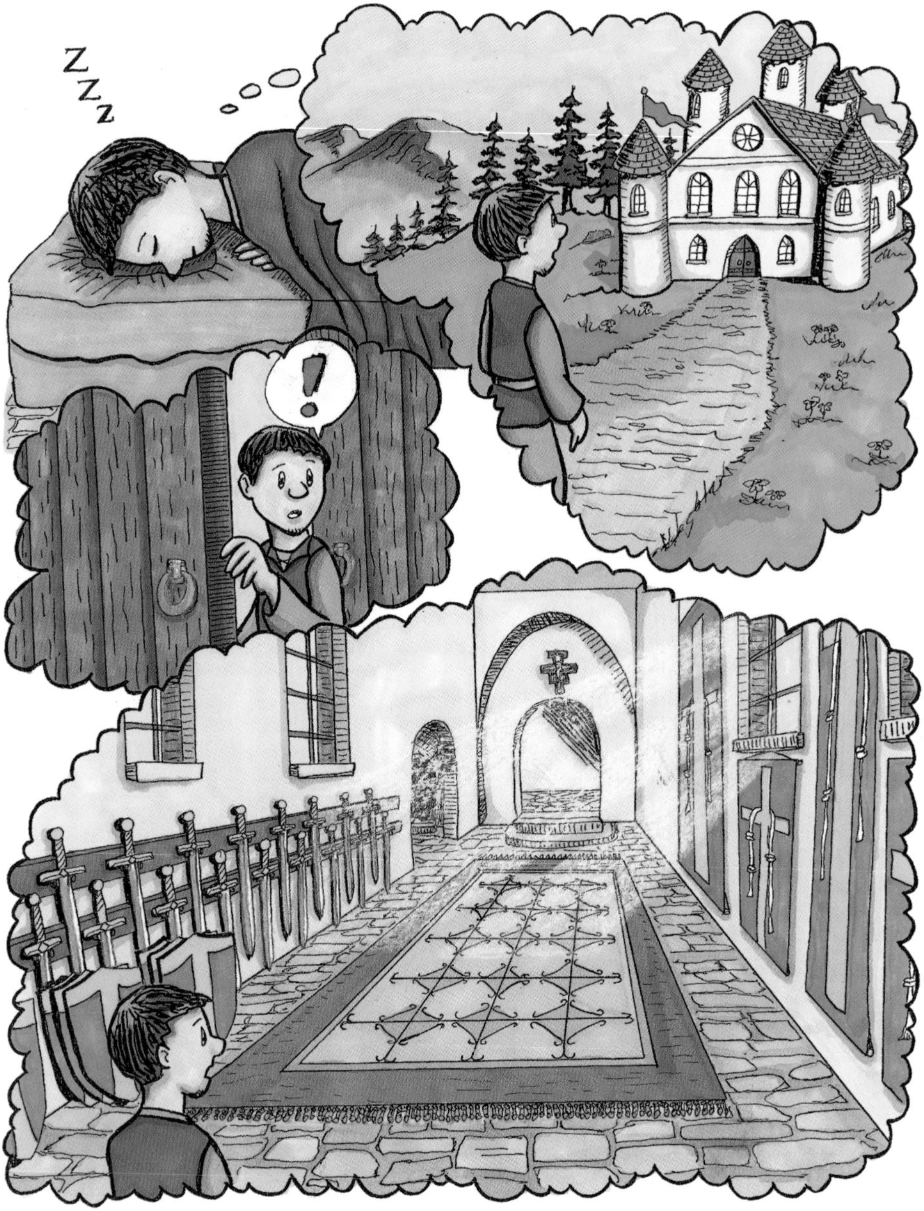
Z Z Z
!

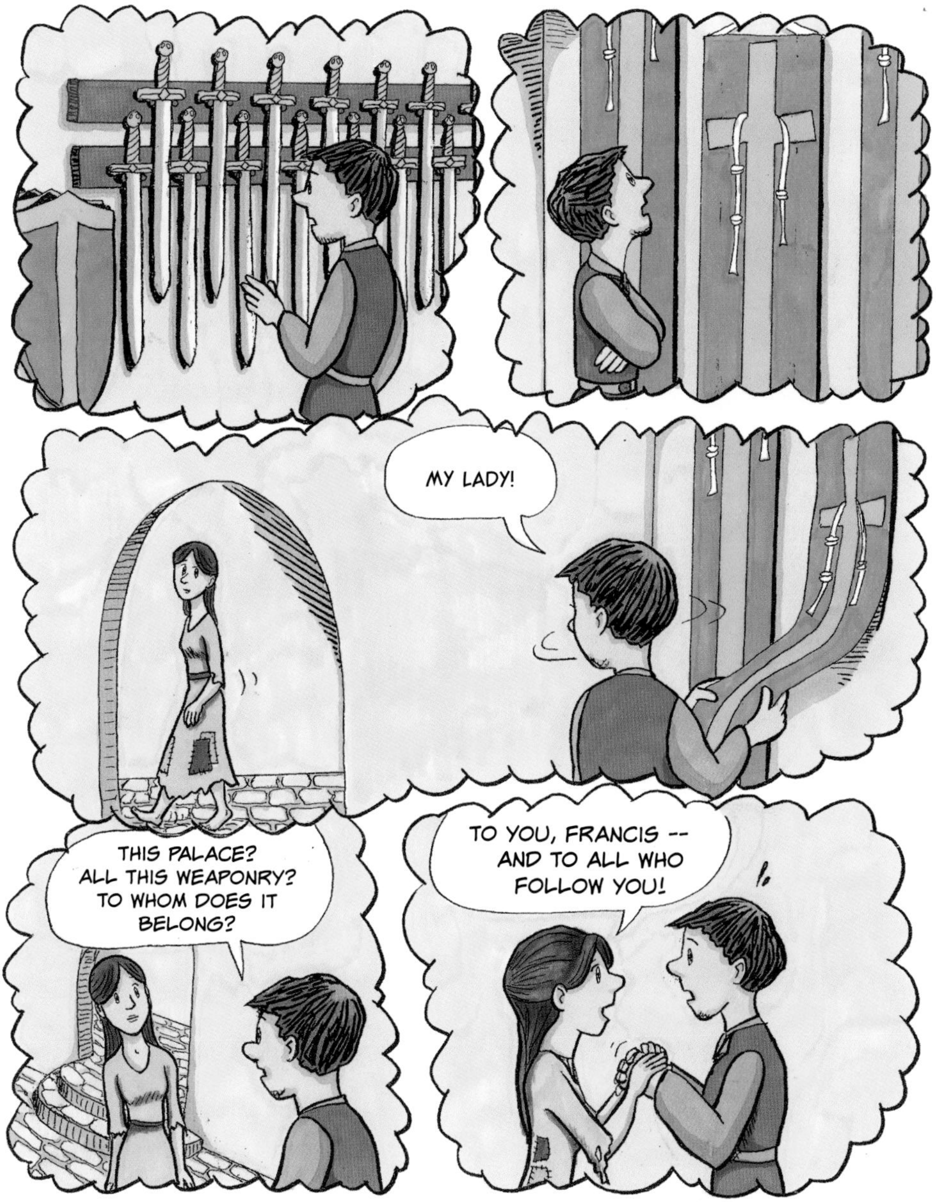
MY LADY!
THIS PALACE? ALL THIS WEAPONRY? TO WHOM DOES IT BELONG?
TO YOU, FRANCIS -- AND TO ALL WHO FOLLOW YOU!

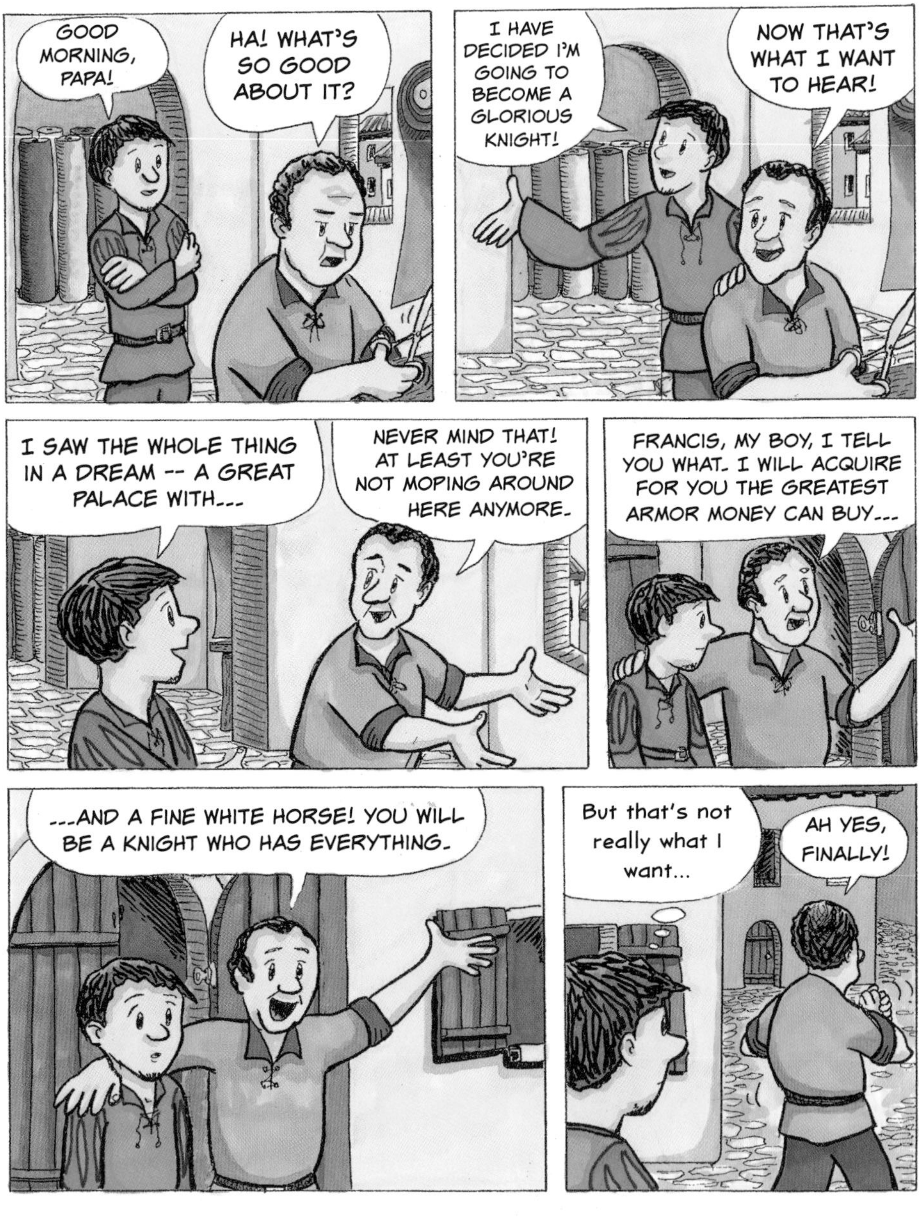
GOOD MORNING, PAPA!
HA! WHAT'S SO GOOD ABOUT IT?
I HAVE DECIDED I'M GOING TO BECOME A GLORIOUS KNIGHT!
NOW THAT'S WHAT I WANT TO HEAR!
I SAW THE WHOLE THING IN A DREAM -- A GREAT PALACE WITH...
NEVER MIND THAT! AT LEAST YOU'RE NOT MOPING AROUND HERE ANYMORE.
FRANCIS, MY BOY, I TELL YOU WHAT. I WILL ACQUIRE FOR YOU THE GREATEST ARMOR MONEY CAN BUY...
...AND A FINE WHITE HORSE! YOU WILL BE A KNIGHT WHO HAS EVERYTHING.
But that's not really what I want...
AH YES, FINALLY!

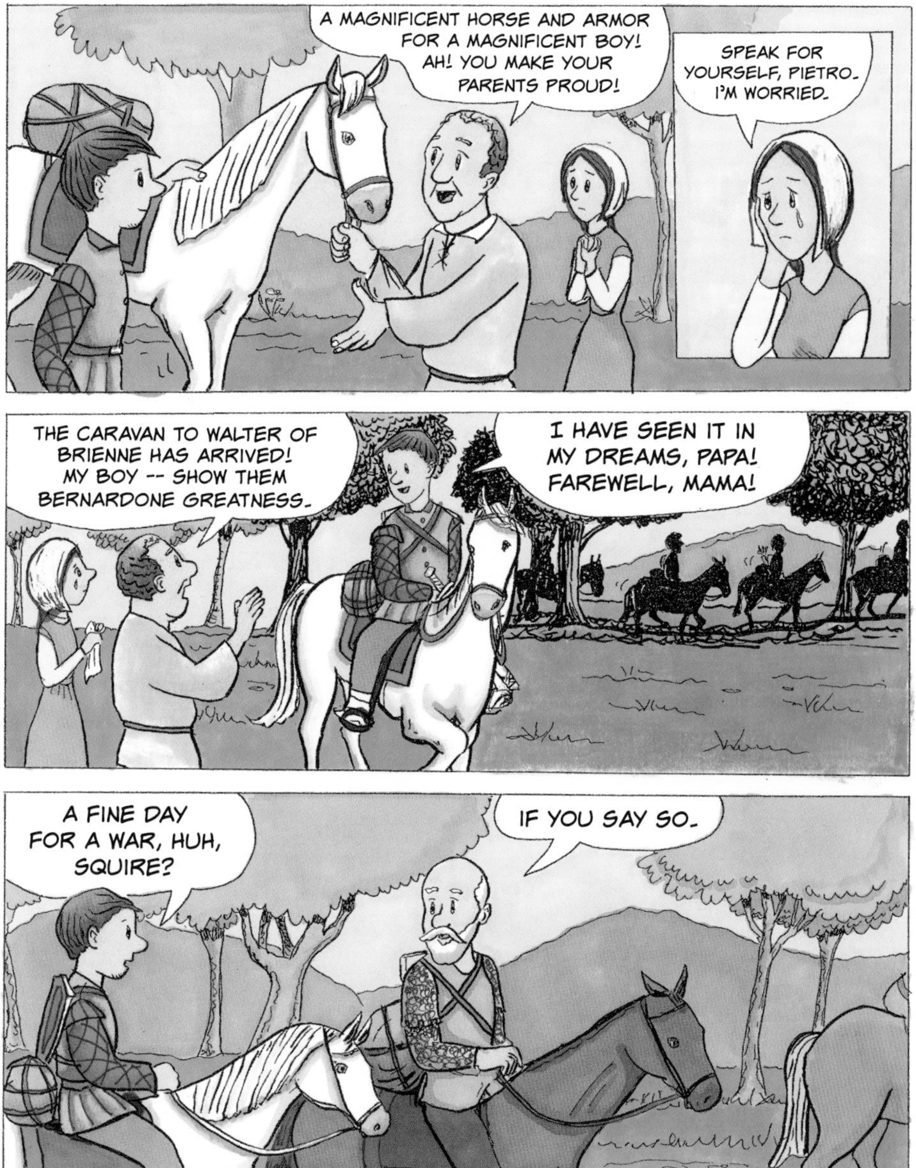
A MAGNIFICENT HORSE AND ARMOR FOR A MAGNIFICENT BOY! AH! YOU MAKE YOUR PARENTS PROUD!
SPEAK FOR YOURSELF, PIETRO. I'M WORRIED.
THE CARAVAN TO WALTER OF BRIENNE HAS ARRIVED! MY BOY -- SHOW THEM BERNARDONE GREATNESS.
I HAVE SEEN IT IN MY DREAMS, PAPA! FAREWELL, MAMA!
A FINE DAY FOR A WAR, HUH, SQUIRE?
IF YOU SAY SO.

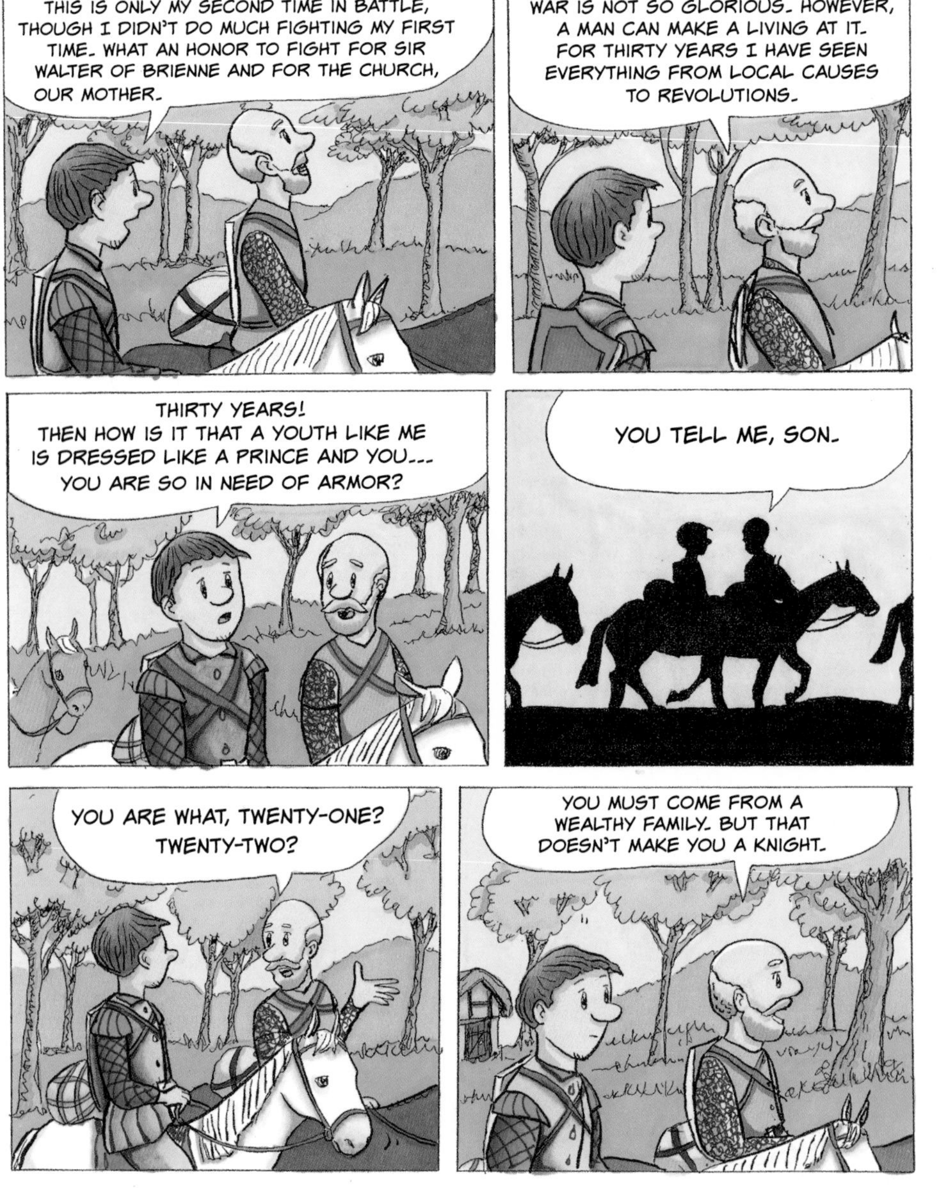
THIS IS ONLY MY SECOND TIME IN BATTLE, THOUGH I DIDN'T DO MUCH FIGHTING MY FIRST TIME. WHAT AN HONOR TO FIGHT FOR SIR WALTER OF BRIENNE AND FOR THE CHURCH, OUR MOTHER.
WAR IS NOT SO GLORIOUS. HOWEVER, A MAN CAN MAKE A LIVING AT IT. FOR THIRTY YEARS I HAVE SEEN EVERYTHING FROM LOCAL CAUSES TO REVOLUTIONS.
THIRTY YEARS! THEN HOW IS IT THAT A YOUTH LIKE ME IS DRESSED LIKE A PRINCE AND YOU... YOU ARE SO IN NEED OF ARMOR?
YOU TELL ME, SON.
YOU ARE WHAT, TWENTY-ONE? TWENTY-TWO?
YOU MUST COME FROM A WEALTHY FAMILY. BUT THAT DOESN'T MAKE YOU A KNIGHT.

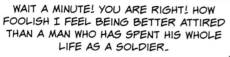

WAIT A MINUTE! YOU ARE RIGHT! HOW FOOLISH I FEEL BEING BETTER ATTIRED THAN A MAN WHO HAS SPENT HIS WHOLE LIFE AS A SOLDIER.

LET'S CHANGE ARMOR.

OH, YOU DON'T HAVE TO DO THAT!

I INSIST! SWORDS, SHIELDS, ALL OF IT!

WE WILL CATCH UP TO THE OTHERS IN NO TIME.

OUR CAMP NEAR SPOLETO WON'T BE FAR AHEAD.

MY FATHER IS A GOOD MAN, BUT HE GIVES ME MORE THAN I DESERVE.

LISTEN! SOMETHING IS HAPPENING UP AHEAD!

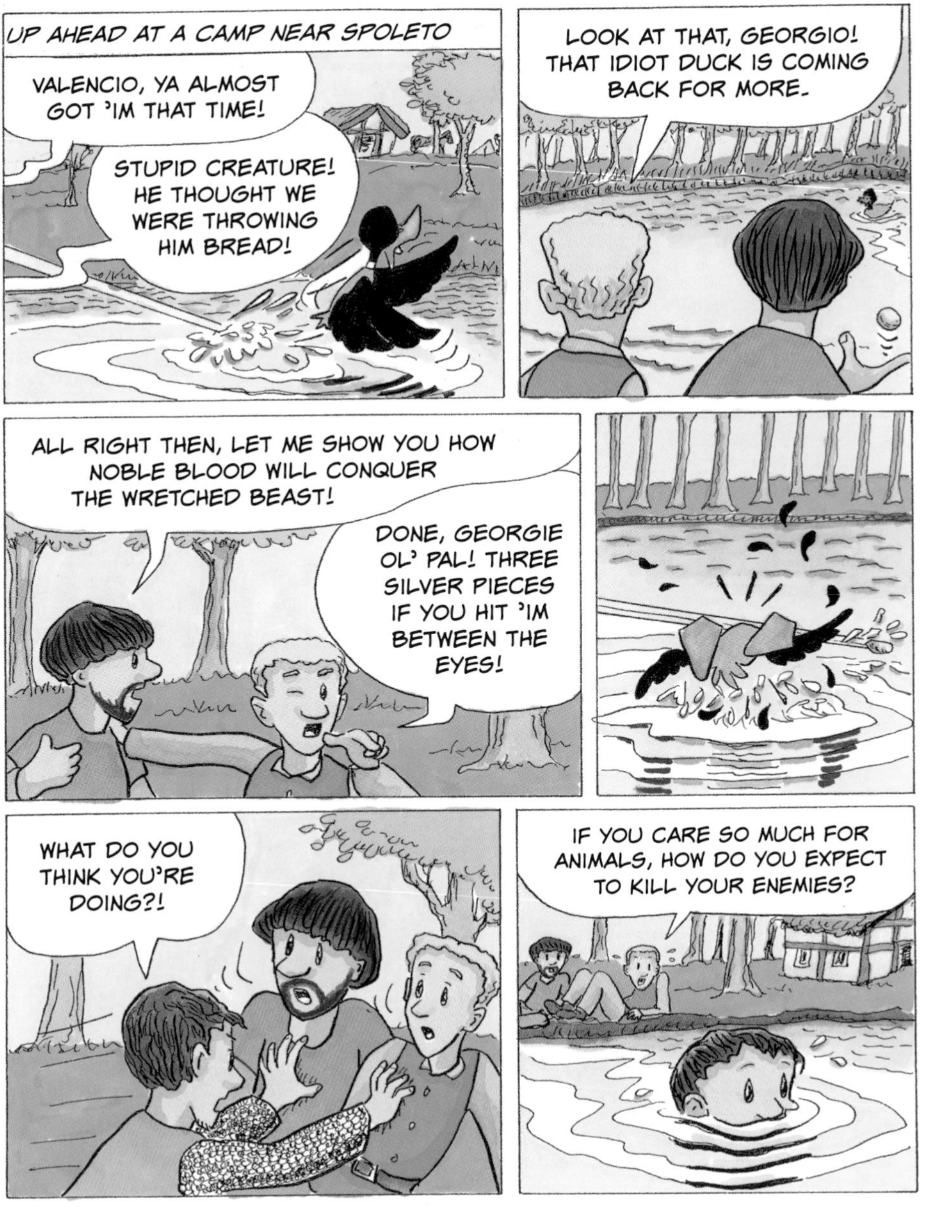

UP AHEAD AT A CAMP NEAR SPOLETO
VALENCIO, YA ALMOST GOT 'IM THAT TIME!
STUPID CREATURE! HE THOUGHT WE WERE THROWING HIM BREAD!
LOOK AT THAT, GEORGIO! THAT IDIOT DUCK IS COMING BACK FOR MORE.
ALL RIGHT THEN, LET ME SHOW YOU HOW NOBLE BLOOD WILL CONQUER THE WRETCHED BEAST!
DONE, GEORGIE OL' PAL! THREE SILVER PIECES IF YOU HIT 'IM BETWEEN THE EYES!
WHAT DO YOU THINK YOU'RE DOING?!
IF YOU CARE SO MUCH FOR ANIMALS, HOW DO YOU EXPECT TO KILL YOUR ENEMIES?

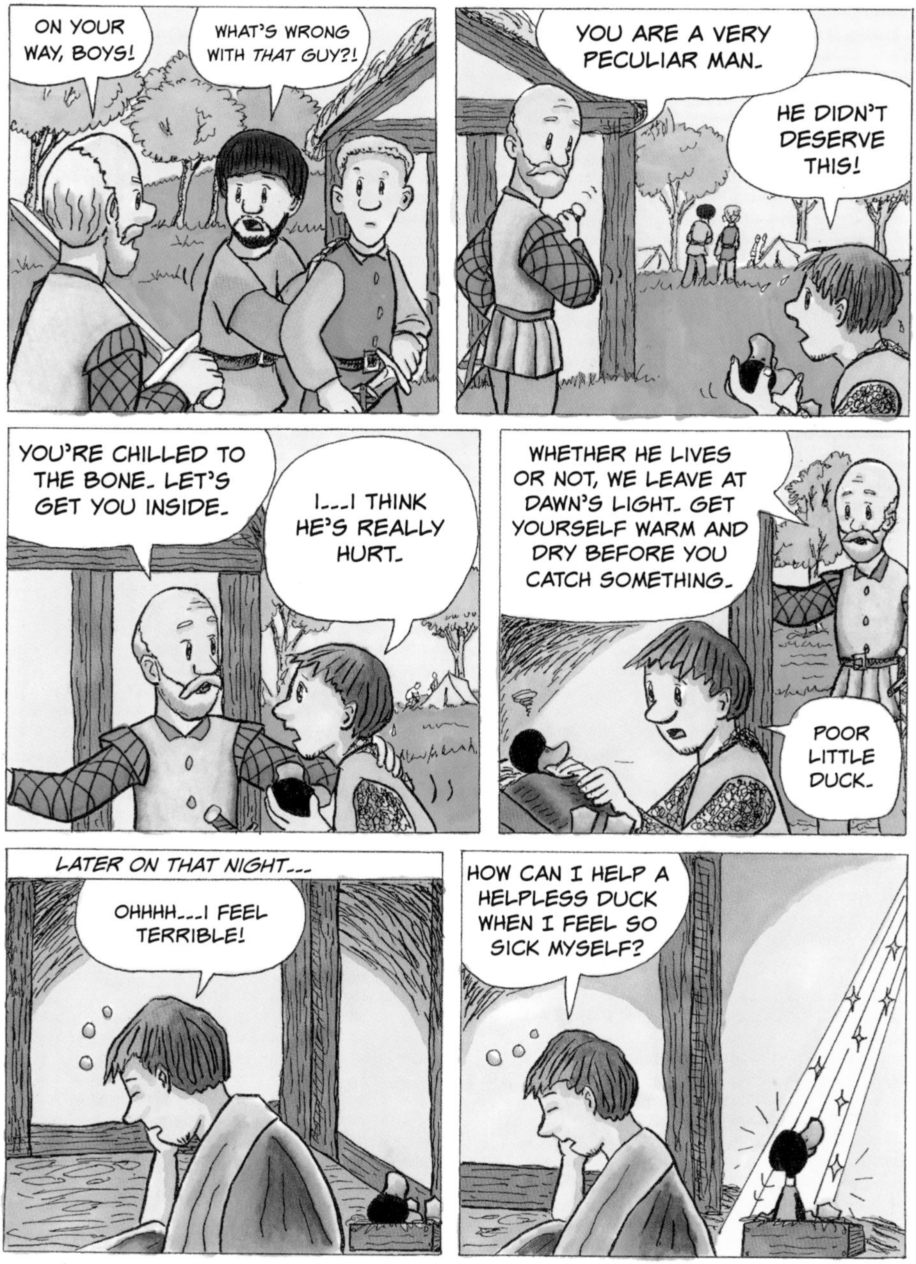
ON YOUR WAY, BOYS!
WHAT'S WRONG WITH *THAT* GUY?!
YOU ARE A VERY PECULIAR MAN.
HE DIDN'T DESERVE THIS!
YOU'RE CHILLED TO THE BONE. LET'S GET YOU INSIDE.
I...I THINK HE'S REALLY HURT.
WHETHER HE LIVES OR NOT, WE LEAVE AT DAWN'S LIGHT. GET YOURSELF WARM AND DRY BEFORE YOU CATCH SOMETHING.
POOR LITTLE DUCK.
LATER ON THAT NIGHT...
OHHHH...I FEEL TERRIBLE!
HOW CAN I HELP A HELPLESS DUCK WHEN I FEEL SO SICK MYSELF?

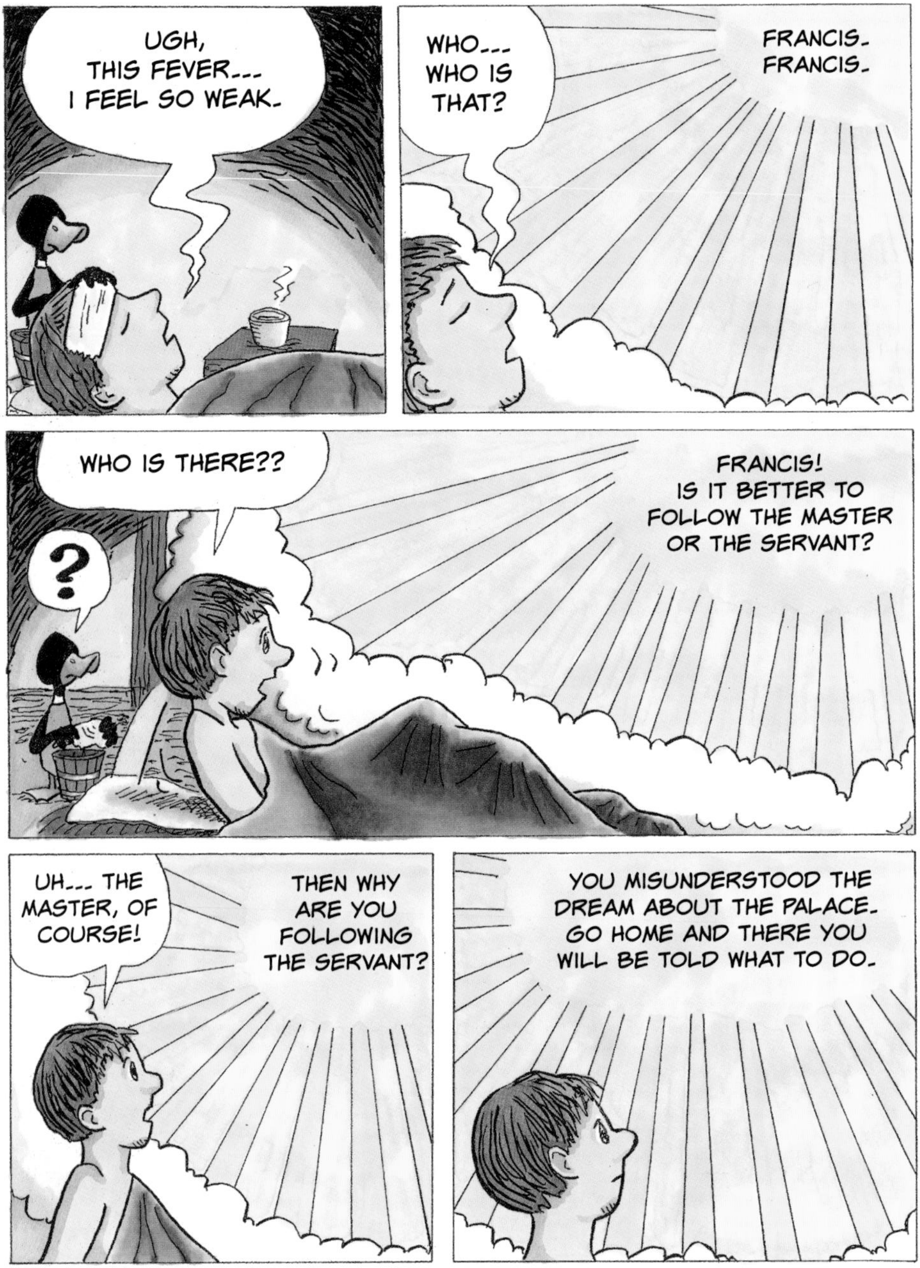
UGH, THIS FEVER... I FEEL SO WEAK.
WHO... WHO IS THAT?
FRANCIS. FRANCIS.
WHO IS THERE??
?
FRANCIS! IS IT BETTER TO FOLLOW THE MASTER OR THE SERVANT?
UH... THE MASTER, OF COURSE!
THEN WHY ARE YOU FOLLOWING THE SERVANT?
YOU MISUNDERSTOOD THE DREAM ABOUT THE PALACE. GO HOME AND THERE YOU WILL BE TOLD WHAT TO DO.

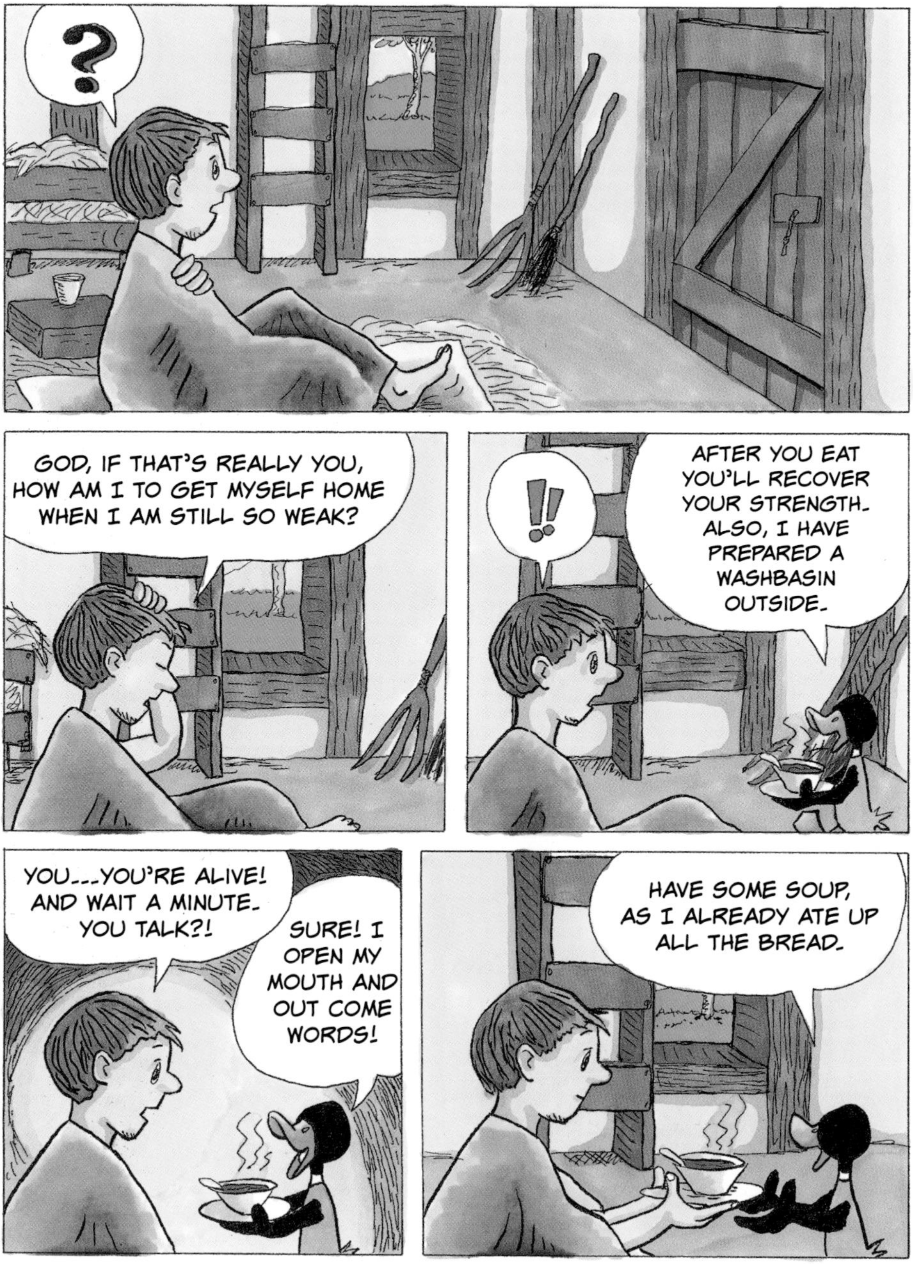
?
GOD, IF THAT'S REALLY YOU, HOW AM I TO GET MYSELF HOME WHEN I AM STILL SO WEAK?
!!
AFTER YOU EAT YOU'LL RECOVER YOUR STRENGTH. ALSO, I HAVE PREPARED A WASHBASIN OUTSIDE.
YOU...YOU'RE ALIVE! AND WAIT A MINUTE. YOU TALK?!
SURE! I OPEN MY MOUTH AND OUT COME WORDS!
HAVE SOME SOUP, AS I ALREADY ATE UP ALL THE BREAD.

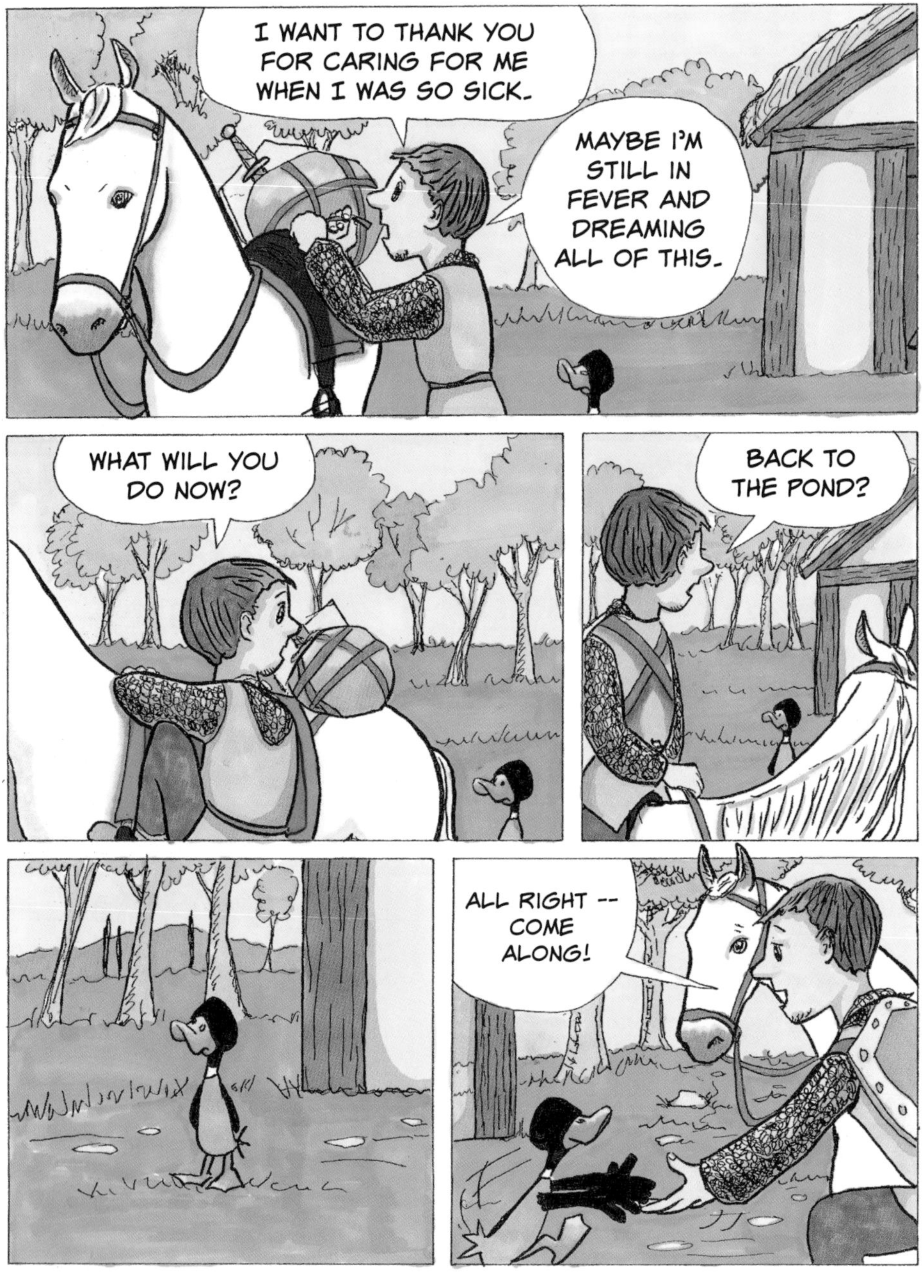
I WANT TO THANK YOU FOR CARING FOR ME WHEN I WAS SO SICK.
MAYBE I'M STILL IN FEVER AND DREAMING ALL OF THIS.
WHAT WILL YOU DO NOW?
BACK TO THE POND?
ALL RIGHT -- COME ALONG!

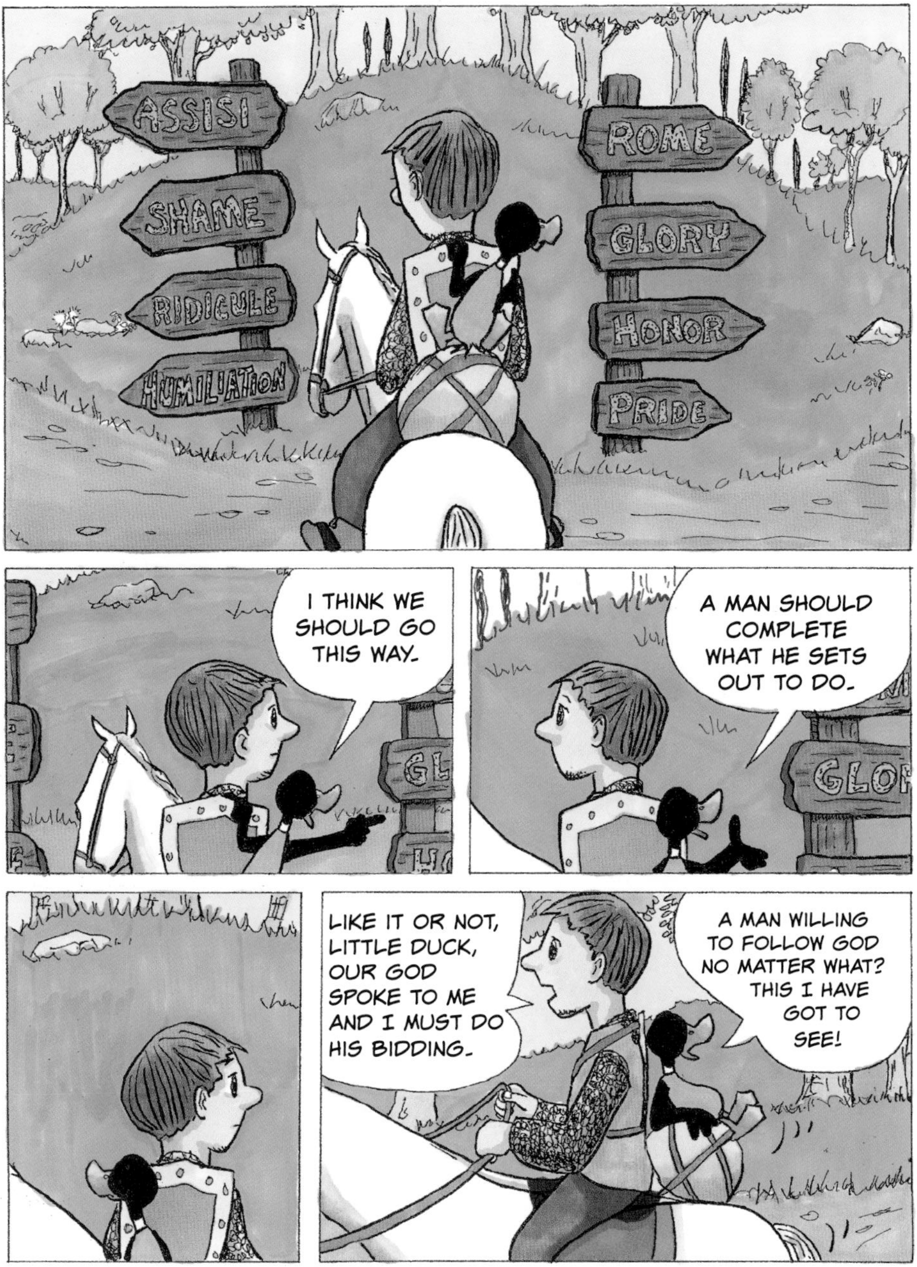
ASSISI
SHAME
RIDICULE
HUMILIATION
ROME
GLORY
HONOR
PRIDE
I THINK WE SHOULD GO THIS WAY.
A MAN SHOULD COMPLETE WHAT HE SETS OUT TO DO.
LIKE IT OR NOT, LITTLE DUCK, OUR GOD SPOKE TO ME AND I MUST DO HIS BIDDING.
A MAN WILLING TO FOLLOW GOD NO MATTER WHAT? THIS I HAVE GOT TO SEE!

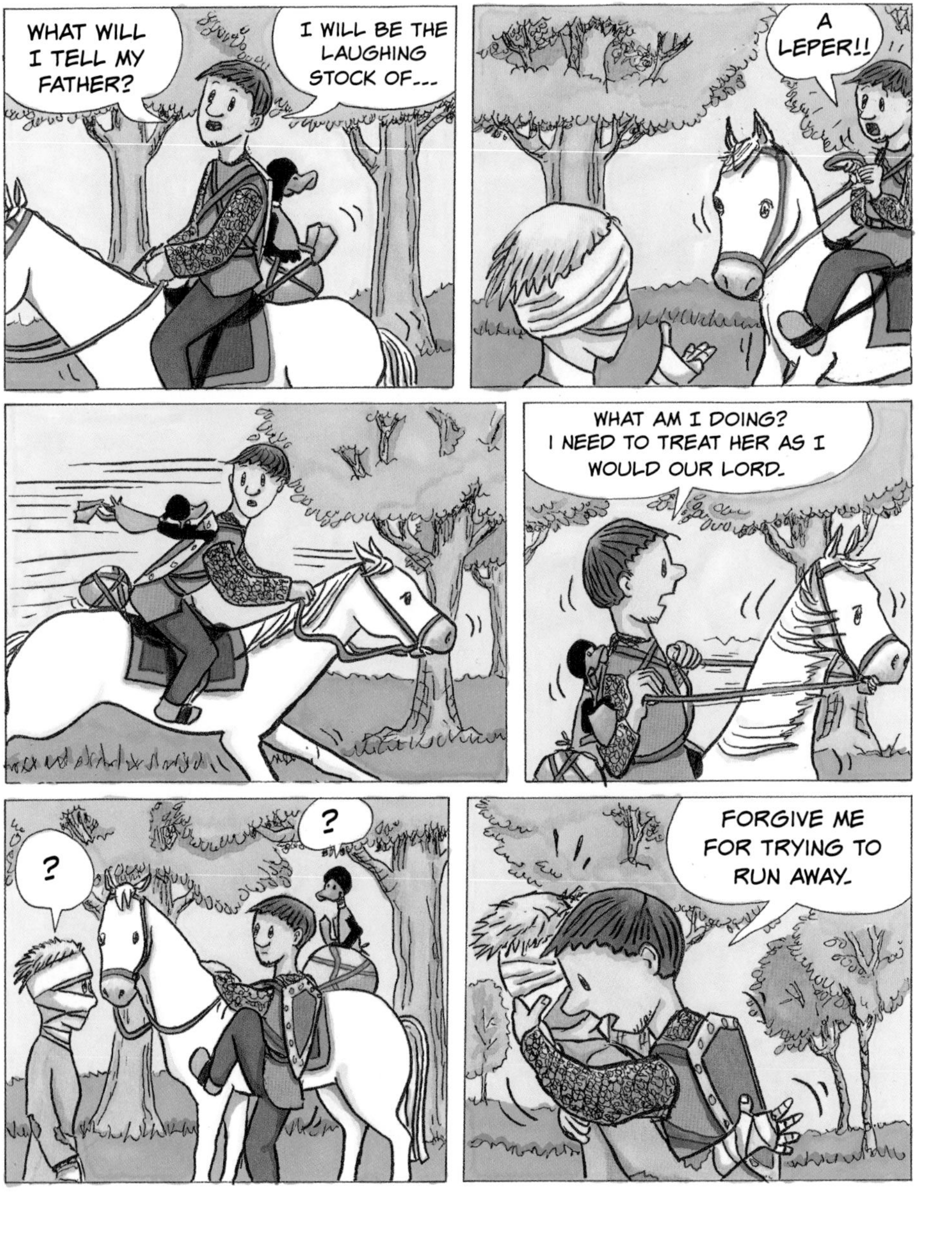
WHAT WILL I TELL MY FATHER?
I WILL BE THE LAUGHING STOCK OF...
A LEPER!!
WHAT AM I DOING? I NEED TO TREAT HER AS I WOULD OUR LORD.
?
?
FORGIVE ME FOR TRYING TO RUN AWAY.

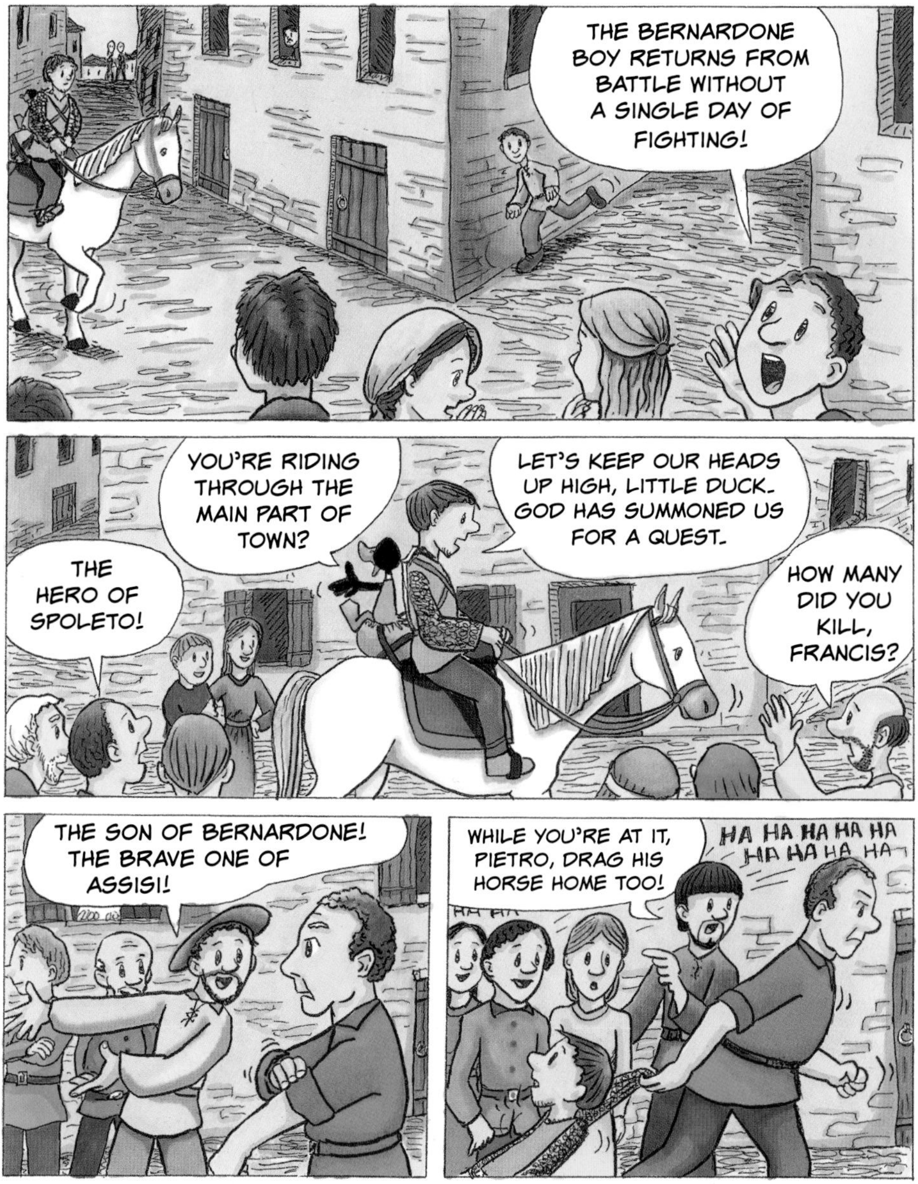
THE BERNARDONE BOY RETURNS FROM BATTLE WITHOUT A SINGLE DAY OF FIGHTING!
YOU'RE RIDING THROUGH THE MAIN PART OF TOWN?
LET'S KEEP OUR HEADS UP HIGH, LITTLE DUCK. GOD HAS SUMMONED US FOR A QUEST.
THE HERO OF SPOLETO!
HOW MANY DID YOU KILL, FRANCIS?
THE SON OF BERNARDONE! THE BRAVE ONE OF ASSISI!
WHILE YOU'RE AT IT, PIETRO, DRAG HIS HORSE HOME TOO!
HA HA HA HA HA HA HA HA HA

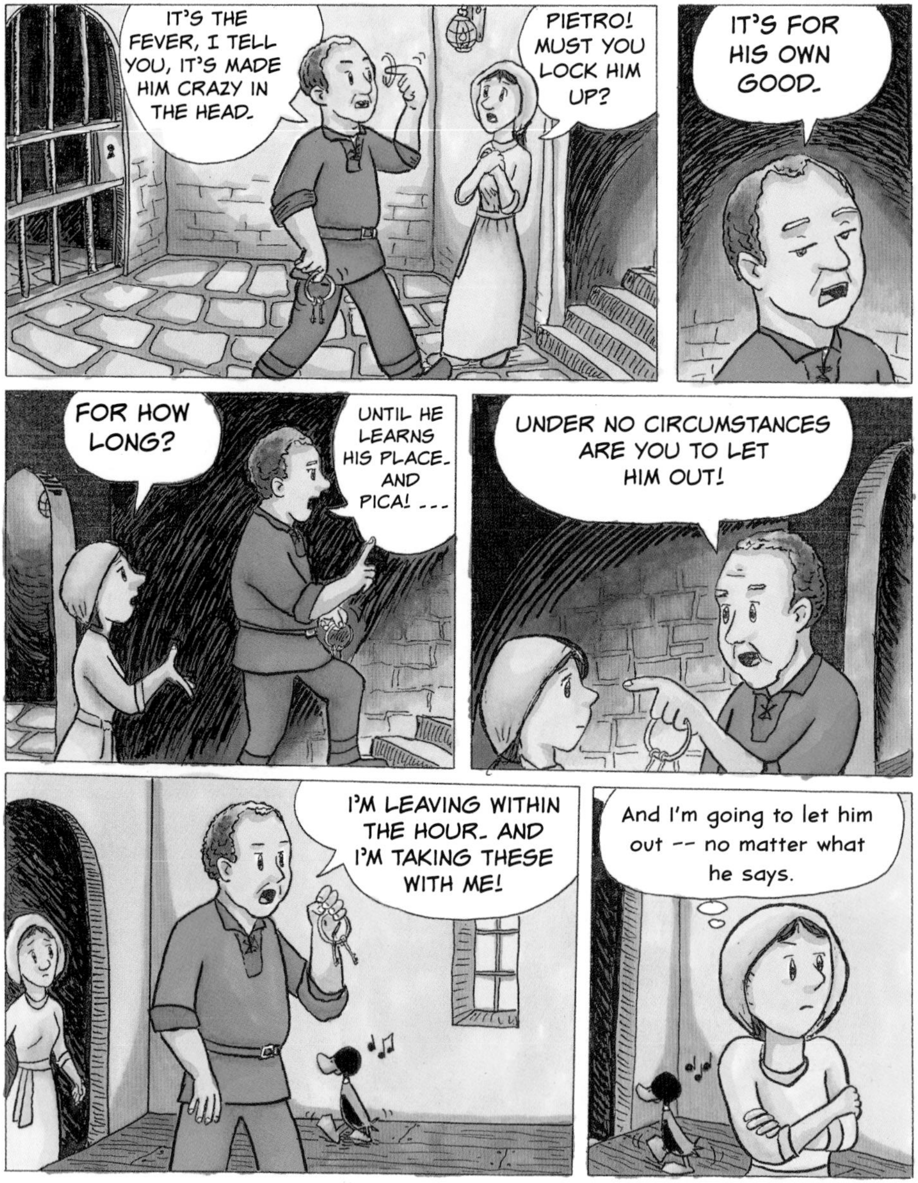
IT'S THE FEVER, I TELL YOU, IT'S MADE HIM CRAZY IN THE HEAD.
PIETRO! MUST YOU LOCK HIM UP?
IT'S FOR HIS OWN GOOD.
FOR HOW LONG?
UNTIL HE LEARNS HIS PLACE. AND PICA! ...
UNDER NO CIRCUMSTANCES ARE YOU TO LET HIM OUT!
I'M LEAVING WITHIN THE HOUR. AND I'M TAKING THESE WITH ME!
And I'm going to let him out -- no matter what he says.

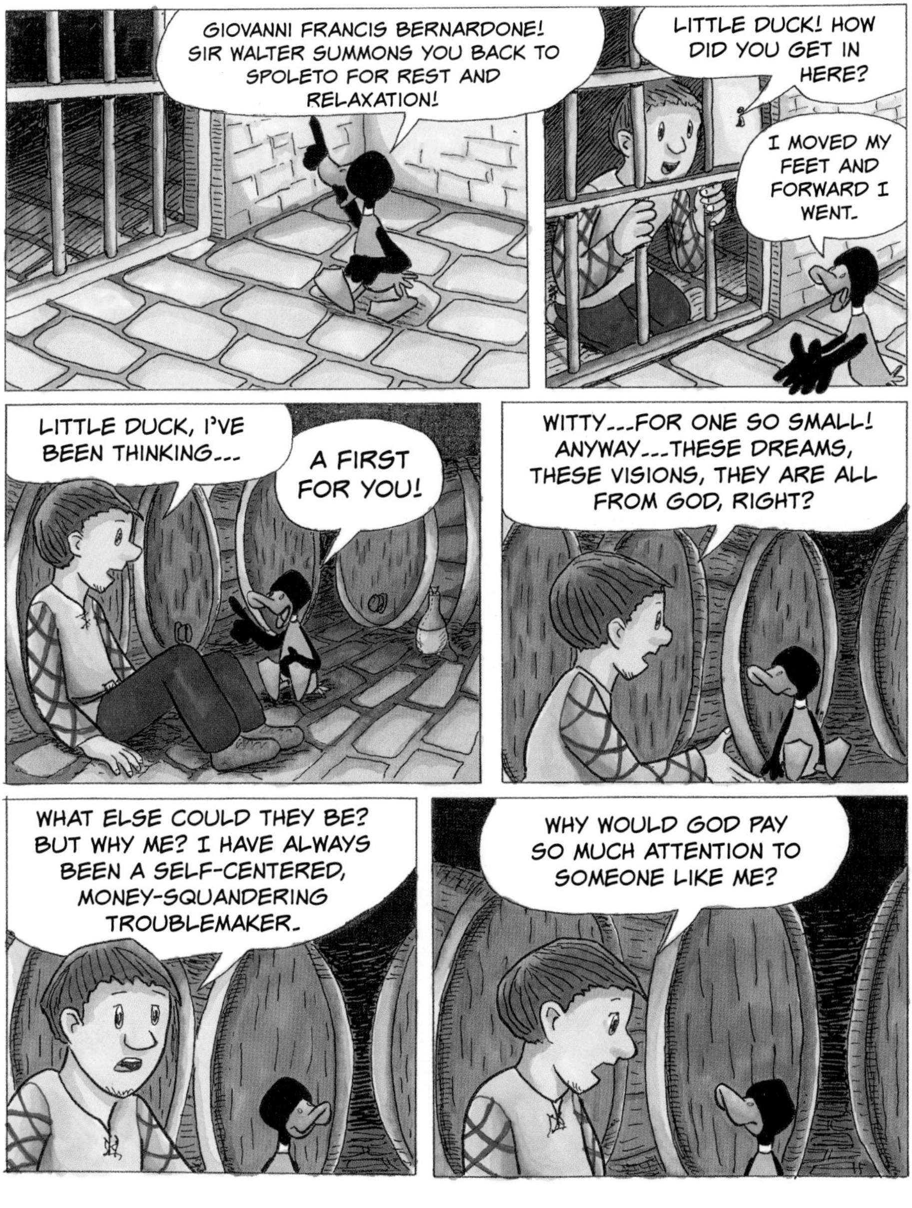
GIOVANNI FRANCIS BERNARDONE! SIR WALTER SUMMONS YOU BACK TO SPOLETO FOR REST AND RELAXATION!
LITTLE DUCK! HOW DID YOU GET IN HERE?
I MOVED MY FEET AND FORWARD I WENT.
LITTLE DUCK, I'VE BEEN THINKING...
A FIRST FOR YOU!
WITTY...FOR ONE SO SMALL! ANYWAY...THESE DREAMS, THESE VISIONS, THEY ARE ALL FROM GOD, RIGHT?
WHAT ELSE COULD THEY BE? BUT WHY ME? I HAVE ALWAYS BEEN A SELF-CENTERED, MONEY-SQUANDERING TROUBLEMAKER.
WHY WOULD GOD PAY SO MUCH ATTENTION TO SOMEONE LIKE ME?

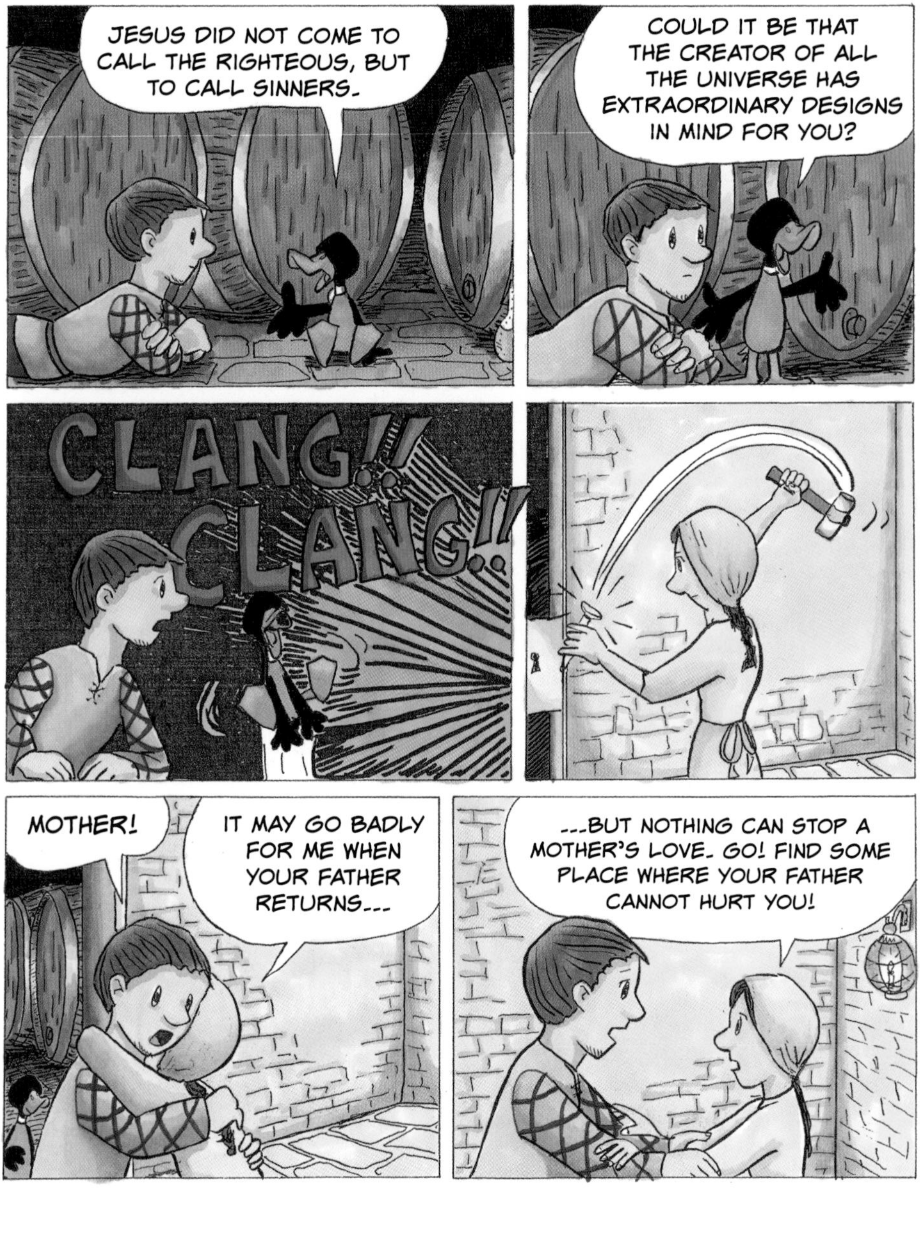
JESUS DID NOT COME TO CALL THE RIGHTEOUS, BUT TO CALL SINNERS.
COULD IT BE THAT THE CREATOR OF ALL THE UNIVERSE HAS EXTRAORDINARY DESIGNS IN MIND FOR YOU?
CLANG!!
CLANG!!
MOTHER!
IT MAY GO BADLY FOR ME WHEN YOUR FATHER RETURNS...
...BUT NOTHING CAN STOP A MOTHER'S LOVE. GO! FIND SOME PLACE WHERE YOUR FATHER CANNOT HURT YOU!

CHAPTER 2
REBUILDING A CHURCH

See the birds under the Heavens
They do not sow, they do not reap,
They do not gather into barns,
Yet their Heavenly Father takes care of them.
—MATTHEW 6:26

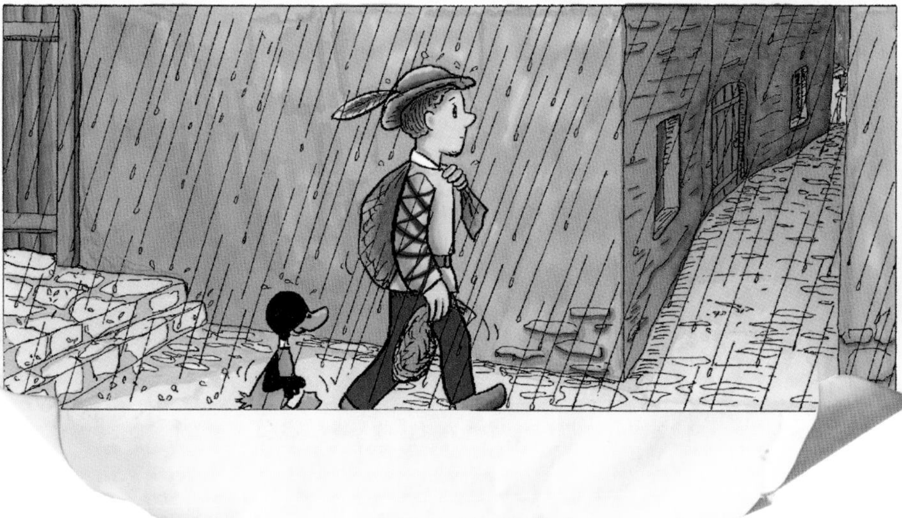

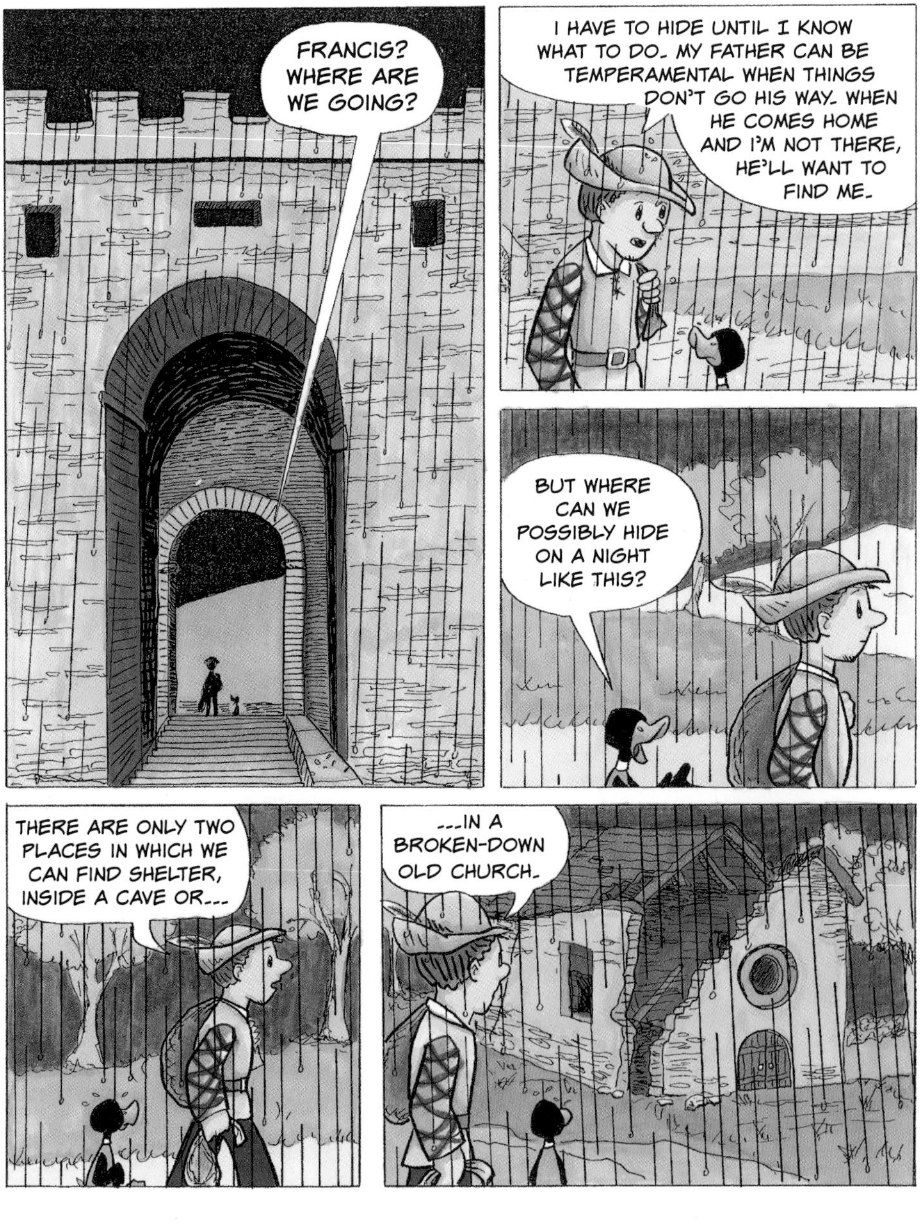
FRANCIS? WHERE ARE WE GOING?
I HAVE TO HIDE UNTIL I KNOW WHAT TO DO. MY FATHER CAN BE TEMPERAMENTAL WHEN THINGS DON'T GO HIS WAY. WHEN HE COMES HOME AND I'M NOT THERE, HE'LL WANT TO FIND ME.
BUT WHERE CAN WE POSSIBLY HIDE ON A NIGHT LIKE THIS?
THERE ARE ONLY TWO PLACES IN WHICH WE CAN FIND SHELTER, INSIDE A CAVE OR...
...IN A BROKEN-DOWN OLD CHURCH.

THE FOLLOWING MORNING...

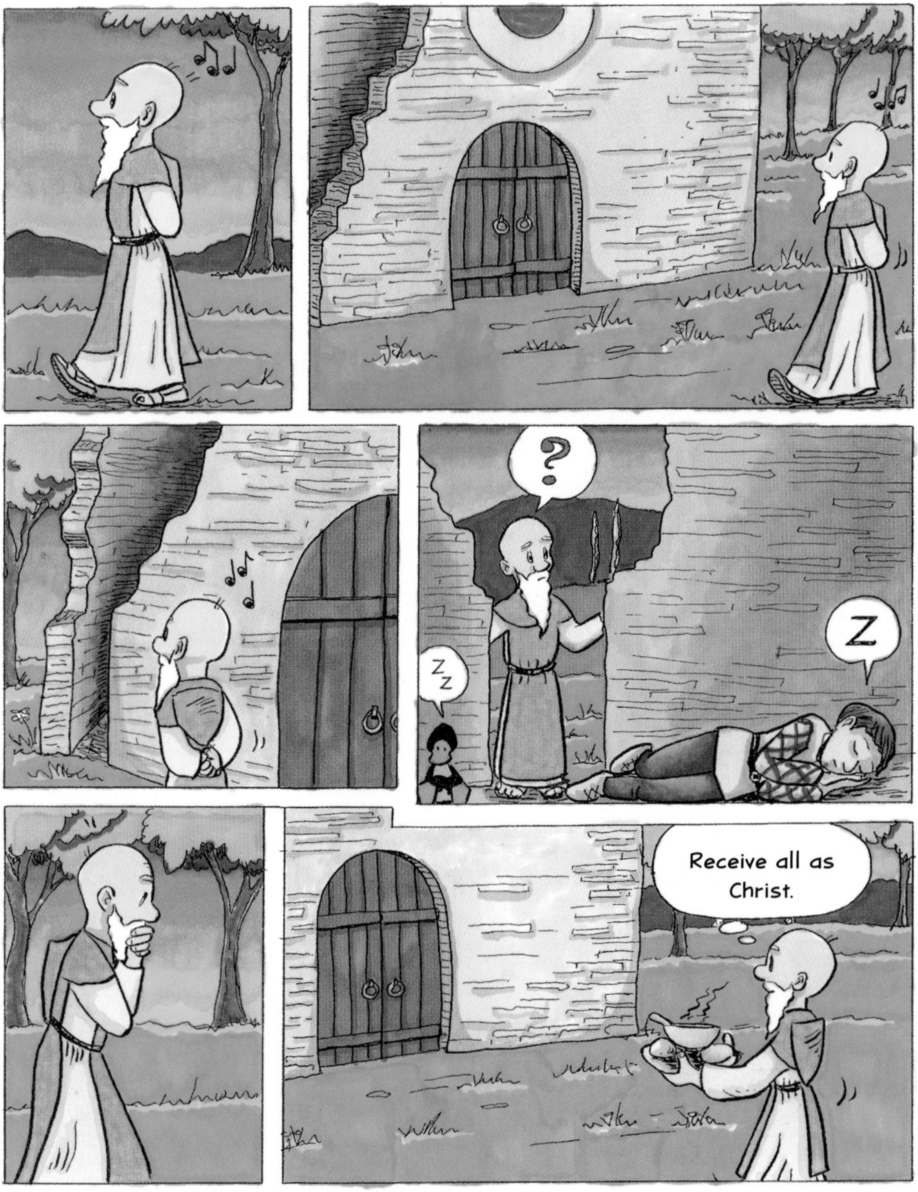
?
Z Z
Z
Receive all as Christ.

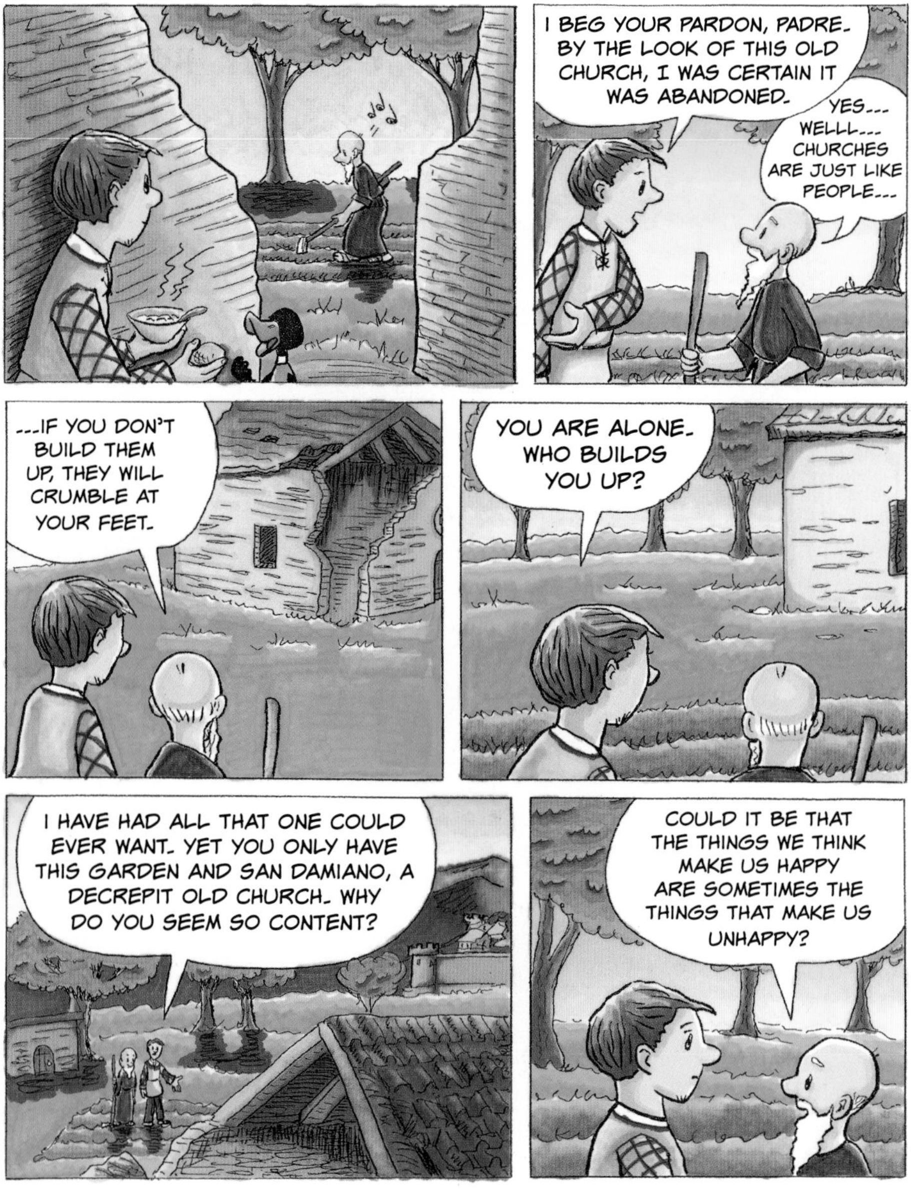
I BEG YOUR PARDON, PADRE. BY THE LOOK OF THIS OLD CHURCH, I WAS CERTAIN IT WAS ABANDONED.
YES... WELLL... CHURCHES ARE JUST LIKE PEOPLE...
...IF YOU DON'T BUILD THEM UP, THEY WILL CRUMBLE AT YOUR FEET.
YOU ARE ALONE. WHO BUILDS YOU UP?
I HAVE HAD ALL THAT ONE COULD EVER WANT. YET YOU ONLY HAVE THIS GARDEN AND SAN DAMIANO, A DECREPIT OLD CHURCH. WHY DO YOU SEEM SO CONTENT?
COULD IT BE THAT THE THINGS WE THINK MAKE US HAPPY ARE SOMETIMES THE THINGS THAT MAKE US UNHAPPY?

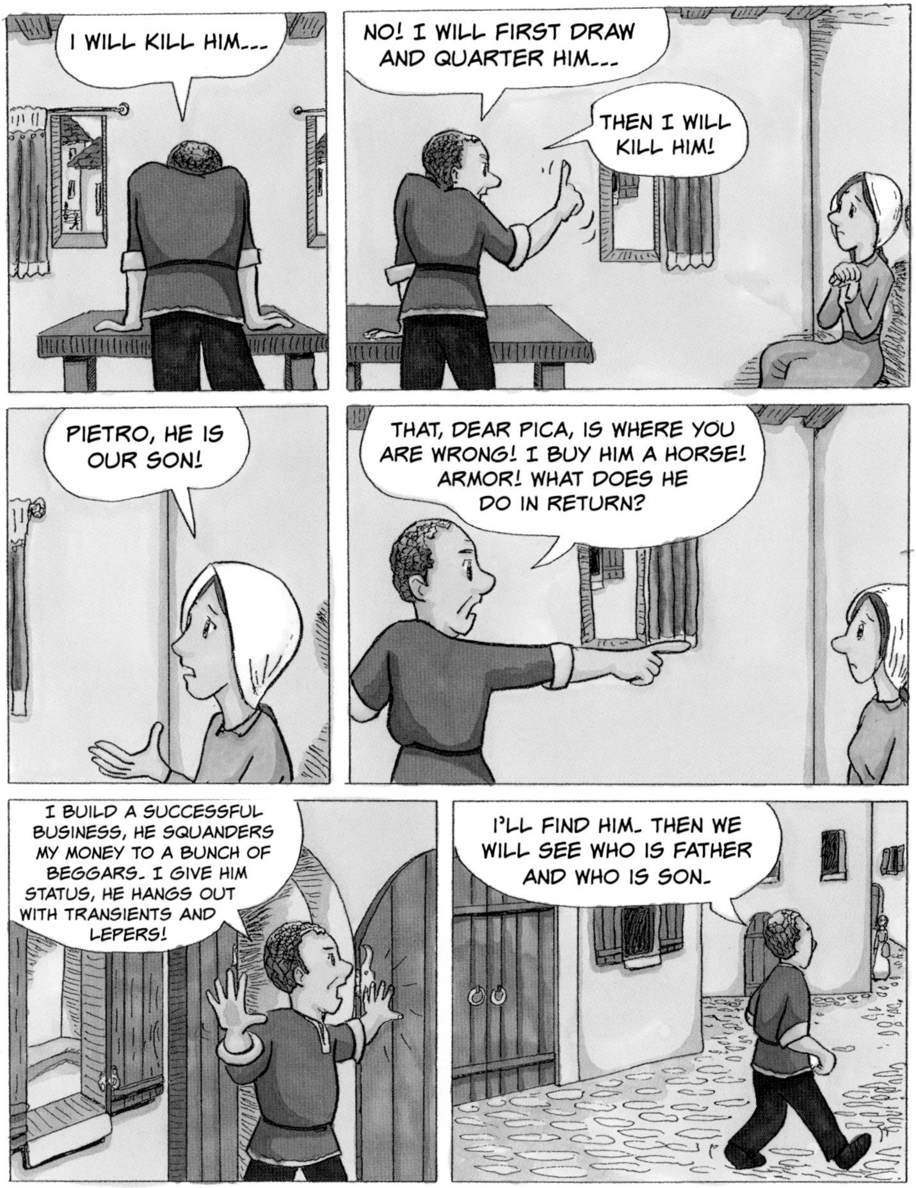
I WILL KILL HIM...
NO! I WILL FIRST DRAW AND QUARTER HIM...
THEN I WILL KILL HIM!
PIETRO, HE IS OUR SON!
THAT, DEAR PICA, IS WHERE YOU ARE WRONG! I BUY HIM A HORSE! ARMOR! WHAT DOES HE DO IN RETURN?
I BUILD A SUCCESSFUL BUSINESS, HE SQUANDERS MY MONEY TO A BUNCH OF BEGGARS. I GIVE HIM STATUS, HE HANGS OUT WITH TRANSIENTS AND LEPERS!
I'LL FIND HIM. THEN WE WILL SEE WHO IS FATHER AND WHO IS SON.

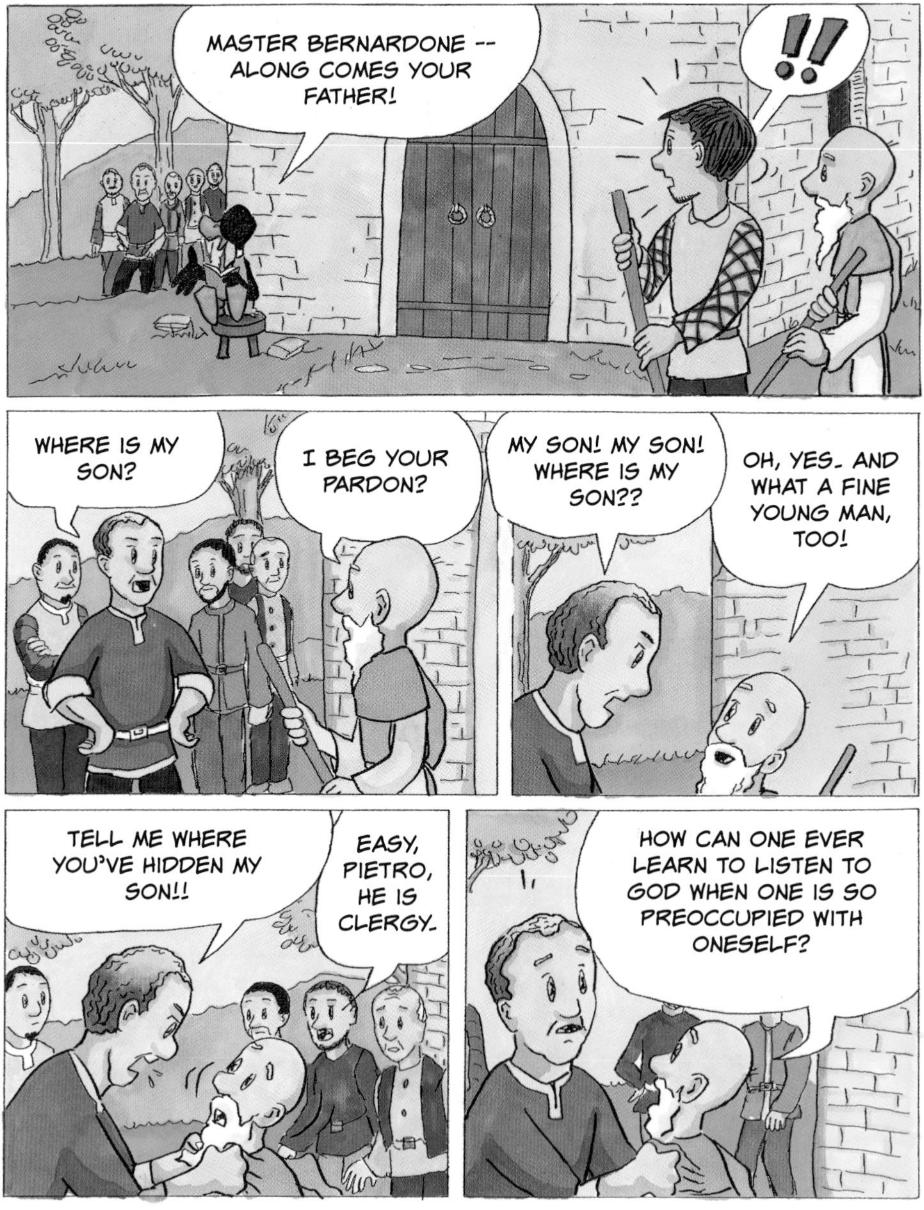
MASTER BERNARDONE -- ALONG COMES YOUR FATHER!
!!
WHERE IS MY SON?
I BEG YOUR PARDON?
MY SON! MY SON! WHERE IS MY SON??
OH, YES. AND WHAT A FINE YOUNG MAN, TOO!
TELL ME WHERE YOU'VE HIDDEN MY SON!!
EASY, PIETRO, HE IS CLERGY.
HOW CAN ONE EVER LEARN TO LISTEN TO GOD WHEN ONE IS SO PREOCCUPIED WITH ONESELF?

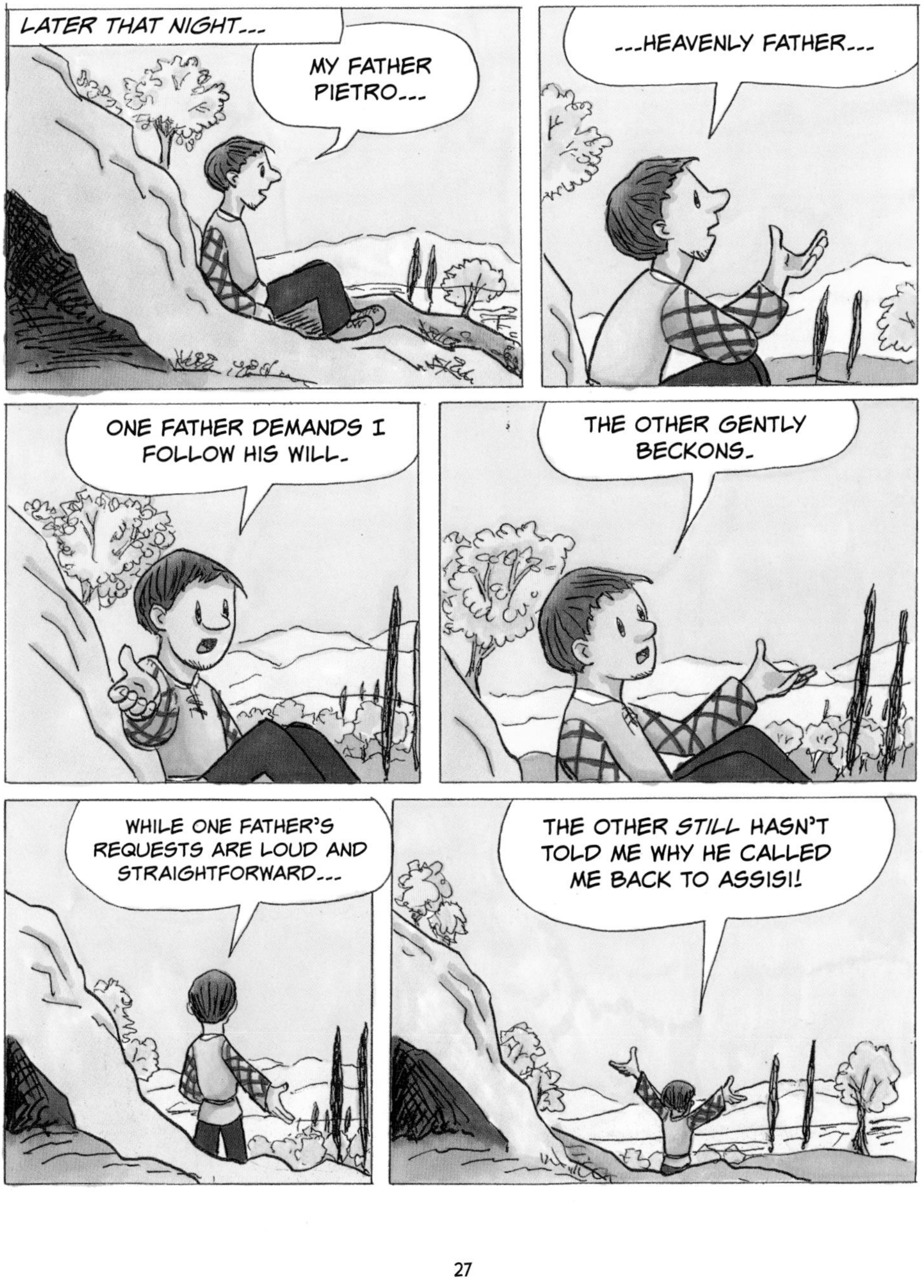
LATER THAT NIGHT...
MY FATHER PIETRO...
...HEAVENLY FATHER...
ONE FATHER DEMANDS I FOLLOW HIS WILL.
THE OTHER GENTLY BECKONS.
WHILE ONE FATHER'S REQUESTS ARE LOUD AND STRAIGHTFORWARD...
THE OTHER *STILL* HASN'T TOLD ME WHY HE CALLED ME BACK TO ASSISI!

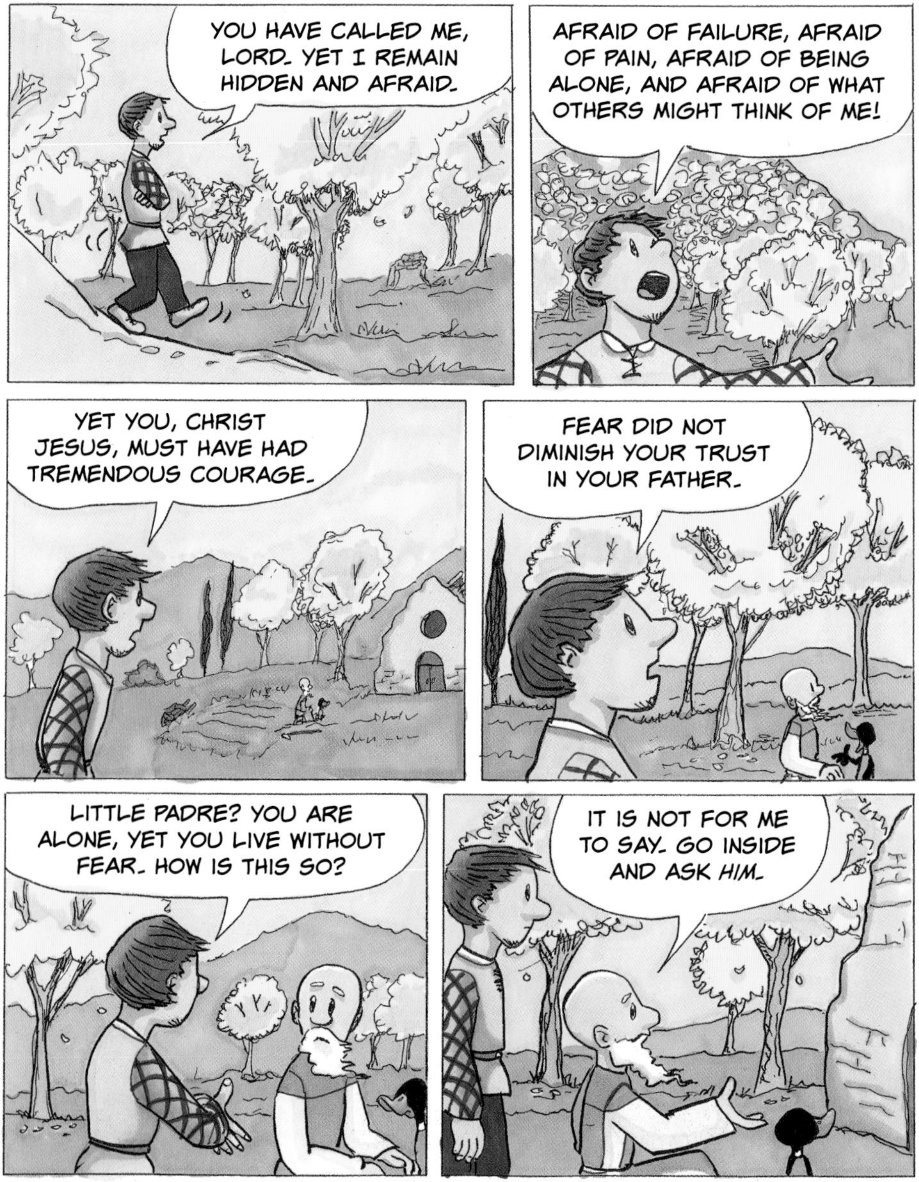
YOU HAVE CALLED ME, LORD. YET I REMAIN HIDDEN AND AFRAID.
AFRAID OF FAILURE, AFRAID OF PAIN, AFRAID OF BEING ALONE, AND AFRAID OF WHAT OTHERS MIGHT THINK OF ME!
YET YOU, CHRIST JESUS, MUST HAVE HAD TREMENDOUS COURAGE.
FEAR DID NOT DIMINISH YOUR TRUST IN YOUR FATHER.
LITTLE PADRE? YOU ARE ALONE, YET YOU LIVE WITHOUT FEAR. HOW IS THIS SO?
IT IS NOT FOR ME TO SAY. GO INSIDE AND ASK *HIM*.

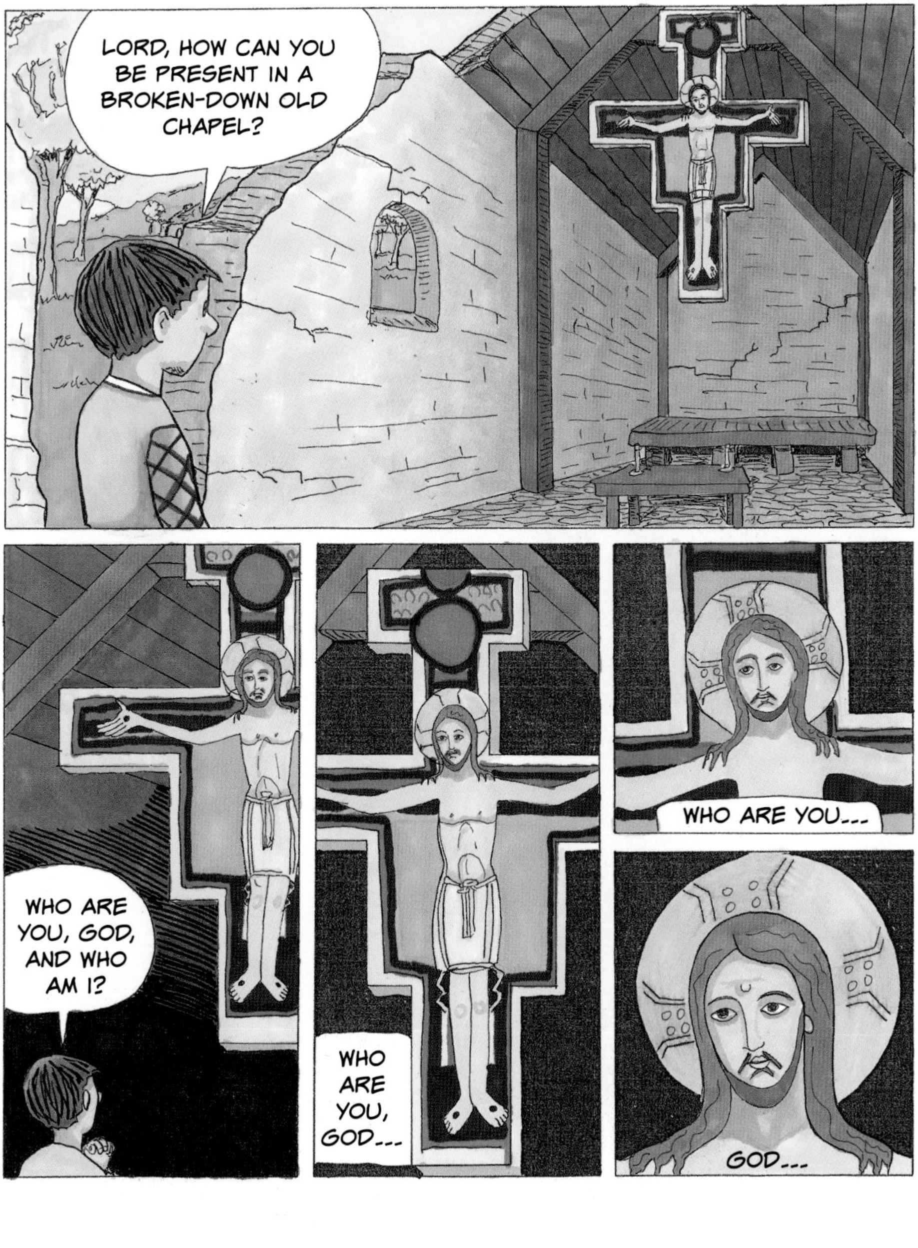
LORD, HOW CAN YOU BE PRESENT IN A BROKEN-DOWN OLD CHAPEL?
WHO ARE YOU, GOD, AND WHO AM I?
WHO ARE YOU, GOD...
WHO ARE YOU...
GOD...

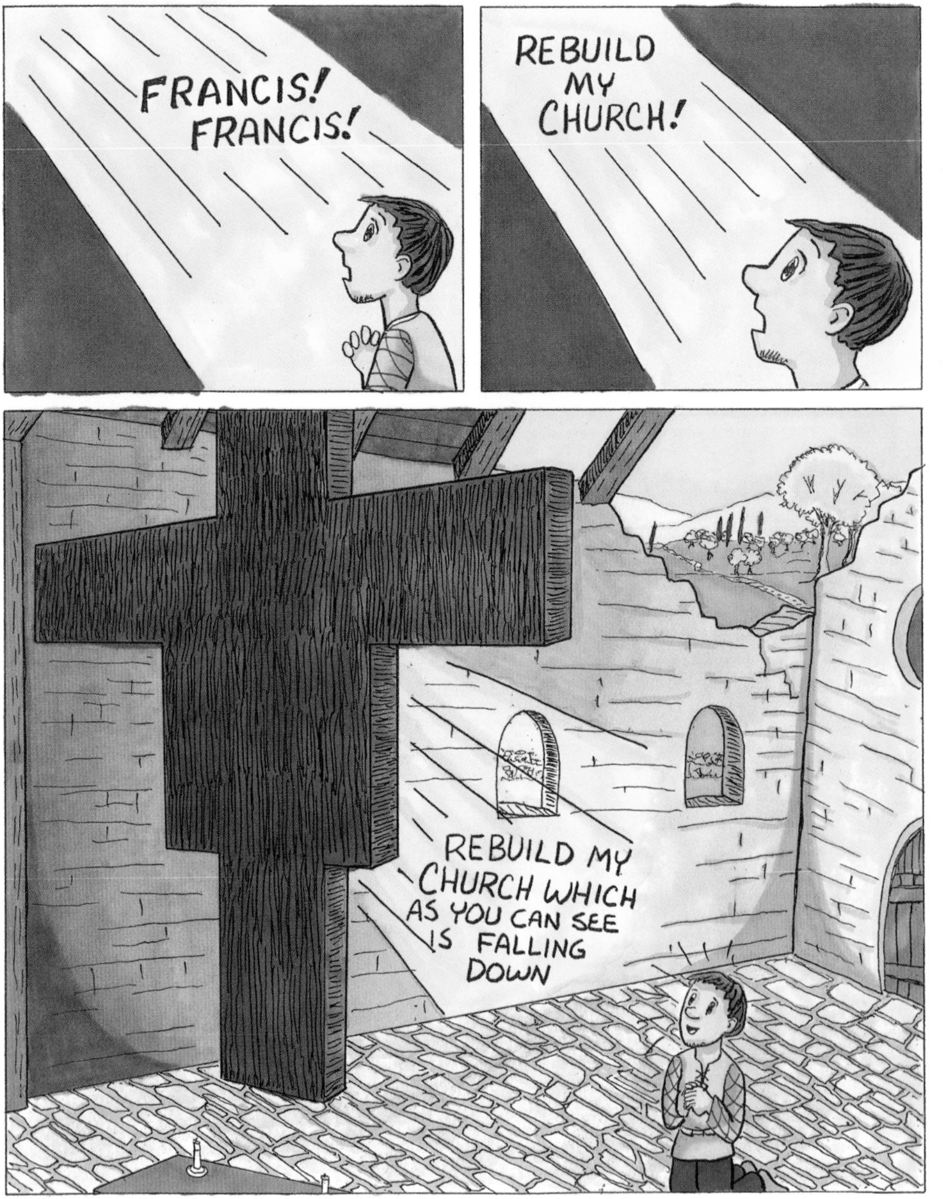
FRANCIS! FRANCIS!
REBUILD MY CHURCH!
REBUILD MY CHURCH WHICH AS YOU CAN SEE IS FALLING DOWN

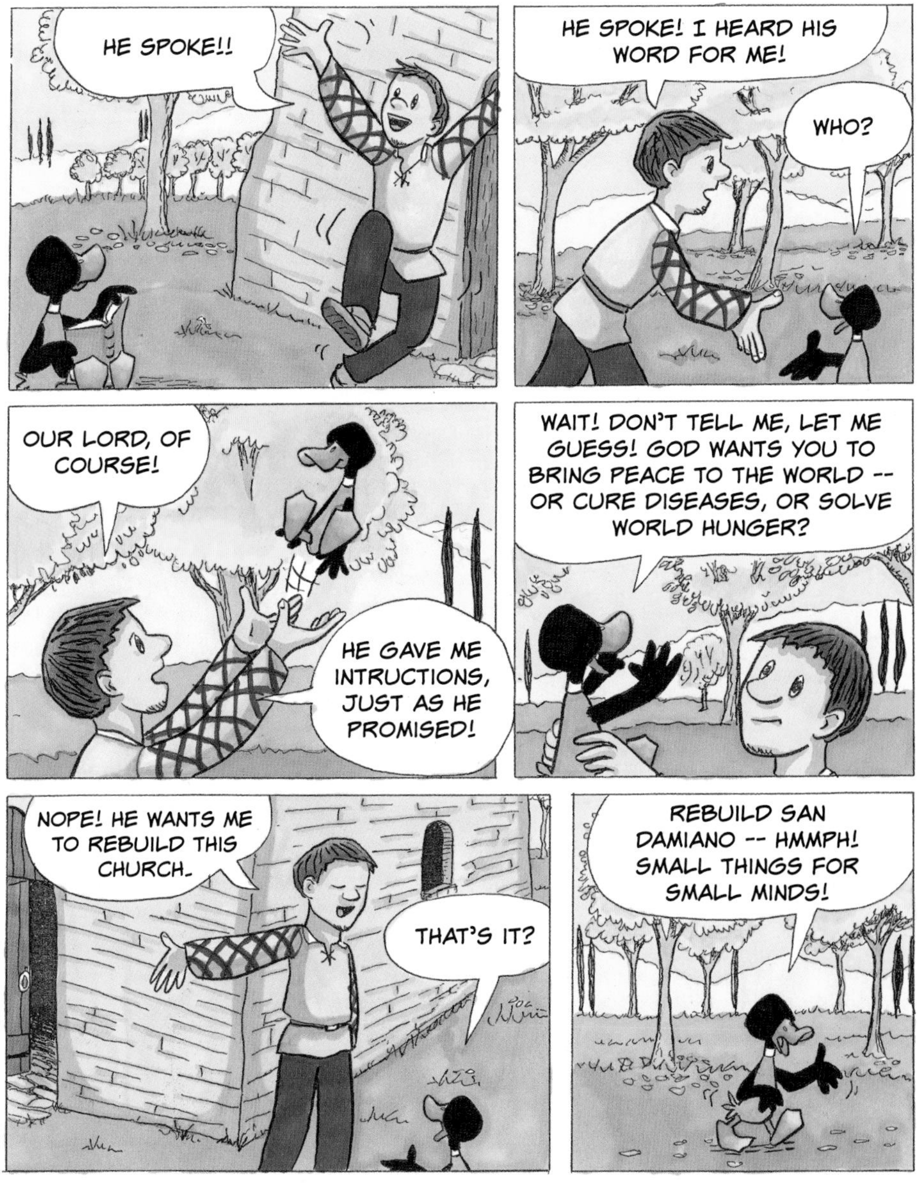
HE SPOKE!!
HE SPOKE! I HEARD HIS WORD FOR ME!
WHO?
OUR LORD, OF COURSE!
HE GAVE ME INTRUCTIONS, JUST AS HE PROMISED!
WAIT! DON'T TELL ME, LET ME GUESS! GOD WANTS YOU TO BRING PEACE TO THE WORLD -- OR CURE DISEASES, OR SOLVE WORLD HUNGER?
NOPE! HE WANTS ME TO REBUILD THIS CHURCH.
THAT'S IT?
REBUILD SAN DAMIANO -- HMMPH! SMALL THINGS FOR SMALL MINDS!

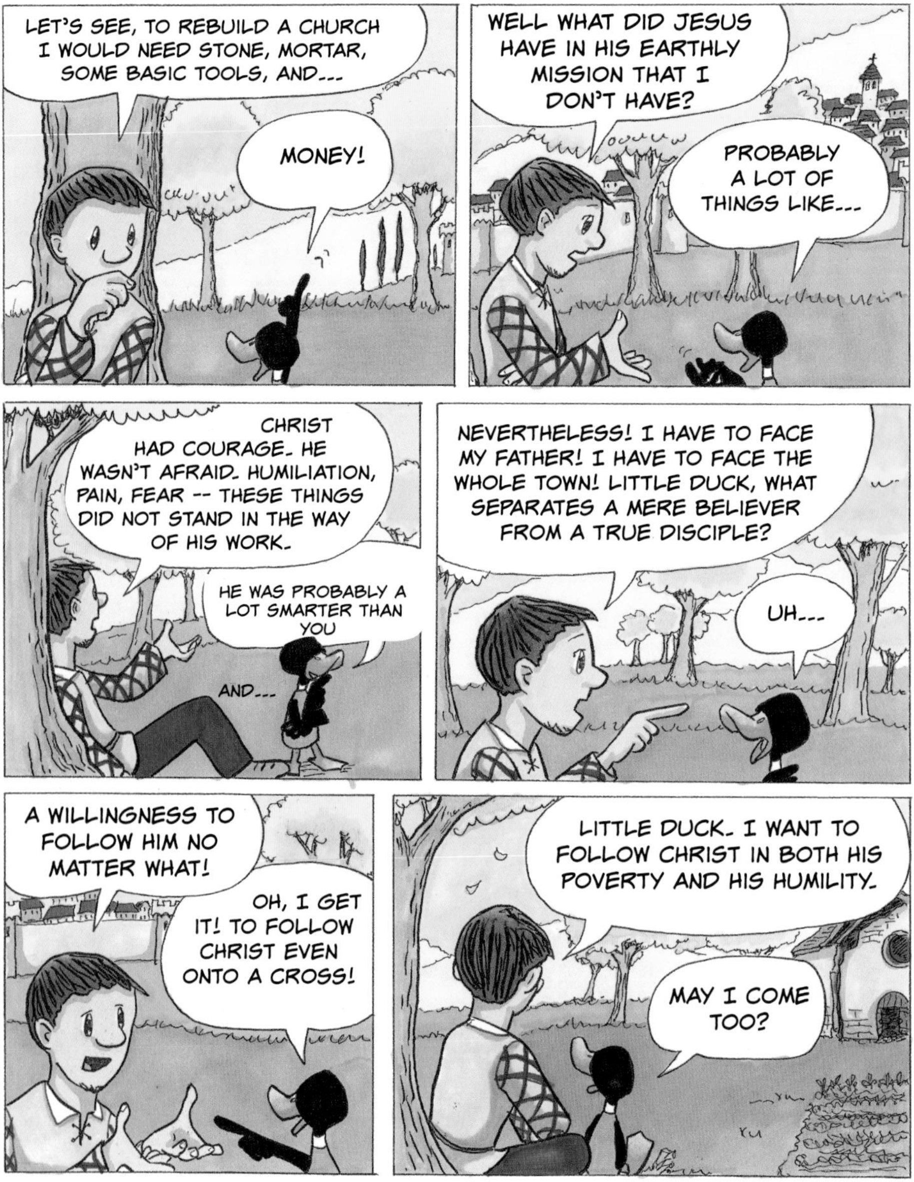
LET'S SEE, TO REBUILD A CHURCH I WOULD NEED STONE, MORTAR, SOME BASIC TOOLS, AND...
MONEY!
WELL WHAT DID JESUS HAVE IN HIS EARTHLY MISSION THAT I DON'T HAVE?
PROBABLY A LOT OF THINGS LIKE...
CHRIST HAD COURAGE. HE WASN'T AFRAID. HUMILIATION, PAIN, FEAR -- THESE THINGS DID NOT STAND IN THE WAY OF HIS WORK.
HE WAS PROBABLY A LOT SMARTER THAN YOU
AND...
NEVERTHELESS! I HAVE TO FACE MY FATHER! I HAVE TO FACE THE WHOLE TOWN! LITTLE DUCK, WHAT SEPARATES A MERE BELIEVER FROM A TRUE DISCIPLE?
UH...
A WILLINGNESS TO FOLLOW HIM NO MATTER WHAT!
OH, I GET IT! TO FOLLOW CHRIST EVEN ONTO A CROSS!
LITTLE DUCK. I WANT TO FOLLOW CHRIST IN BOTH HIS POVERTY AND HIS HUMILITY.
MAY I COME TOO?

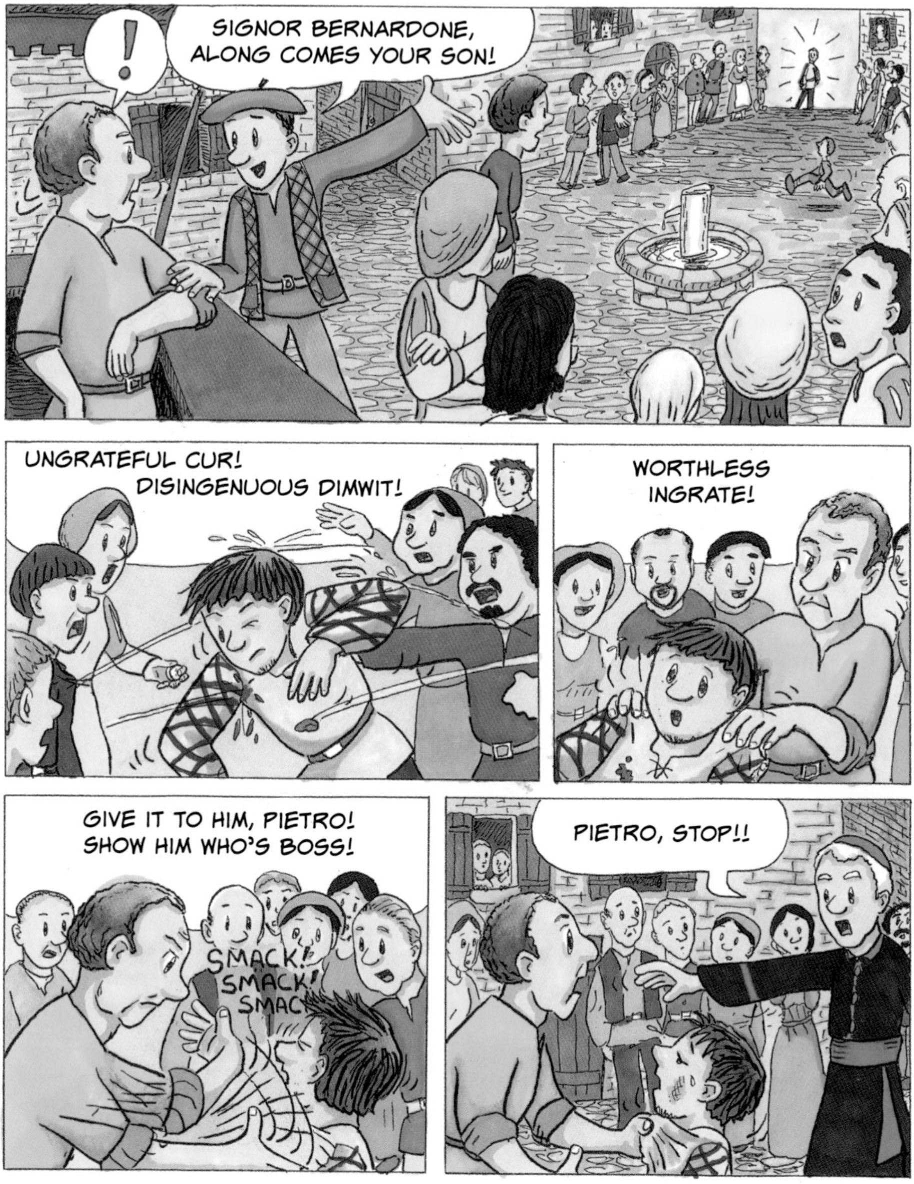
!
SIGNOR BERNARDONE, ALONG COMES YOUR SON!
UNGRATEFUL CUR!
DISINGENUOUS DIMWIT!
WORTHLESS INGRATE!
GIVE IT TO HIM, PIETRO! SHOW HIM WHO'S BOSS!
SMACK! SMACK!
PIETRO, STOP!!

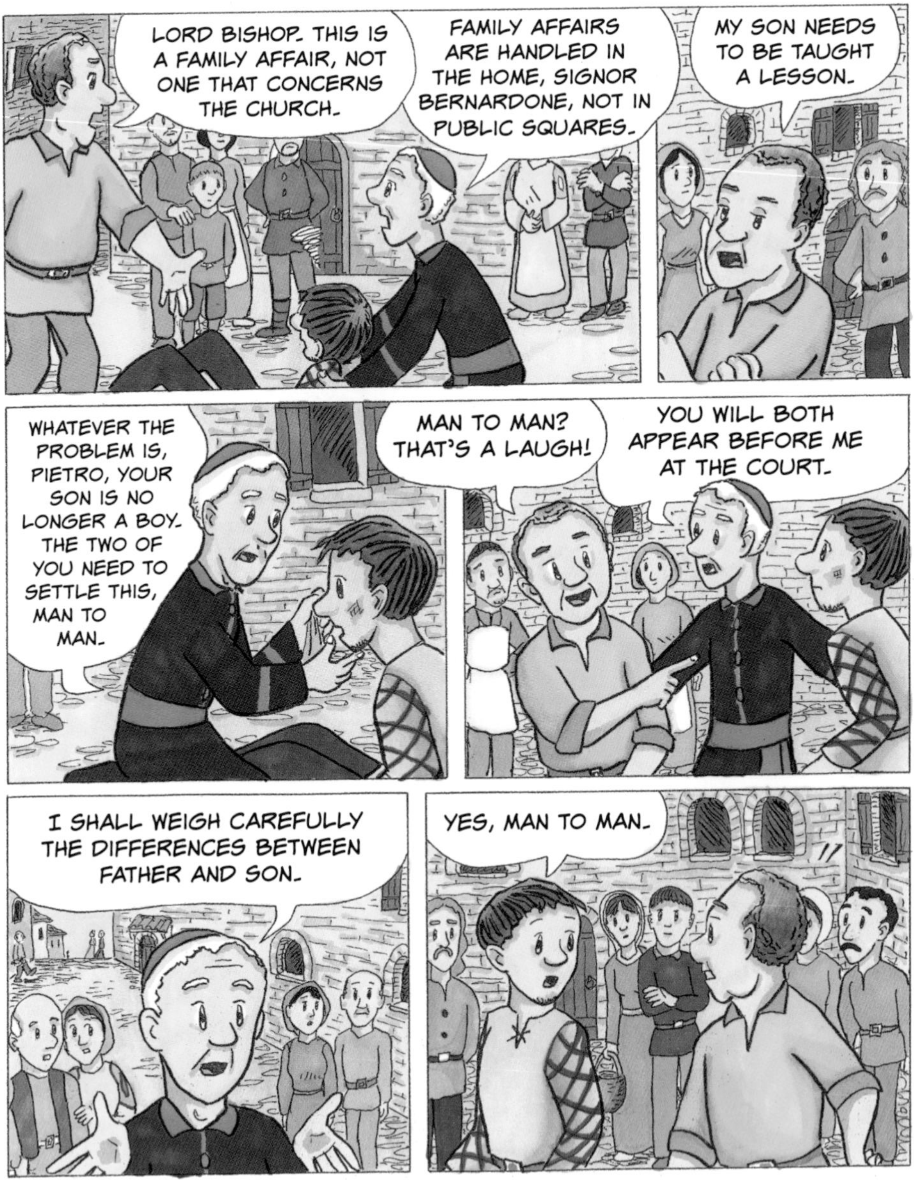
LORD BISHOP. THIS IS A FAMILY AFFAIR, NOT ONE THAT CONCERNS THE CHURCH.
FAMILY AFFAIRS ARE HANDLED IN THE HOME, SIGNOR BERNARDONE, NOT IN PUBLIC SQUARES.
MY SON NEEDS TO BE TAUGHT A LESSON.
WHATEVER THE PROBLEM IS, PIETRO, YOUR SON IS NO LONGER A BOY. THE TWO OF YOU NEED TO SETTLE THIS, MAN TO MAN.
MAN TO MAN? THAT'S A LAUGH!
YOU WILL BOTH APPEAR BEFORE ME AT THE COURT.
I SHALL WEIGH CAREFULLY THE DIFFERENCES BETWEEN FATHER AND SON.
YES, MAN TO MAN.

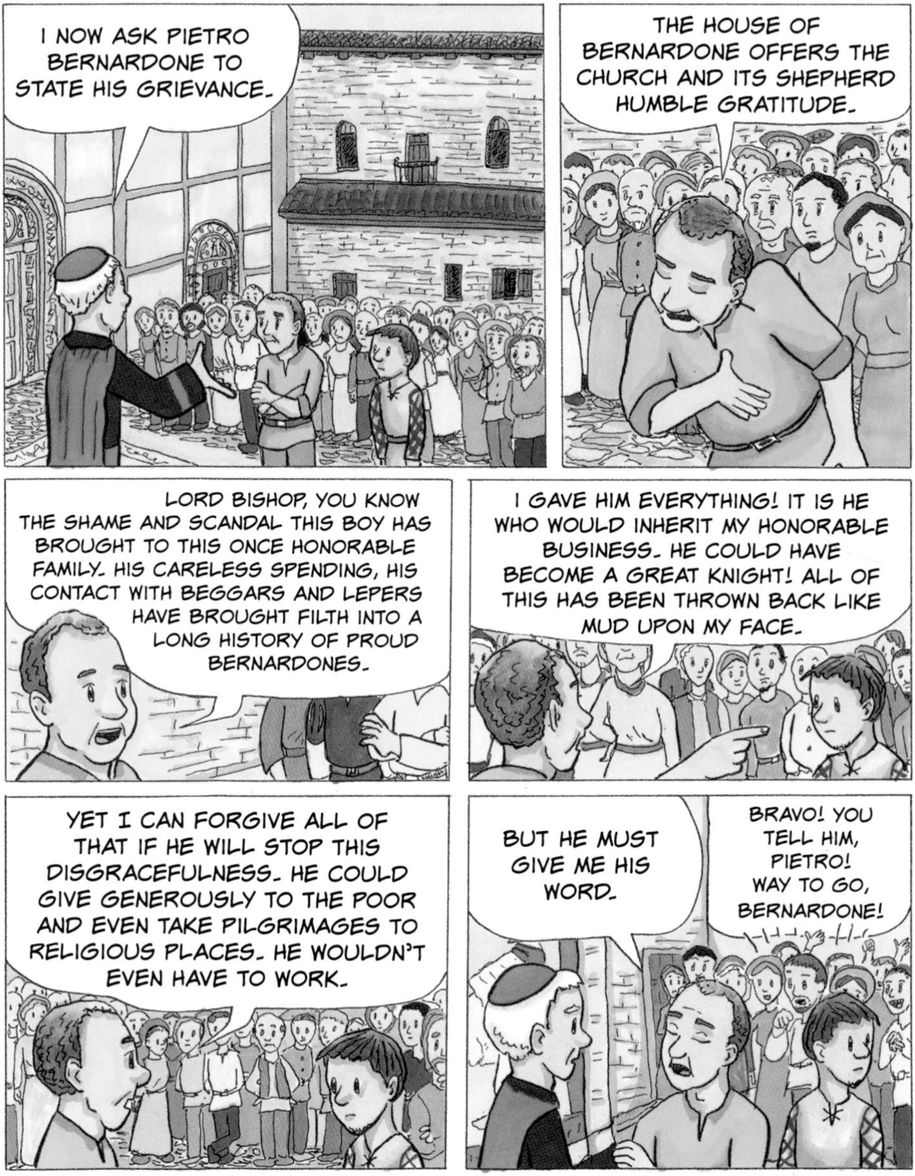
I NOW ASK PIETRO BERNARDONE TO STATE HIS GRIEVANCE.
THE HOUSE OF BERNARDONE OFFERS THE CHURCH AND ITS SHEPHERD HUMBLE GRATITUDE.
LORD BISHOP, YOU KNOW THE SHAME AND SCANDAL THIS BOY HAS BROUGHT TO THIS ONCE HONORABLE FAMILY. HIS CARELESS SPENDING, HIS CONTACT WITH BEGGARS AND LEPERS HAVE BROUGHT FILTH INTO A LONG HISTORY OF PROUD BERNARDONES.
I GAVE HIM EVERYTHING! IT IS HE WHO WOULD INHERIT MY HONORABLE BUSINESS. HE COULD HAVE BECOME A GREAT KNIGHT! ALL OF THIS HAS BEEN THROWN BACK LIKE MUD UPON MY FACE.
YET I CAN FORGIVE ALL OF THAT IF HE WILL STOP THIS DISGRACEFULNESS. HE COULD GIVE GENEROUSLY TO THE POOR AND EVEN TAKE PILGRIMAGES TO RELIGIOUS PLACES. HE WOULDN'T EVEN HAVE TO WORK.
BUT HE MUST GIVE ME HIS WORD.
BRAVO! YOU TELL HIM, PIETRO! WAY TO GO, BERNARDONE!

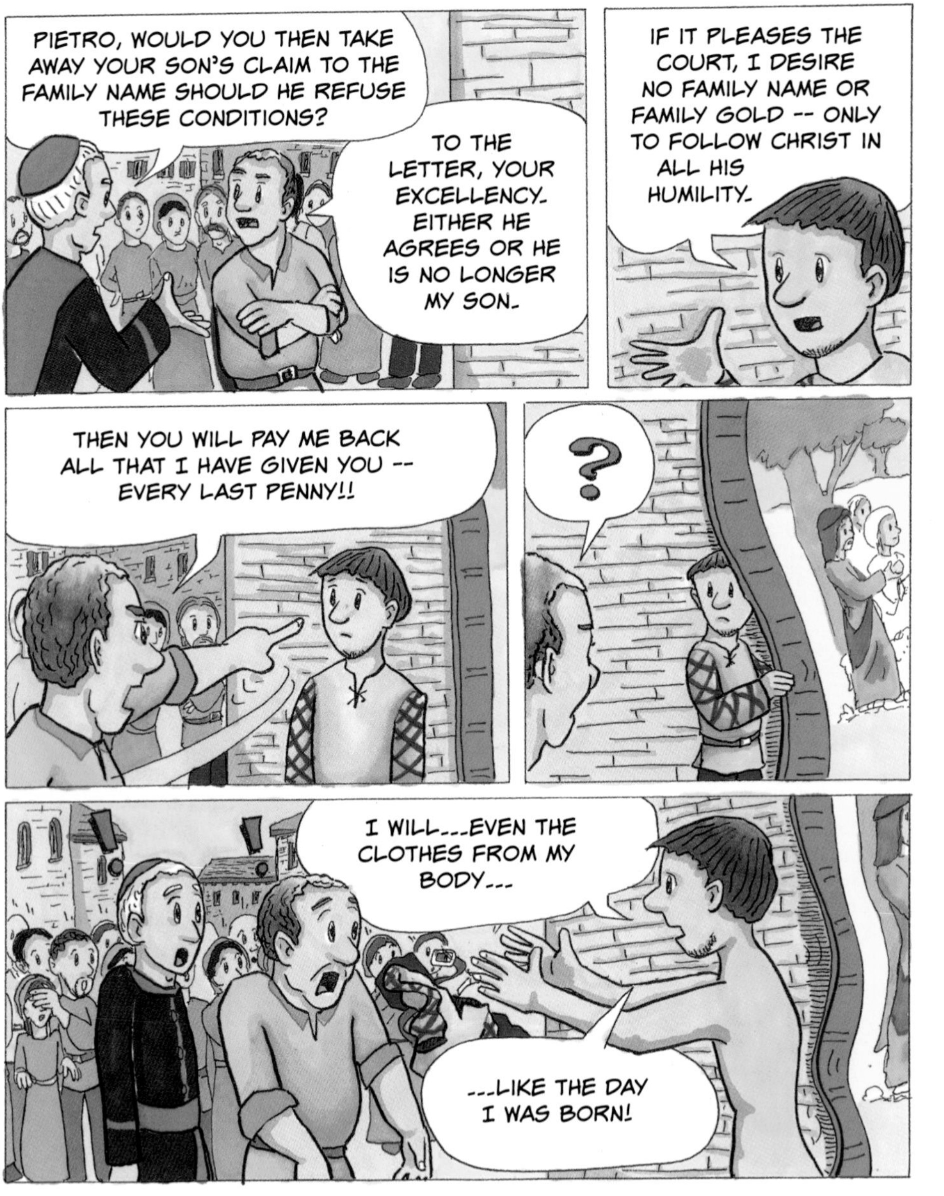
PIETRO, WOULD YOU THEN TAKE AWAY YOUR SON'S CLAIM TO THE FAMILY NAME SHOULD HE REFUSE THESE CONDITIONS?
TO THE LETTER, YOUR EXCELLENCY. EITHER HE AGREES OR HE IS NO LONGER MY SON.
IF IT PLEASES THE COURT, I DESIRE NO FAMILY NAME OR FAMILY GOLD -- ONLY TO FOLLOW CHRIST IN ALL HIS HUMILITY.
THEN YOU WILL PAY ME BACK ALL THAT I HAVE GIVEN YOU -- EVERY LAST PENNY!!
?
I WILL...EVEN THE CLOTHES FROM MY BODY...
...LIKE THE DAY I WAS BORN!

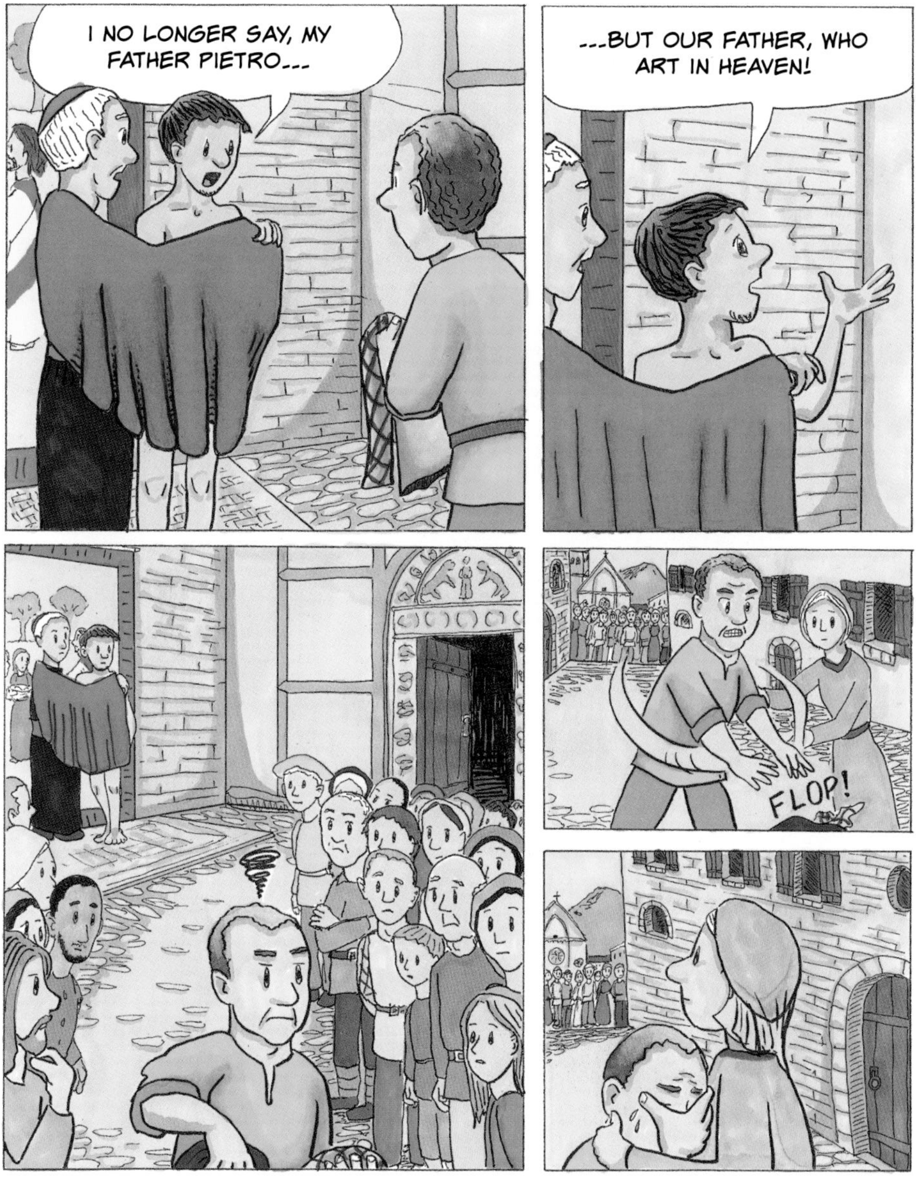
I NO LONGER SAY, MY FATHER PIETRO...
...BUT OUR FATHER, WHO ART IN HEAVEN!
FLOP!

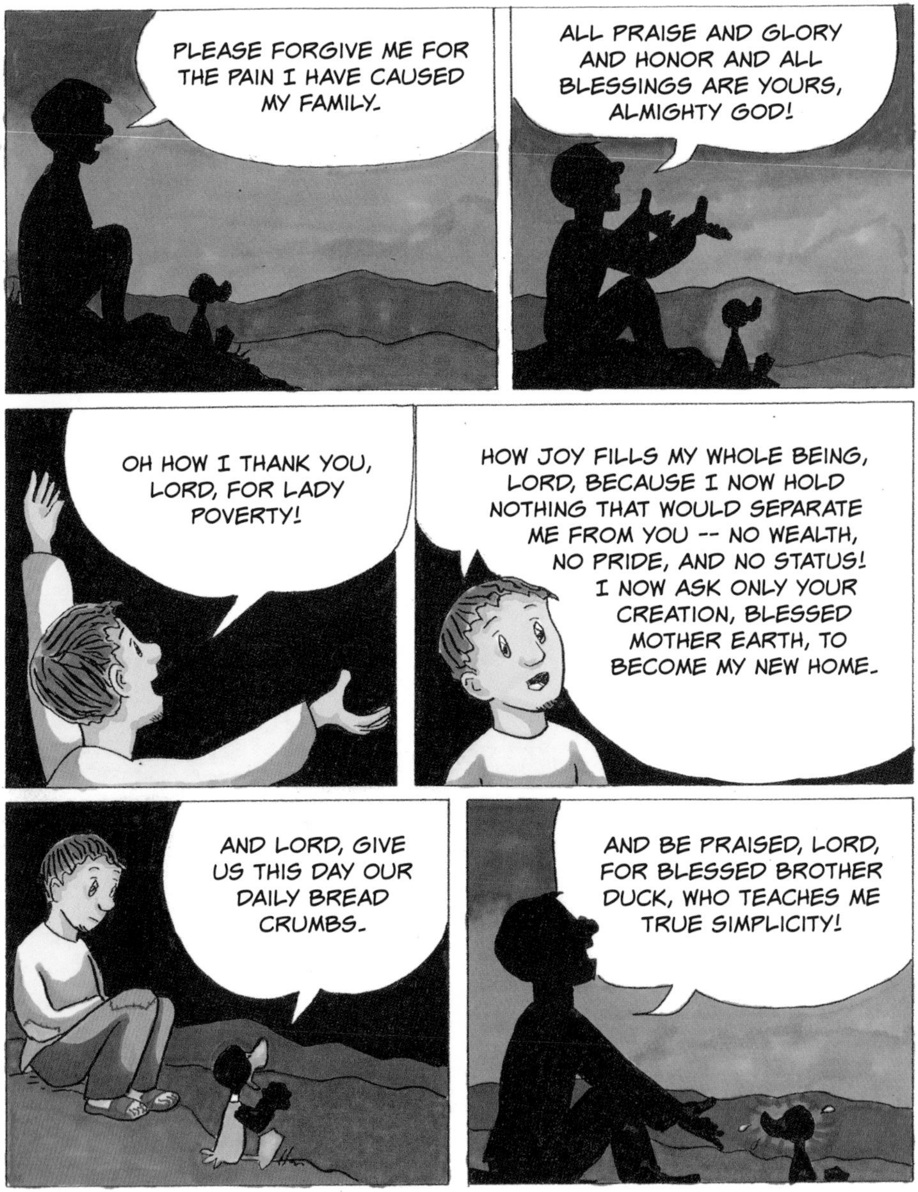
PLEASE FORGIVE ME FOR THE PAIN I HAVE CAUSED MY FAMILY.
ALL PRAISE AND GLORY AND HONOR AND ALL BLESSINGS ARE YOURS, ALMIGHTY GOD!
OH HOW I THANK YOU, LORD, FOR LADY POVERTY!
HOW JOY FILLS MY WHOLE BEING, LORD, BECAUSE I NOW HOLD NOTHING THAT WOULD SEPARATE ME FROM YOU -- NO WEALTH, NO PRIDE, AND NO STATUS! I NOW ASK ONLY YOUR CREATION, BLESSED MOTHER EARTH, TO BECOME MY NEW HOME.
AND LORD, GIVE US THIS DAY OUR DAILY BREAD CRUMBS.
AND BE PRAISED, LORD, FOR BLESSED BROTHER DUCK, WHO TEACHES ME TRUE SIMPLICITY!

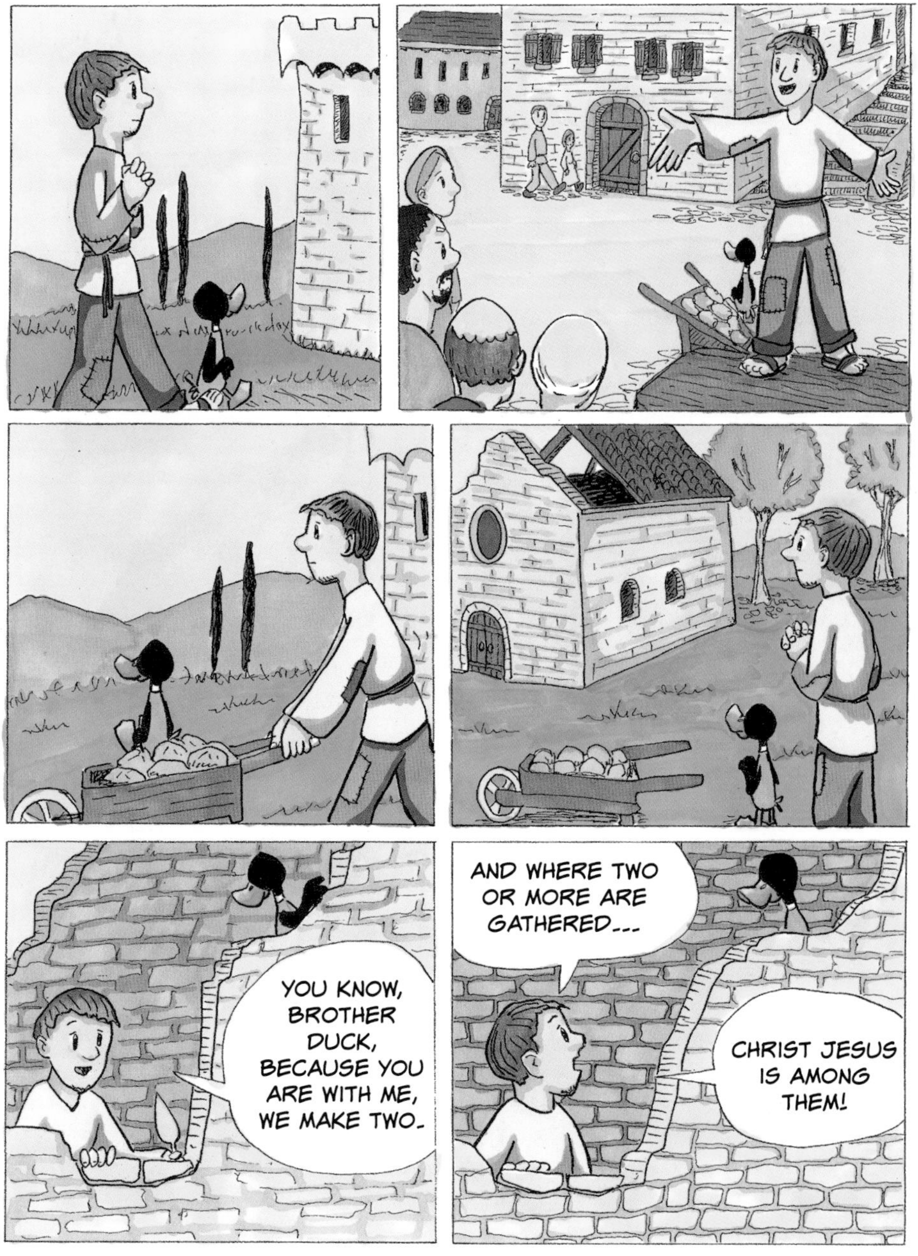
YOU KNOW, BROTHER DUCK, BECAUSE YOU ARE WITH ME, WE MAKE TWO.
AND WHERE TWO OR MORE ARE GATHERED...
CHRIST JESUS IS AMONG THEM!

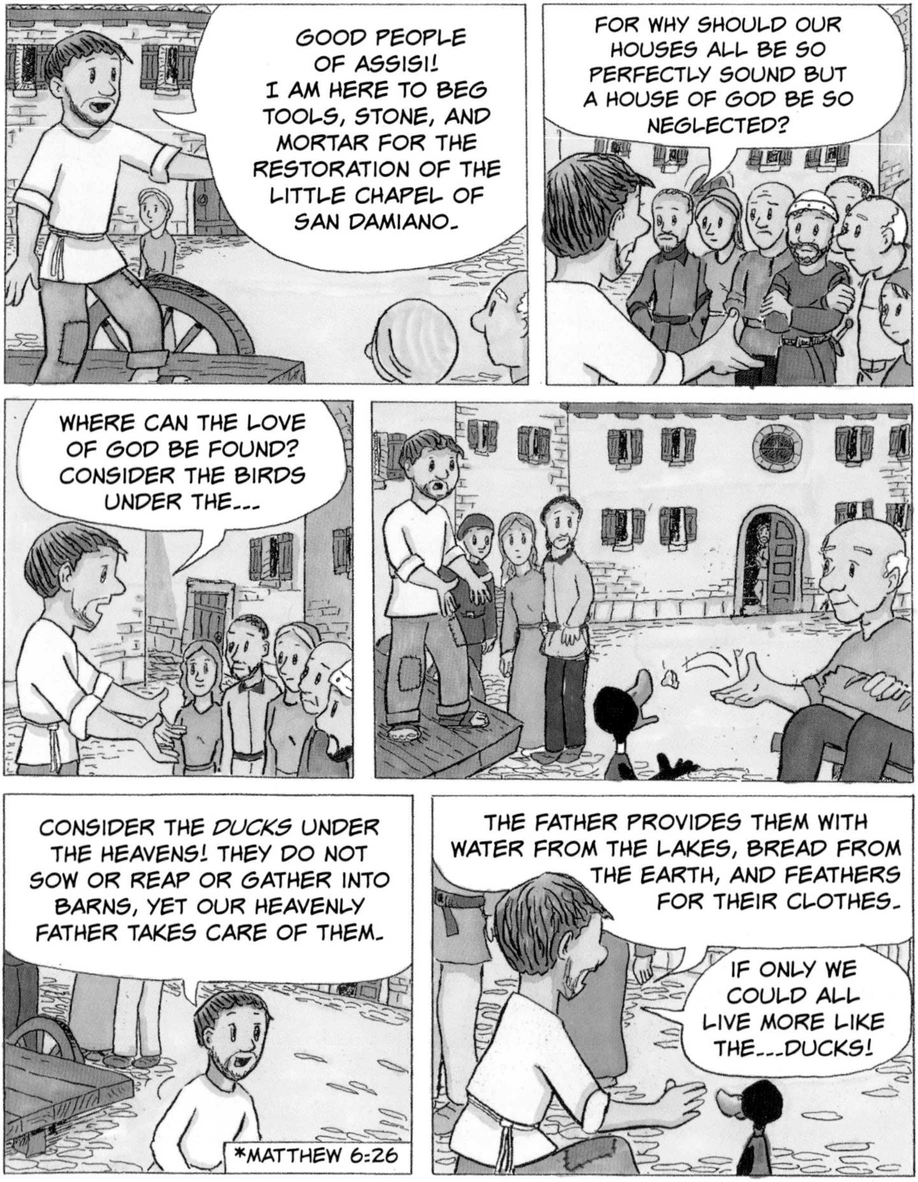
GOOD PEOPLE OF ASSISI! I AM HERE TO BEG TOOLS, STONE, AND MORTAR FOR THE RESTORATION OF THE LITTLE CHAPEL OF SAN DAMIANO.
FOR WHY SHOULD OUR HOUSES ALL BE SO PERFECTLY SOUND BUT A HOUSE OF GOD BE SO NEGLECTED?
WHERE CAN THE LOVE OF GOD BE FOUND? CONSIDER THE BIRDS UNDER THE...
CONSIDER THE *DUCKS* UNDER THE HEAVENS! THEY DO NOT SOW OR REAP OR GATHER INTO BARNS, YET OUR HEAVENLY FATHER TAKES CARE OF THEM.
*MATTHEW 6:26
THE FATHER PROVIDES THEM WITH WATER FROM THE LAKES, BREAD FROM THE EARTH, AND FEATHERS FOR THEIR CLOTHES.
IF ONLY WE COULD ALL LIVE MORE LIKE THE...DUCKS!

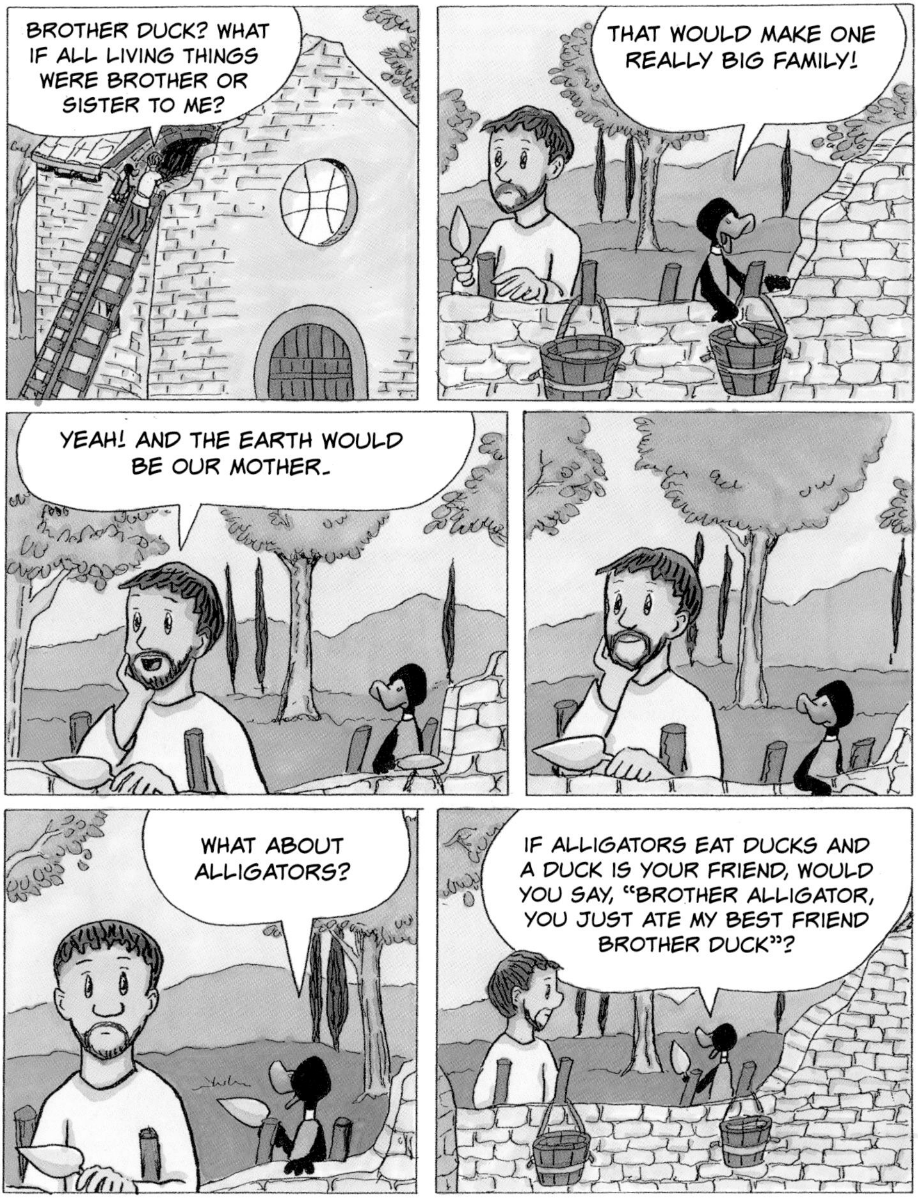
BROTHER DUCK? WHAT IF ALL LIVING THINGS WERE BROTHER OR SISTER TO ME?
THAT WOULD MAKE ONE REALLY BIG FAMILY!
YEAH! AND THE EARTH WOULD BE OUR MOTHER.
WHAT ABOUT ALLIGATORS?
IF ALLIGATORS EAT DUCKS AND A DUCK IS YOUR FRIEND, WOULD YOU SAY, "BROTHER ALLIGATOR, YOU JUST ATE MY BEST FRIEND BROTHER DUCK"?

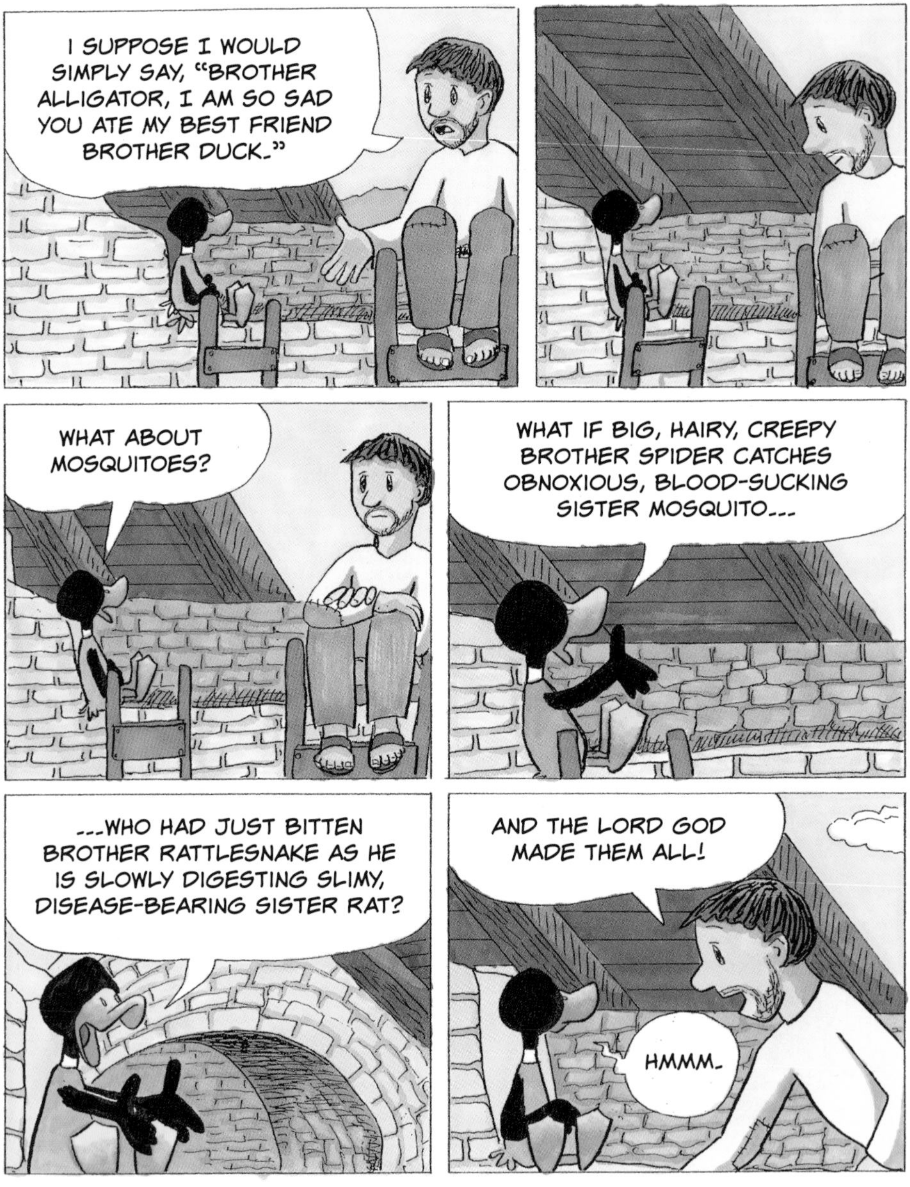
I SUPPOSE I WOULD SIMPLY SAY, "BROTHER ALLIGATOR, I AM SO SAD YOU ATE MY BEST FRIEND BROTHER DUCK."
WHAT ABOUT MOSQUITOES?
WHAT IF BIG, HAIRY, CREEPY BROTHER SPIDER CATCHES OBNOXIOUS, BLOOD-SUCKING SISTER MOSQUITO...
...WHO HAD JUST BITTEN BROTHER RATTLESNAKE AS HE IS SLOWLY DIGESTING SLIMY, DISEASE-BEARING SISTER RAT?
AND THE LORD GOD MADE THEM ALL!
HMMM.

CHAPTER 3

THE FIRST FOLLOWERS OF FRANCIS

For I know well the plans
I have in mind for you, says the Lord
Plans for your welfare, not for woe!
Plans to give you a future full of hope
When you call me, when you go to pray,
I will listen to you.
—JEREMIAH 29:11-12

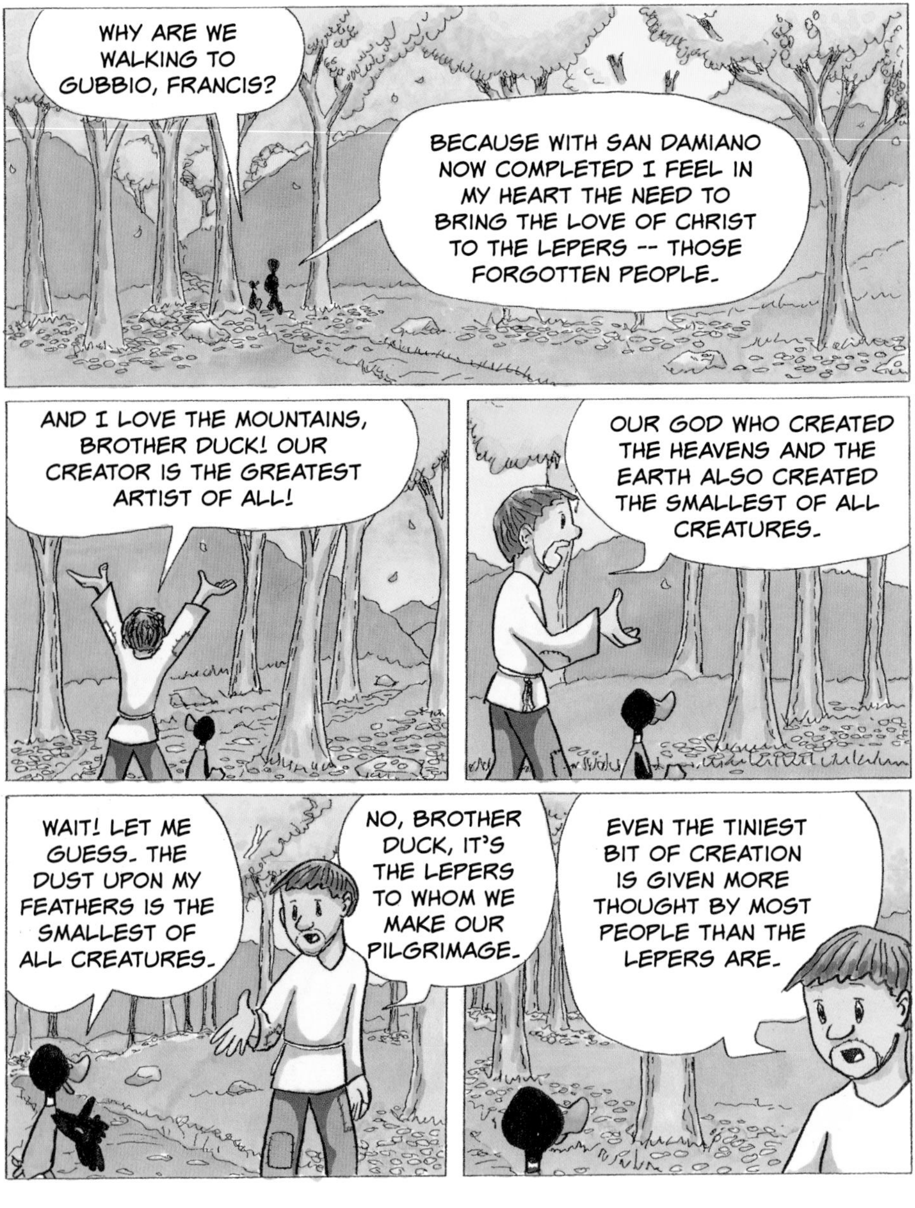
WHY ARE WE WALKING TO GUBBIO, FRANCIS?
BECAUSE WITH SAN DAMIANO NOW COMPLETED I FEEL IN MY HEART THE NEED TO BRING THE LOVE OF CHRIST TO THE LEPERS -- THOSE FORGOTTEN PEOPLE.
AND I LOVE THE MOUNTAINS, BROTHER DUCK! OUR CREATOR IS THE GREATEST ARTIST OF ALL!
OUR GOD WHO CREATED THE HEAVENS AND THE EARTH ALSO CREATED THE SMALLEST OF ALL CREATURES.
WAIT! LET ME GUESS. THE DUST UPON MY FEATHERS IS THE SMALLEST OF ALL CREATURES.
NO, BROTHER DUCK, IT'S THE LEPERS TO WHOM WE MAKE OUR PILGRIMAGE.
EVEN THE TINIEST BIT OF CREATION IS GIVEN MORE THOUGHT BY MOST PEOPLE THAN THE LEPERS ARE.

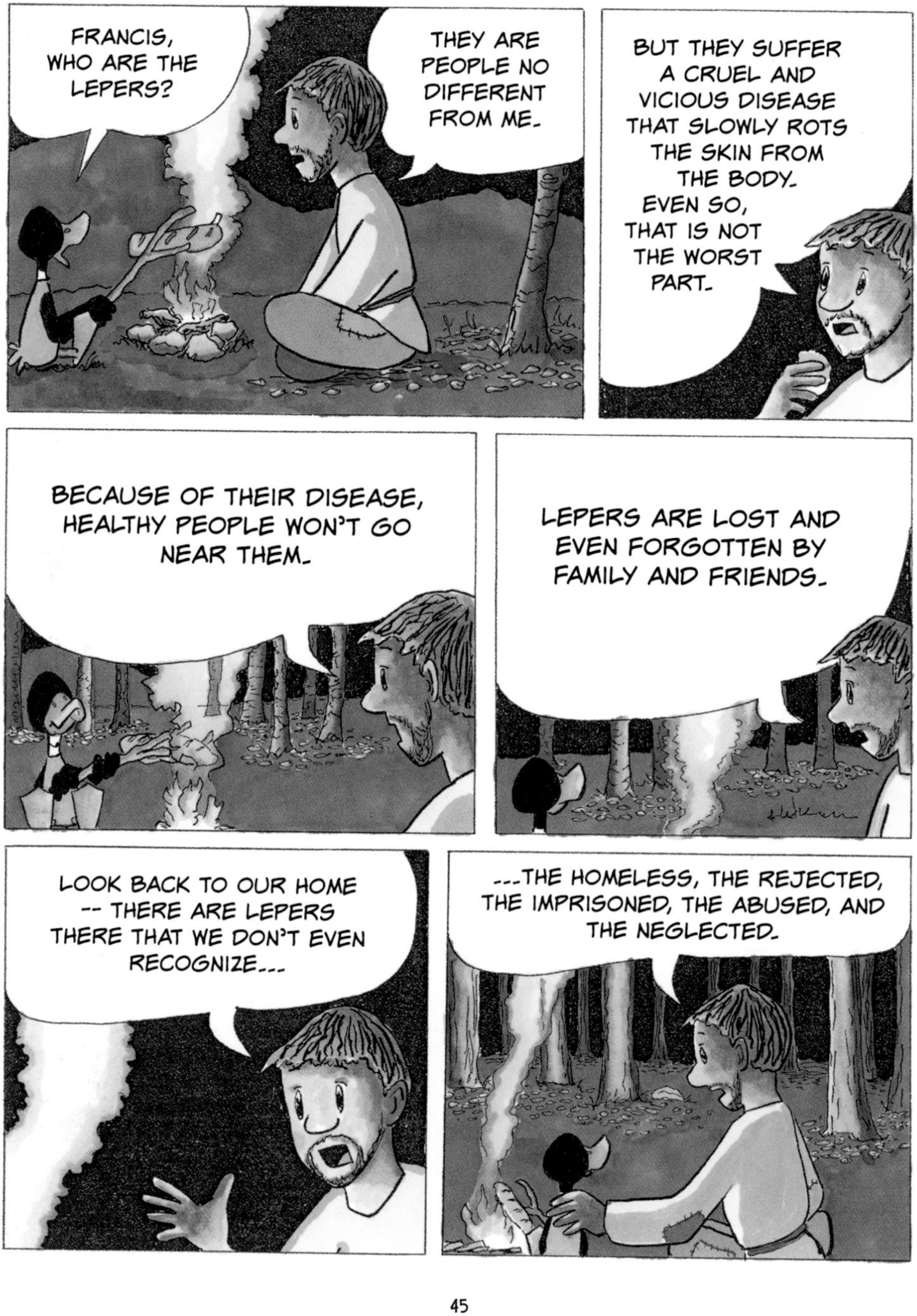
FRANCIS, WHO ARE THE LEPERS?
THEY ARE PEOPLE NO DIFFERENT FROM ME.
BUT THEY SUFFER A CRUEL AND VICIOUS DISEASE THAT SLOWLY ROTS THE SKIN FROM THE BODY. EVEN SO, THAT IS NOT THE WORST PART.
BECAUSE OF THEIR DISEASE, HEALTHY PEOPLE WON'T GO NEAR THEM.
LEPERS ARE LOST AND EVEN FORGOTTEN BY FAMILY AND FRIENDS.
LOOK BACK TO OUR HOME -- THERE ARE LEPERS THERE THAT WE DON'T EVEN RECOGNIZE...
...THE HOMELESS, THE REJECTED, THE IMPRISONED, THE ABUSED, AND THE NEGLECTED.

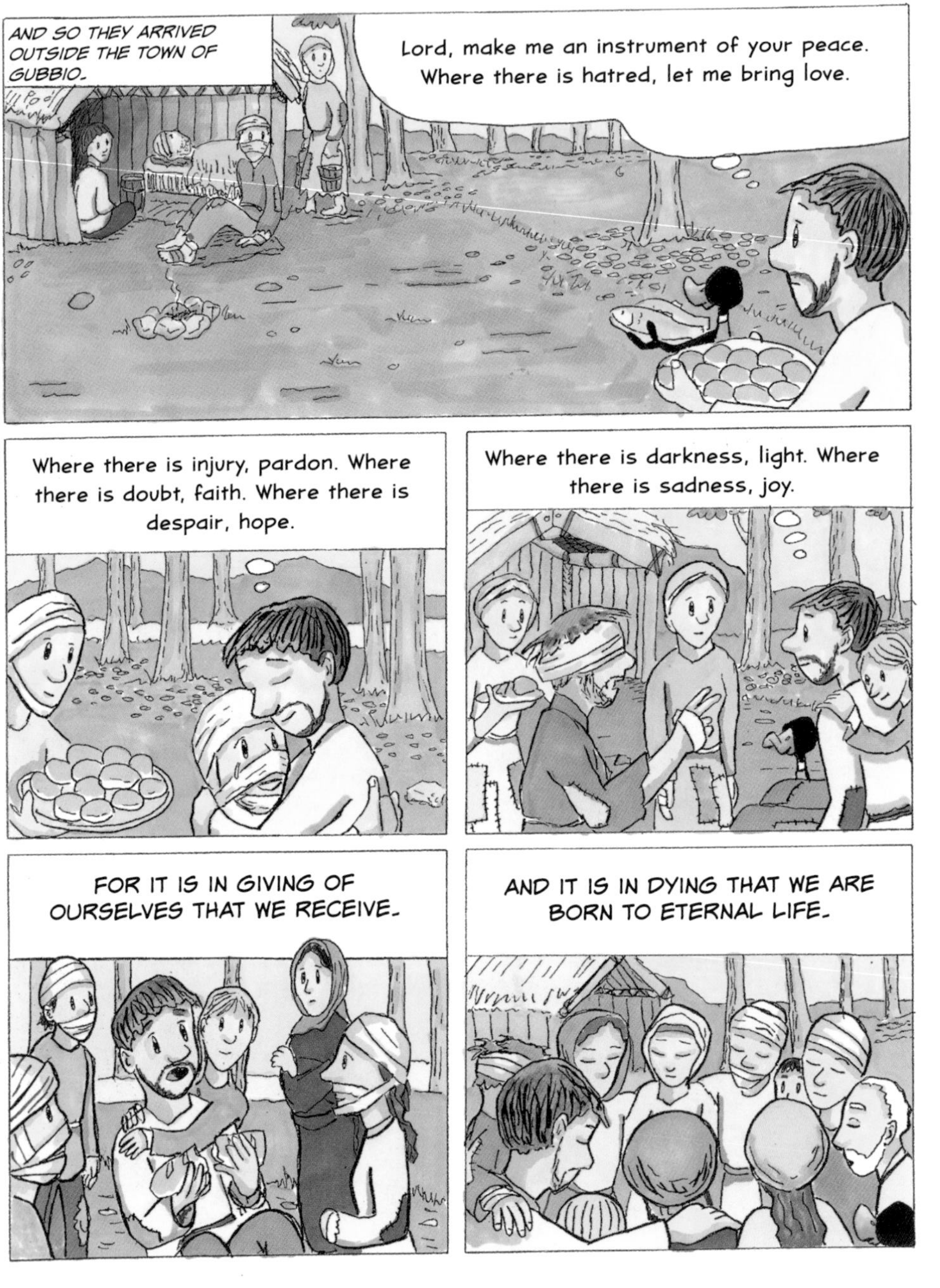
AND SO THEY ARRIVED OUTSIDE THE TOWN OF GUBBIO.
Lord, make me an instrument of your peace. Where there is hatred, let me bring love.
Where there is injury, pardon. Where there is doubt, faith. Where there is despair, hope.
Where there is darkness, light. Where there is sadness, joy.
FOR IT IS IN GIVING OF OURSELVES THAT WE RECEIVE.
AND IT IS IN DYING THAT WE ARE BORN TO ETERNAL LIFE.

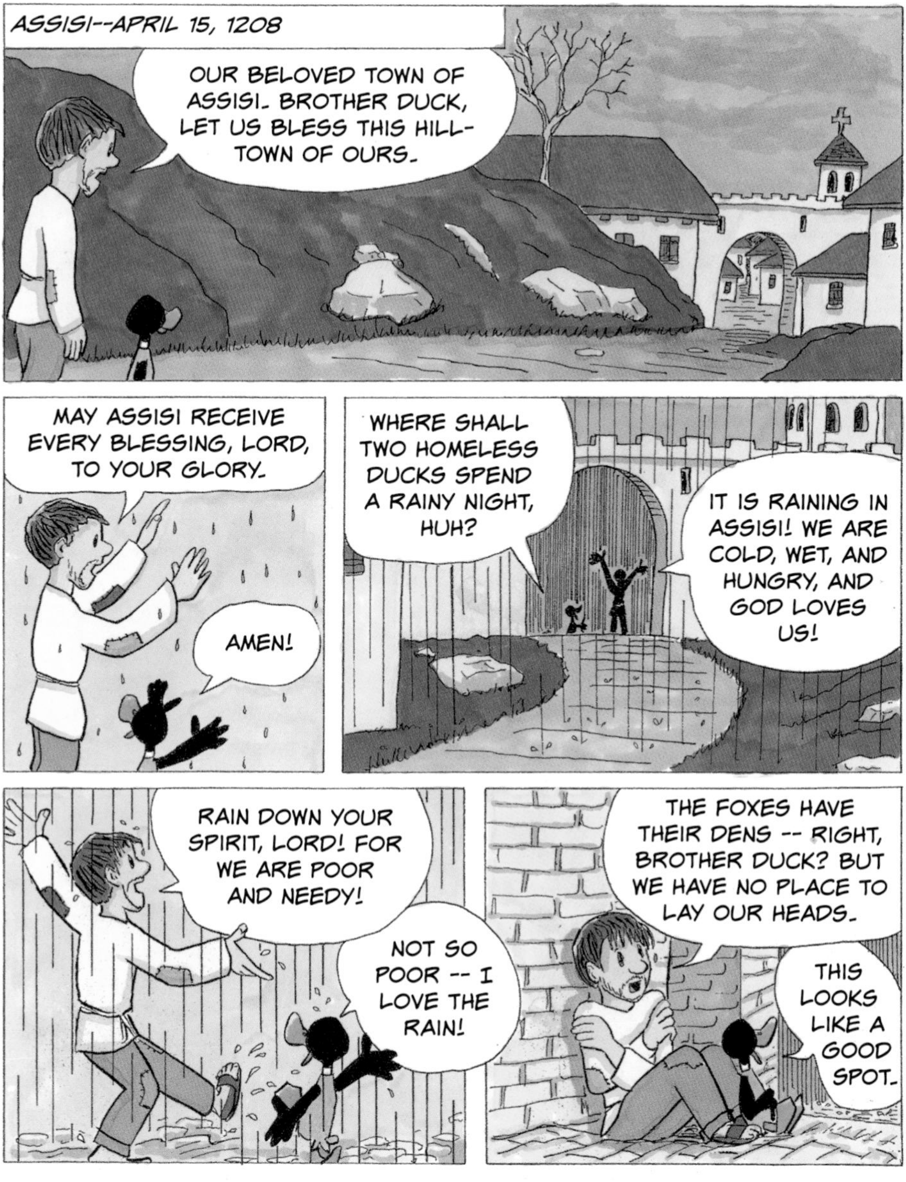
ASSISI--APRIL 15, 1208
OUR BELOVED TOWN OF ASSISI. BROTHER DUCK, LET US BLESS THIS HILL-TOWN OF OURS.
MAY ASSISI RECEIVE EVERY BLESSING, LORD, TO YOUR GLORY.
AMEN!
WHERE SHALL TWO HOMELESS DUCKS SPEND A RAINY NIGHT, HUH?
IT IS RAINING IN ASSISI! WE ARE COLD, WET, AND HUNGRY, AND GOD LOVES US!
RAIN DOWN YOUR SPIRIT, LORD! FOR WE ARE POOR AND NEEDY!
NOT SO POOR -- I LOVE THE RAIN!
THE FOXES HAVE THEIR DENS -- RIGHT, BROTHER DUCK? BUT WE HAVE NO PLACE TO LAY OUR HEADS.
THIS LOOKS LIKE A GOOD SPOT.

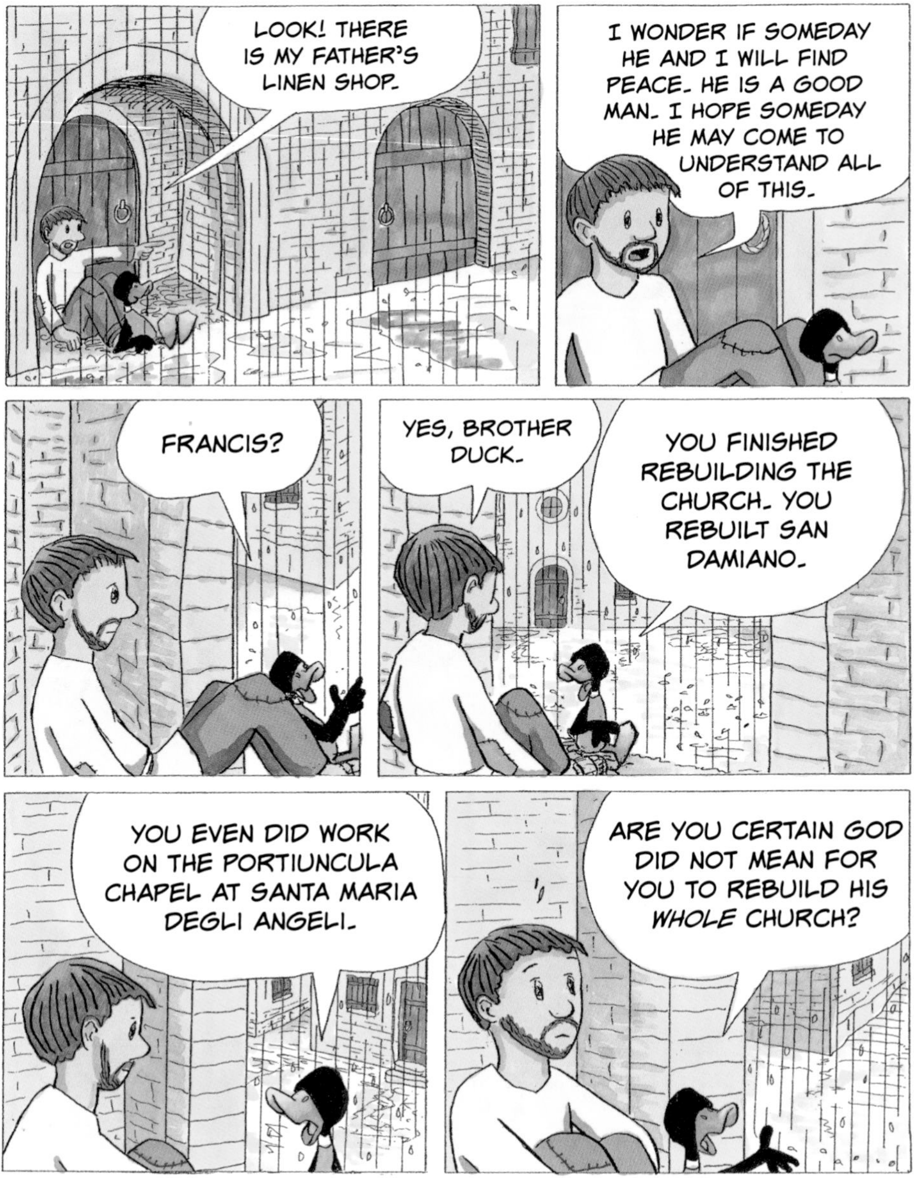
LOOK! THERE IS MY FATHER'S LINEN SHOP.
I WONDER IF SOMEDAY HE AND I WILL FIND PEACE. HE IS A GOOD MAN. I HOPE SOMEDAY HE MAY COME TO UNDERSTAND ALL OF THIS.
FRANCIS?
YES, BROTHER DUCK.
YOU FINISHED REBUILDING THE CHURCH. YOU REBUILT SAN DAMIANO.
YOU EVEN DID WORK ON THE PORTIUNCULA CHAPEL AT SANTA MARIA DEGLI ANGELI.
ARE YOU CERTAIN GOD DID NOT MEAN FOR YOU TO REBUILD HIS *WHOLE* CHURCH?

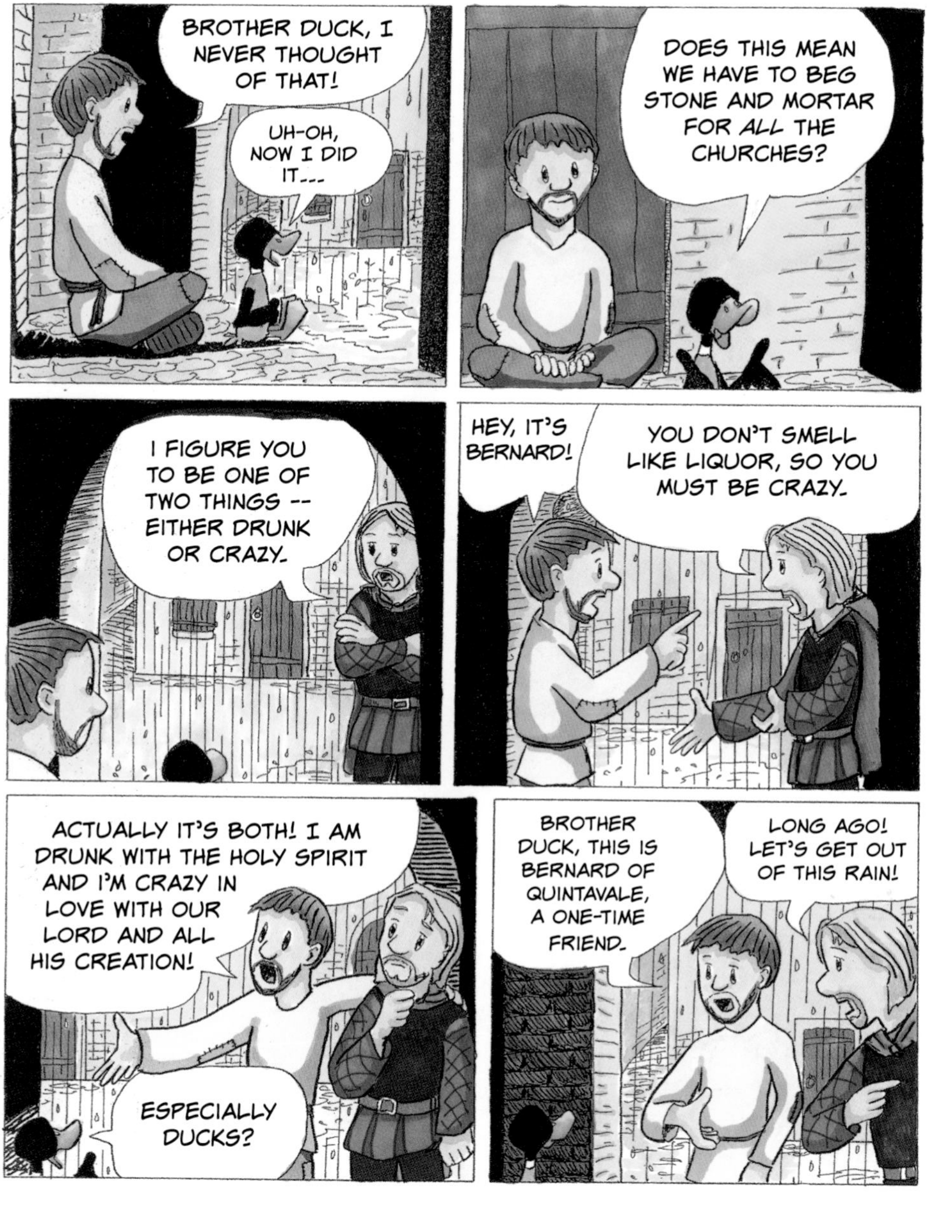
BROTHER DUCK, I NEVER THOUGHT OF THAT!
UH-OH, NOW I DID IT...
DOES THIS MEAN WE HAVE TO BEG STONE AND MORTAR FOR *ALL* THE CHURCHES?
I FIGURE YOU TO BE ONE OF TWO THINGS -- EITHER DRUNK OR CRAZY.
HEY, IT'S BERNARD!
YOU DON'T SMELL LIKE LIQUOR, SO YOU MUST BE CRAZY.
ACTUALLY IT'S BOTH! I AM DRUNK WITH THE HOLY SPIRIT AND I'M CRAZY IN LOVE WITH OUR LORD AND ALL HIS CREATION!
ESPECIALLY DUCKS?
BROTHER DUCK, THIS IS BERNARD OF QUINTAVALE, A ONE-TIME FRIEND.
LONG AGO! LET'S GET OUT OF THIS RAIN!

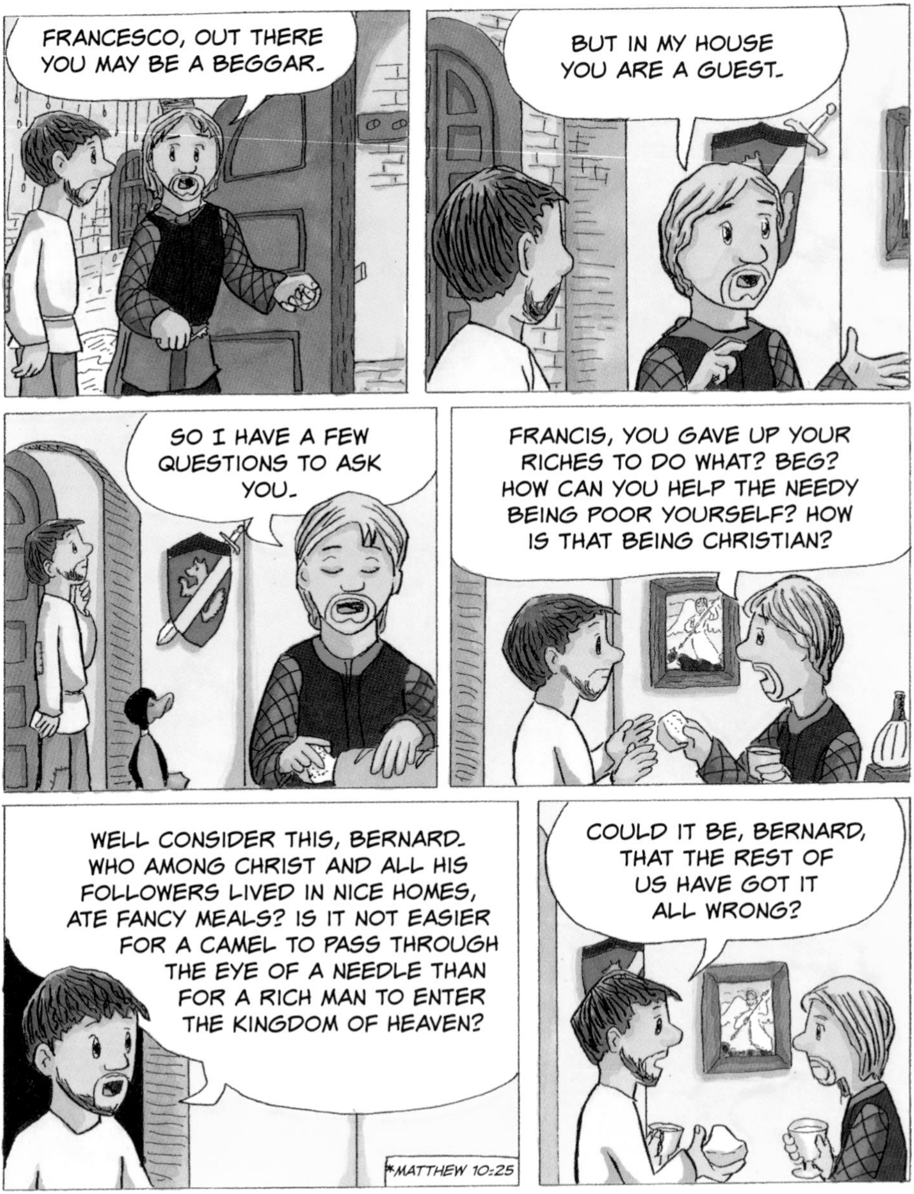
FRANCESCO, OUT THERE YOU MAY BE A BEGGAR.
BUT IN MY HOUSE YOU ARE A GUEST.
SO I HAVE A FEW QUESTIONS TO ASK YOU.
FRANCIS, YOU GAVE UP YOUR RICHES TO DO WHAT? BEG? HOW CAN YOU HELP THE NEEDY BEING POOR YOURSELF? HOW IS THAT BEING CHRISTIAN?
WELL CONSIDER THIS, BERNARD. WHO AMONG CHRIST AND ALL HIS FOLLOWERS LIVED IN NICE HOMES, ATE FANCY MEALS? IS IT NOT EASIER FOR A CAMEL TO PASS THROUGH THE EYE OF A NEEDLE THAN FOR A RICH MAN TO ENTER THE KINGDOM OF HEAVEN?
*MATTHEW 10:25
COULD IT BE, BERNARD, THAT THE REST OF US HAVE GOT IT ALL WRONG?

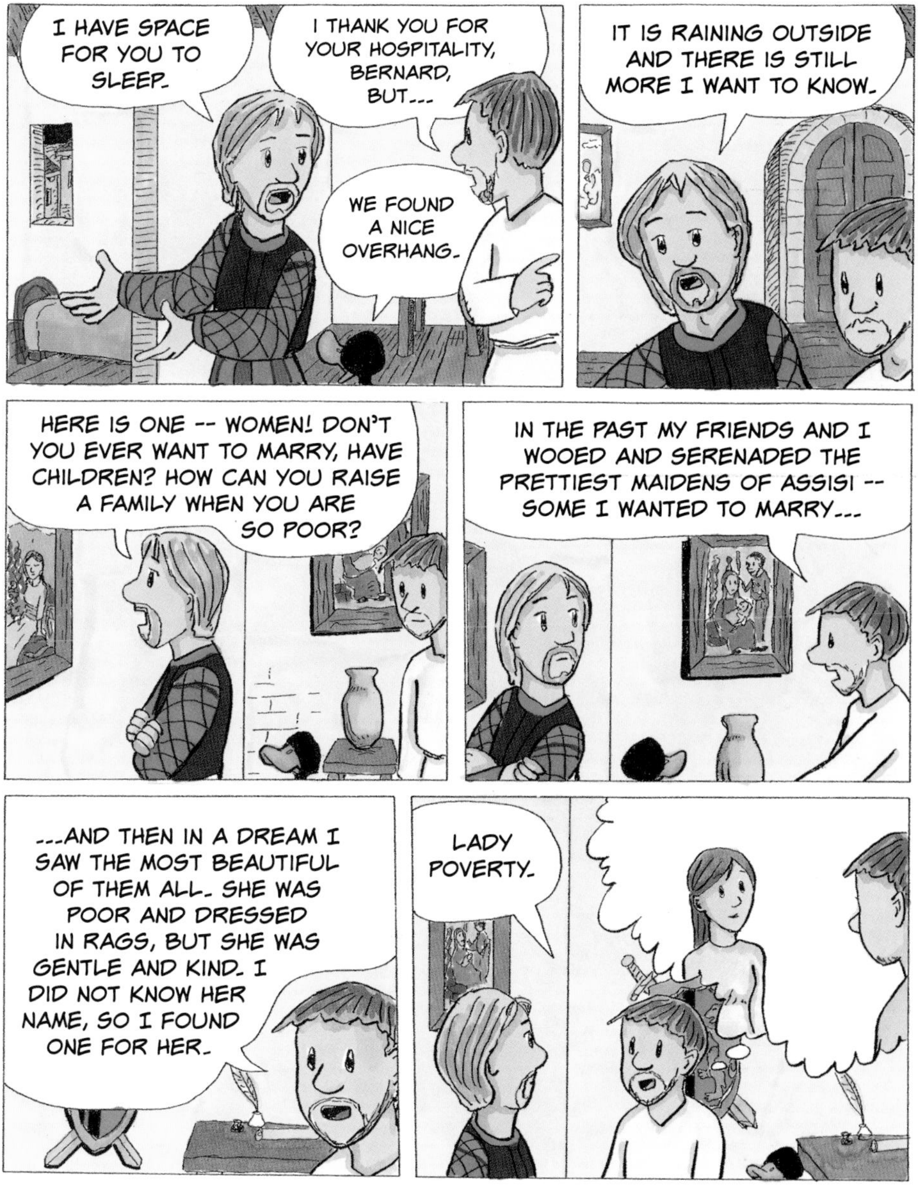
I HAVE SPACE FOR YOU TO SLEEP.
I THANK YOU FOR YOUR HOSPITALITY, BERNARD, BUT...
WE FOUND A NICE OVERHANG.
IT IS RAINING OUTSIDE AND THERE IS STILL MORE I WANT TO KNOW.
HERE IS ONE -- WOMEN! DON'T YOU EVER WANT TO MARRY, HAVE CHILDREN? HOW CAN YOU RAISE A FAMILY WHEN YOU ARE SO POOR?
IN THE PAST MY FRIENDS AND I WOOED AND SERENADED THE PRETTIEST MAIDENS OF ASSISI -- SOME I WANTED TO MARRY...
...AND THEN IN A DREAM I SAW THE MOST BEAUTIFUL OF THEM ALL. SHE WAS POOR AND DRESSED IN RAGS, BUT SHE WAS GENTLE AND KIND. I DID NOT KNOW HER NAME, SO I FOUND ONE FOR HER.
LADY POVERTY.

LADY POVERTY? SHE IS FROM A DREAM, FRANCESCO, SHE'S NOT REAL.

SHE IS MORE REAL, BERNARD, THAN EVEN YOU OR ME. SHE TEACHES US THE WISDOM THAT JOY CAN ONLY COME FROM CARRYING NOTHING THAT WOULD KEEP US FROM OUR FATHER'S LOVE. FOR POSSESSING NOTHING WE BELONG ENTIRELY TO GOD.

*FROM SACRUM COMMERCIUM, THE ROMANCE OF ST. FRANCIS TO LADY POVERTY.

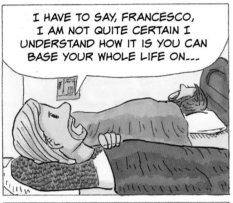

I HAVE TO SAY, FRANCESCO, I AM NOT QUITE CERTAIN I UNDERSTAND HOW IT IS YOU CAN BASE YOUR WHOLE LIFE ON...

WELL I AM AMAZED -- ASLEEP ALREADY.

NNNNNNNN

SOMETIME LATER THAT NIGHT...

?

...GOD...
AND...
ALL...

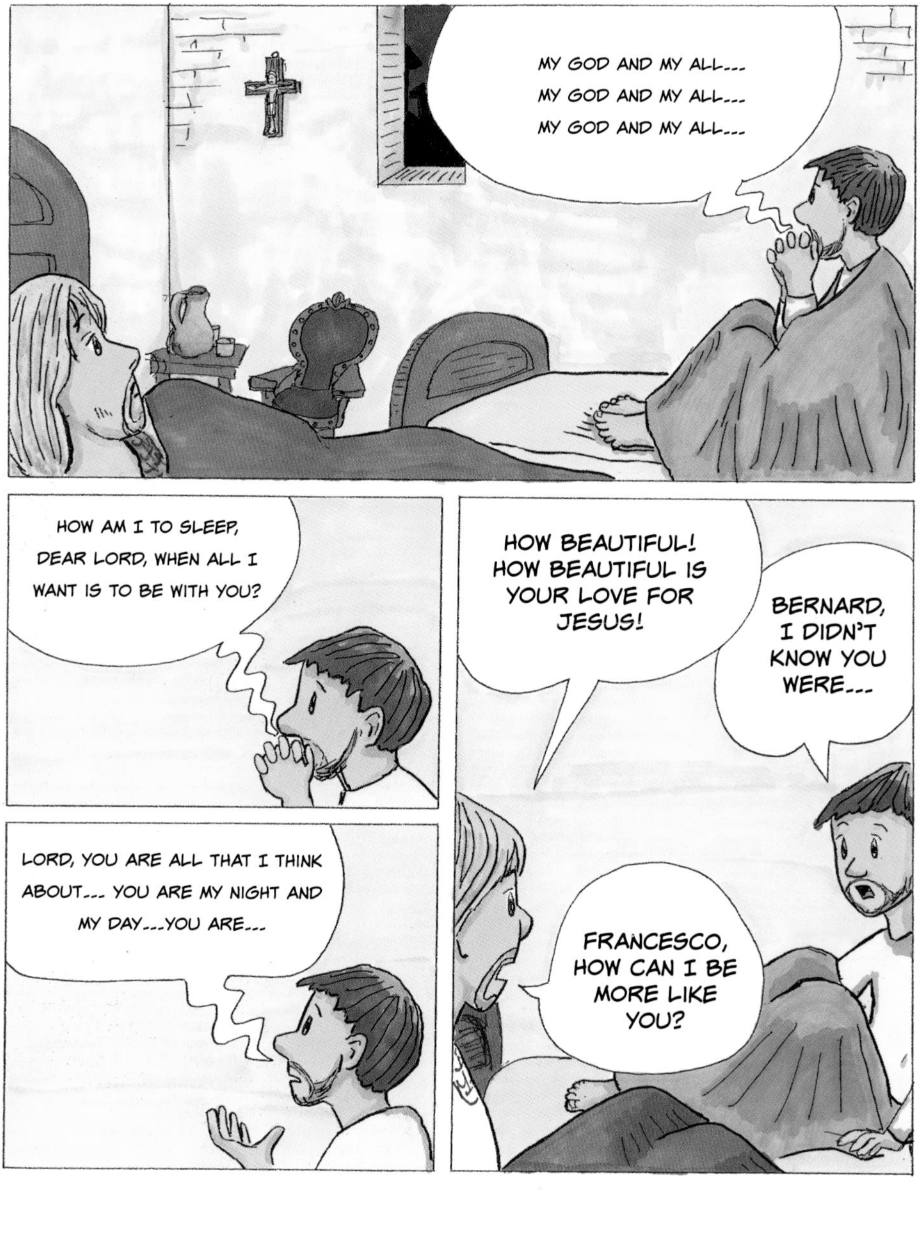
MY GOD AND MY ALL...
MY GOD AND MY ALL...
MY GOD AND MY ALL...
HOW AM I TO SLEEP, DEAR LORD, WHEN ALL I WANT IS TO BE WITH YOU?
LORD, YOU ARE ALL THAT I THINK ABOUT... YOU ARE MY NIGHT AND MY DAY...YOU ARE...
HOW BEAUTIFUL! HOW BEAUTIFUL IS YOUR LOVE FOR JESUS!
BERNARD, I DIDN'T KNOW YOU WERE...
FRANCESCO, HOW CAN I BE MORE LIKE YOU?

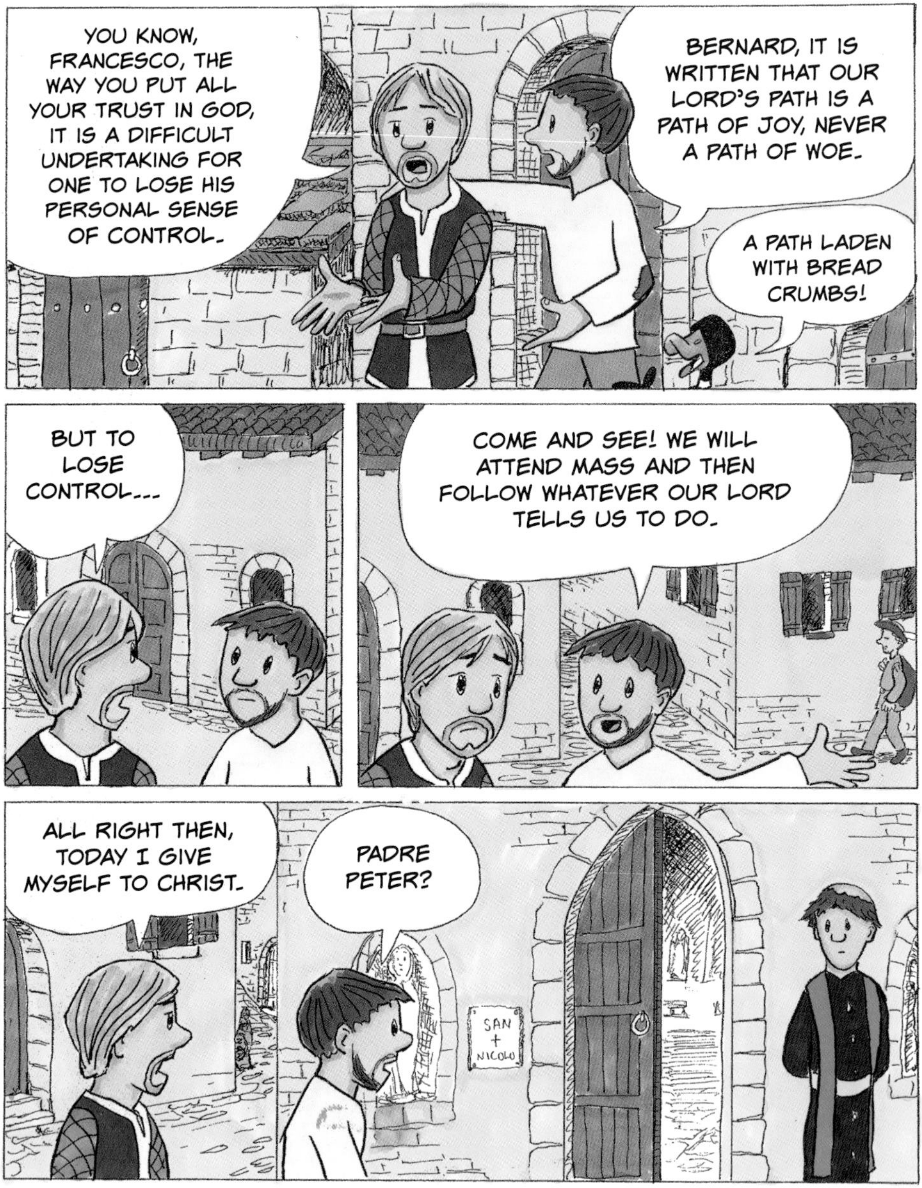
YOU KNOW, FRANCESCO, THE WAY YOU PUT ALL YOUR TRUST IN GOD, IT IS A DIFFICULT UNDERTAKING FOR ONE TO LOSE HIS PERSONAL SENSE OF CONTROL.
BERNARD, IT IS WRITTEN THAT OUR LORD'S PATH IS A PATH OF JOY, NEVER A PATH OF WOE.
A PATH LADEN WITH BREAD CRUMBS!
BUT TO LOSE CONTROL...
COME AND SEE! WE WILL ATTEND MASS AND THEN FOLLOW WHATEVER OUR LORD TELLS US TO DO.
ALL RIGHT THEN, TODAY I GIVE MYSELF TO CHRIST.
PADRE PETER?
SAN + NICOLO

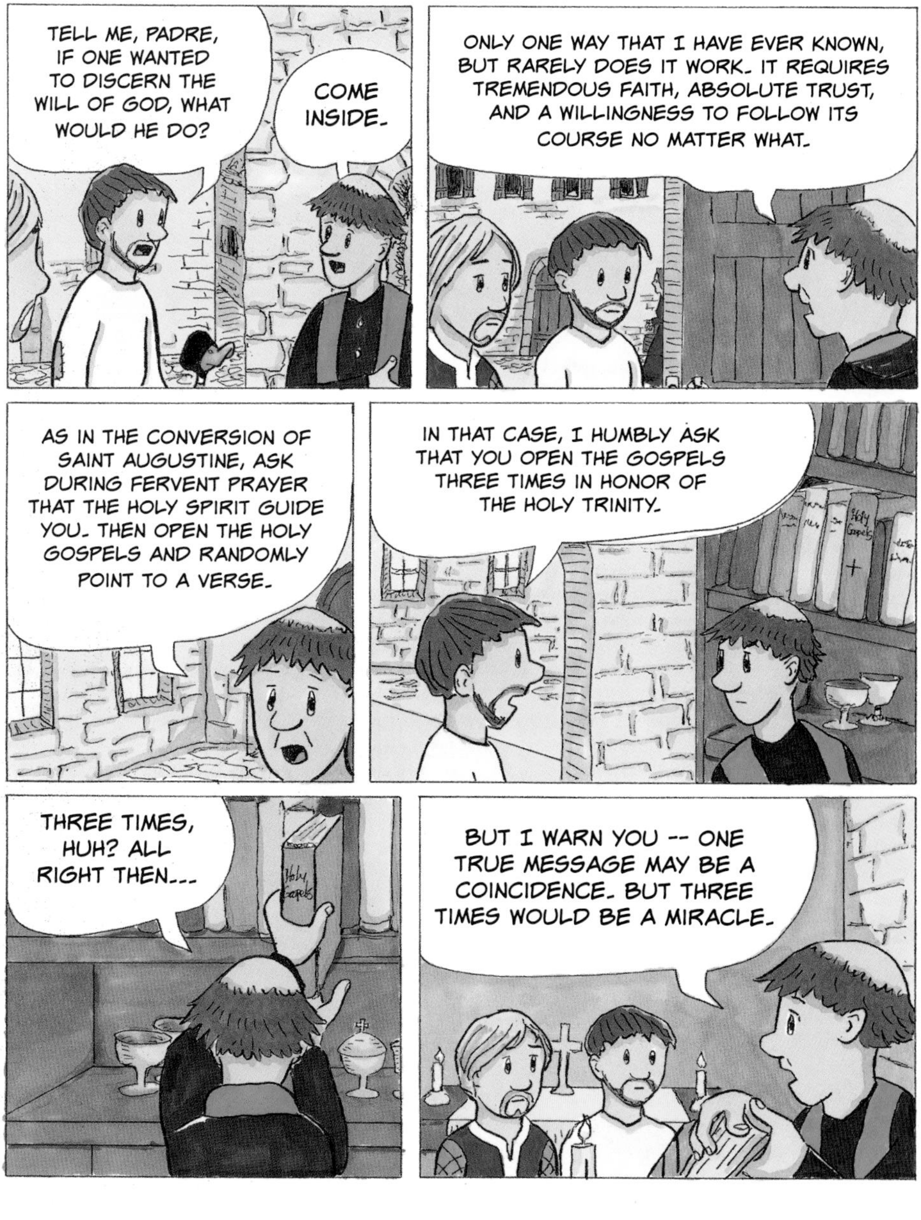
TELL ME, PADRE, IF ONE WANTED TO DISCERN THE WILL OF GOD, WHAT WOULD HE DO?
COME INSIDE.
ONLY ONE WAY THAT I HAVE EVER KNOWN, BUT RARELY DOES IT WORK. IT REQUIRES TREMENDOUS FAITH, ABSOLUTE TRUST, AND A WILLINGNESS TO FOLLOW ITS COURSE NO MATTER WHAT.
AS IN THE CONVERSION OF SAINT AUGUSTINE, ASK DURING FERVENT PRAYER THAT THE HOLY SPIRIT GUIDE YOU. THEN OPEN THE HOLY GOSPELS AND RANDOMLY POINT TO A VERSE.
IN THAT CASE, I HUMBLY ASK THAT YOU OPEN THE GOSPELS THREE TIMES IN HONOR OF THE HOLY TRINITY.
THREE TIMES, HUH? ALL RIGHT THEN...
Holy Gospels
BUT I WARN YOU -- ONE TRUE MESSAGE MAY BE A COINCIDENCE. BUT THREE TIMES WOULD BE A MIRACLE.

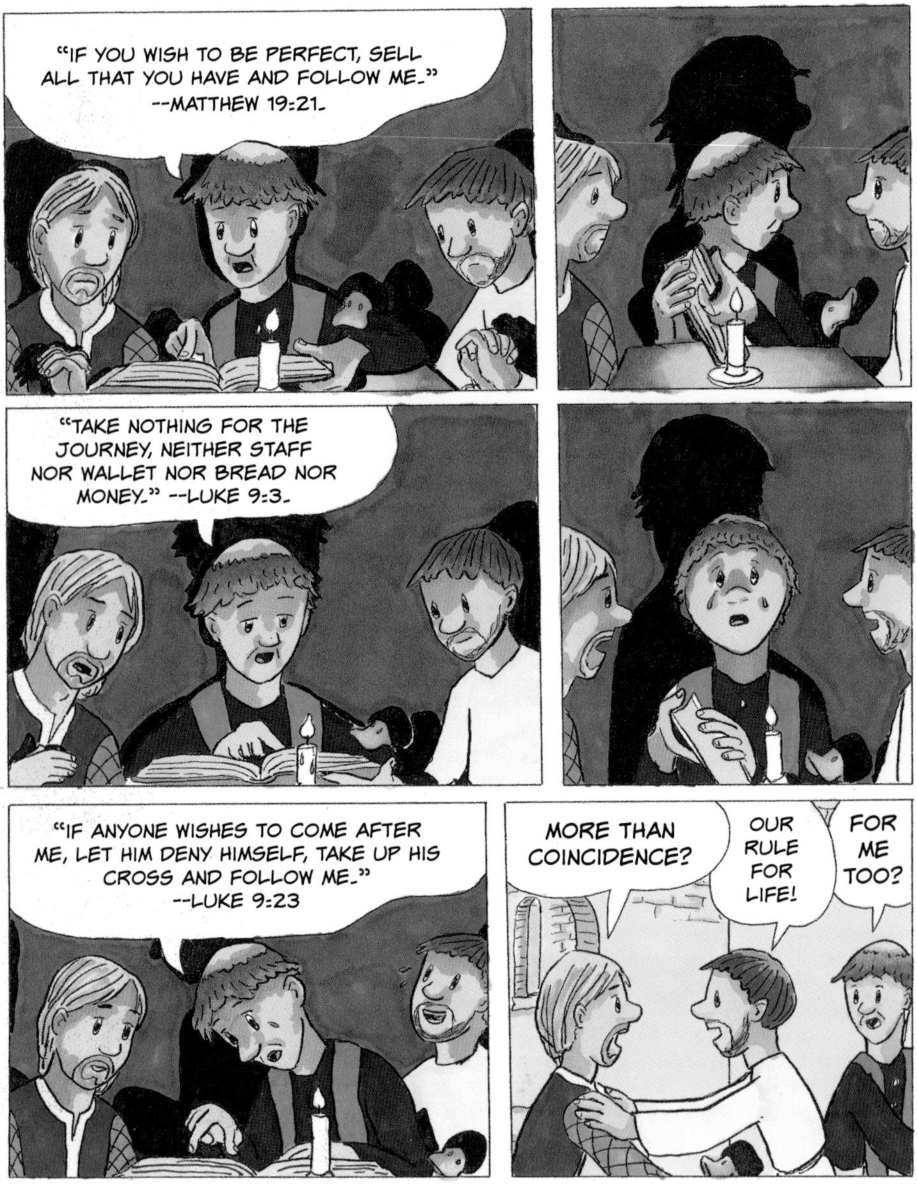
"IF YOU WISH TO BE PERFECT, SELL ALL THAT YOU HAVE AND FOLLOW ME." --MATTHEW 19:21.
"TAKE NOTHING FOR THE JOURNEY, NEITHER STAFF NOR WALLET NOR BREAD NOR MONEY." --LUKE 9:3.
"IF ANYONE WISHES TO COME AFTER ME, LET HIM DENY HIMSELF, TAKE UP HIS CROSS AND FOLLOW ME." --LUKE 9:23
MORE THAN COINCIDENCE?
OUR RULE FOR LIFE!
FOR ME TOO?

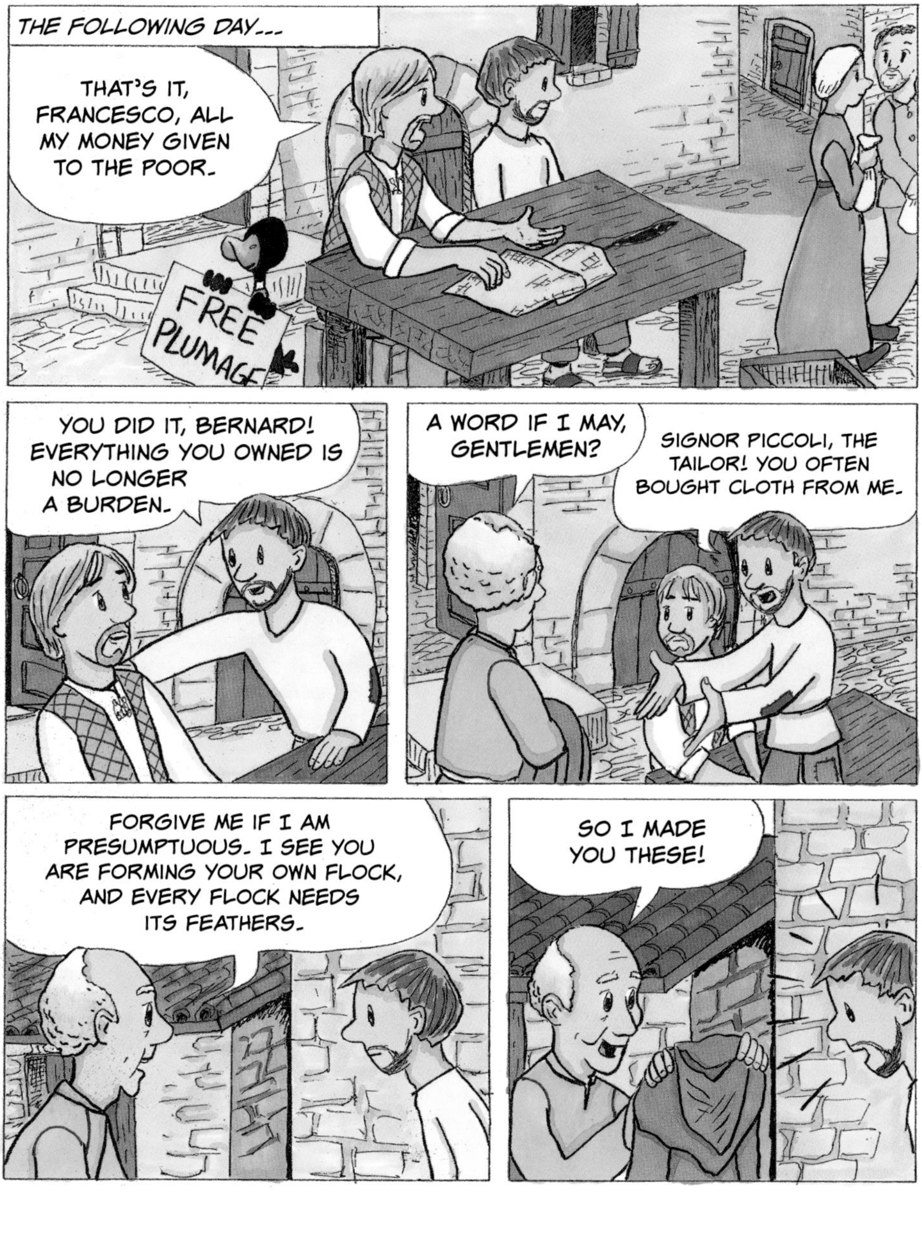
THE FOLLOWING DAY...
THAT'S IT, FRANCESCO, ALL MY MONEY GIVEN TO THE POOR.
FREE PLUMAGE
YOU DID IT, BERNARD! EVERYTHING YOU OWNED IS NO LONGER A BURDEN.
A WORD IF I MAY, GENTLEMEN?
SIGNOR PICCOLI, THE TAILOR! YOU OFTEN BOUGHT CLOTH FROM ME.
FORGIVE ME IF I AM PRESUMPTUOUS. I SEE YOU ARE FORMING YOUR OWN FLOCK, AND EVERY FLOCK NEEDS ITS FEATHERS.
SO I MADE YOU THESE!

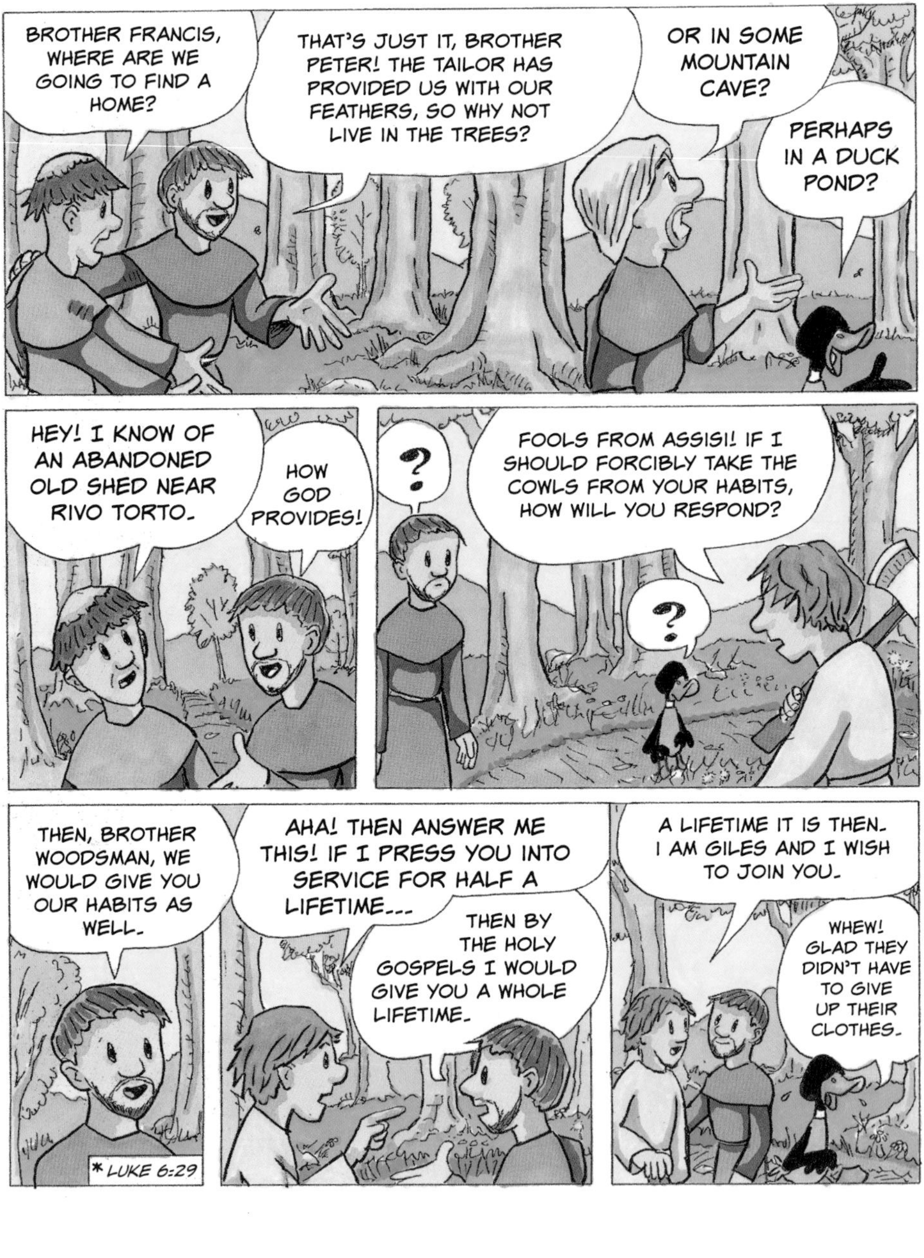
BROTHER FRANCIS, WHERE ARE WE GOING TO FIND A HOME?
THAT'S JUST IT, BROTHER PETER! THE TAILOR HAS PROVIDED US WITH OUR FEATHERS, SO WHY NOT LIVE IN THE TREES?
OR IN SOME MOUNTAIN CAVE?
PERHAPS IN A DUCK POND?
HEY! I KNOW OF AN ABANDONED OLD SHED NEAR RIVO TORTO.
HOW GOD PROVIDES!
?
FOOLS FROM ASSISI! IF I SHOULD FORCIBLY TAKE THE COWLS FROM YOUR HABITS, HOW WILL YOU RESPOND?
?
THEN, BROTHER WOODSMAN, WE WOULD GIVE YOU OUR HABITS AS WELL.
* LUKE 6:29
AHA! THEN ANSWER ME THIS! IF I PRESS YOU INTO SERVICE FOR HALF A LIFETIME...
THEN BY THE HOLY GOSPELS I WOULD GIVE YOU A WHOLE LIFETIME.
A LIFETIME IT IS THEN. I AM GILES AND I WISH TO JOIN YOU.
WHEW! GLAD THEY DIDN'T HAVE TO GIVE UP THEIR CLOTHES.

CHAPTER 4
FOLLOWERS OF THE WAY

Let the children come to me and do not prevent them;
For the Kingdom of God belongs to such as these.
Amen I say to you, whoever does not accept the Kingdom of God like a child
Will not enter it.
— LUKE 18:16-17

RIVO TORTO, NEAR ASSISI, 1210

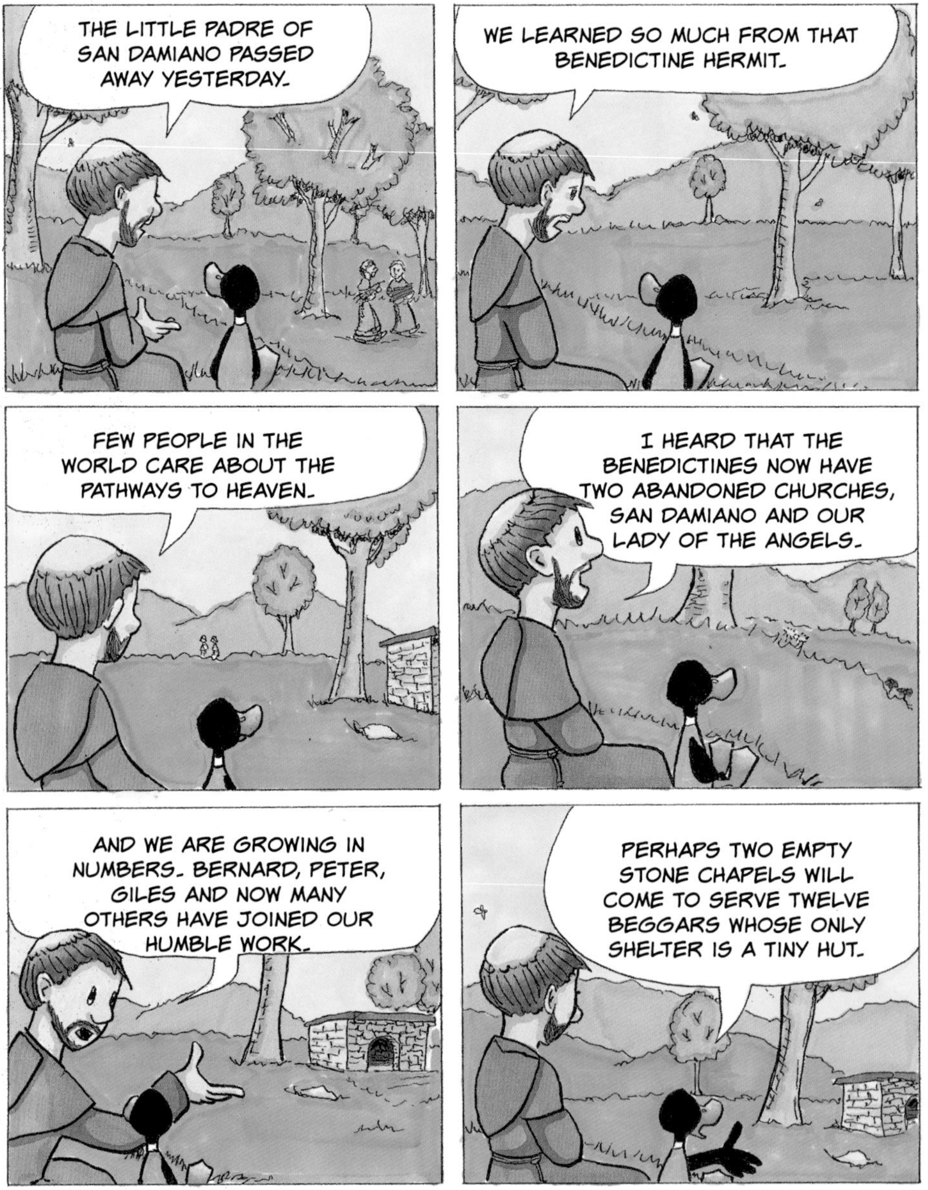
THE LITTLE PADRE OF SAN DAMIANO PASSED AWAY YESTERDAY.
WE LEARNED SO MUCH FROM THAT BENEDICTINE HERMIT.
FEW PEOPLE IN THE WORLD CARE ABOUT THE PATHWAYS TO HEAVEN.
I HEARD THAT THE BENEDICTINES NOW HAVE TWO ABANDONED CHURCHES, SAN DAMIANO AND OUR LADY OF THE ANGELS.
AND WE ARE GROWING IN NUMBERS. BERNARD, PETER, GILES AND NOW MANY OTHERS HAVE JOINED OUR HUMBLE WORK.
PERHAPS TWO EMPTY STONE CHAPELS WILL COME TO SERVE TWELVE BEGGARS WHOSE ONLY SHELTER IS A TINY HUT.

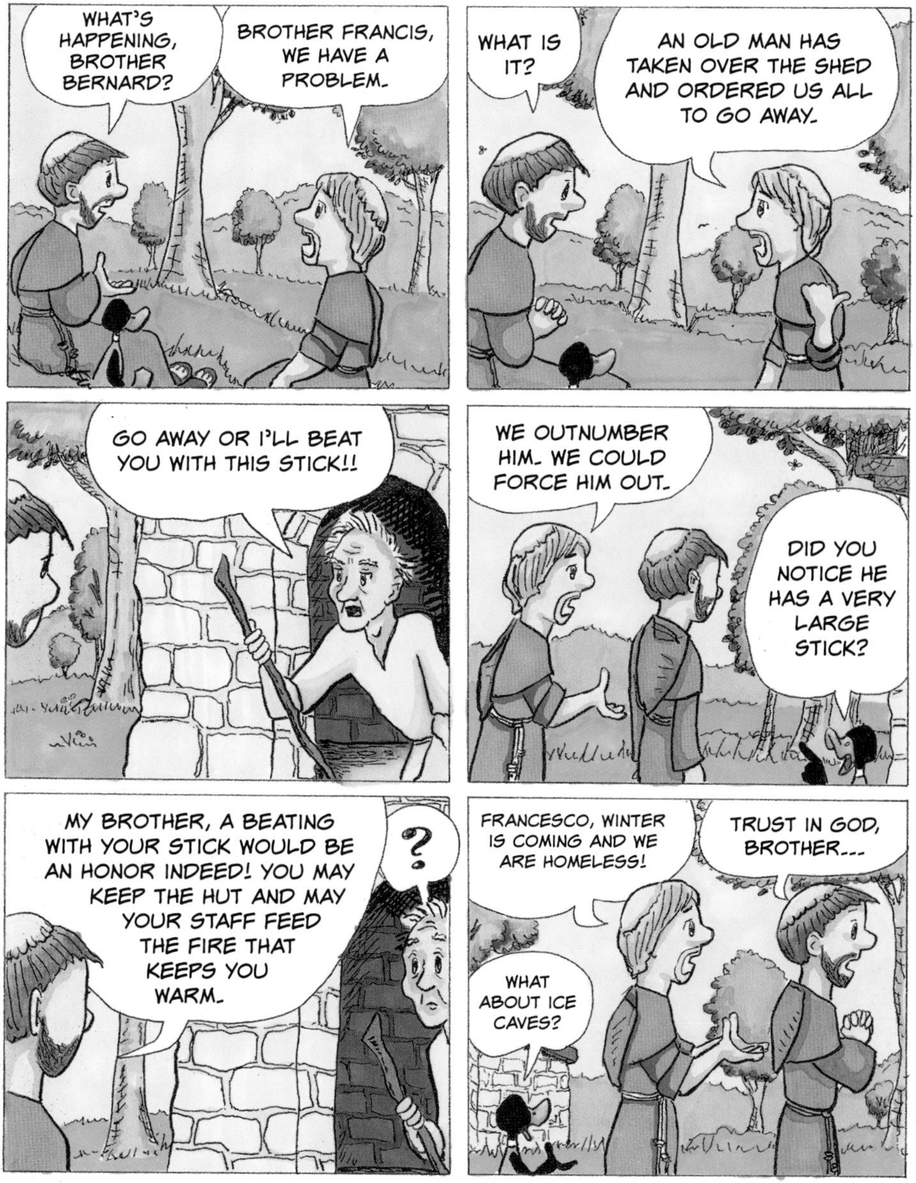
WHAT'S HAPPENING, BROTHER BERNARD?
BROTHER FRANCIS, WE HAVE A PROBLEM.
WHAT IS IT?
AN OLD MAN HAS TAKEN OVER THE SHED AND ORDERED US ALL TO GO AWAY.
GO AWAY OR I'LL BEAT YOU WITH THIS STICK!!
WE OUTNUMBER HIM. WE COULD FORCE HIM OUT.
DID YOU NOTICE HE HAS A VERY LARGE STICK?
MY BROTHER, A BEATING WITH YOUR STICK WOULD BE AN HONOR INDEED! YOU MAY KEEP THE HUT AND MAY YOUR STAFF FEED THE FIRE THAT KEEPS YOU WARM.
?
FRANCESCO, WINTER IS COMING AND WE ARE HOMELESS!
TRUST IN GOD, BROTHER...
WHAT ABOUT ICE CAVES?

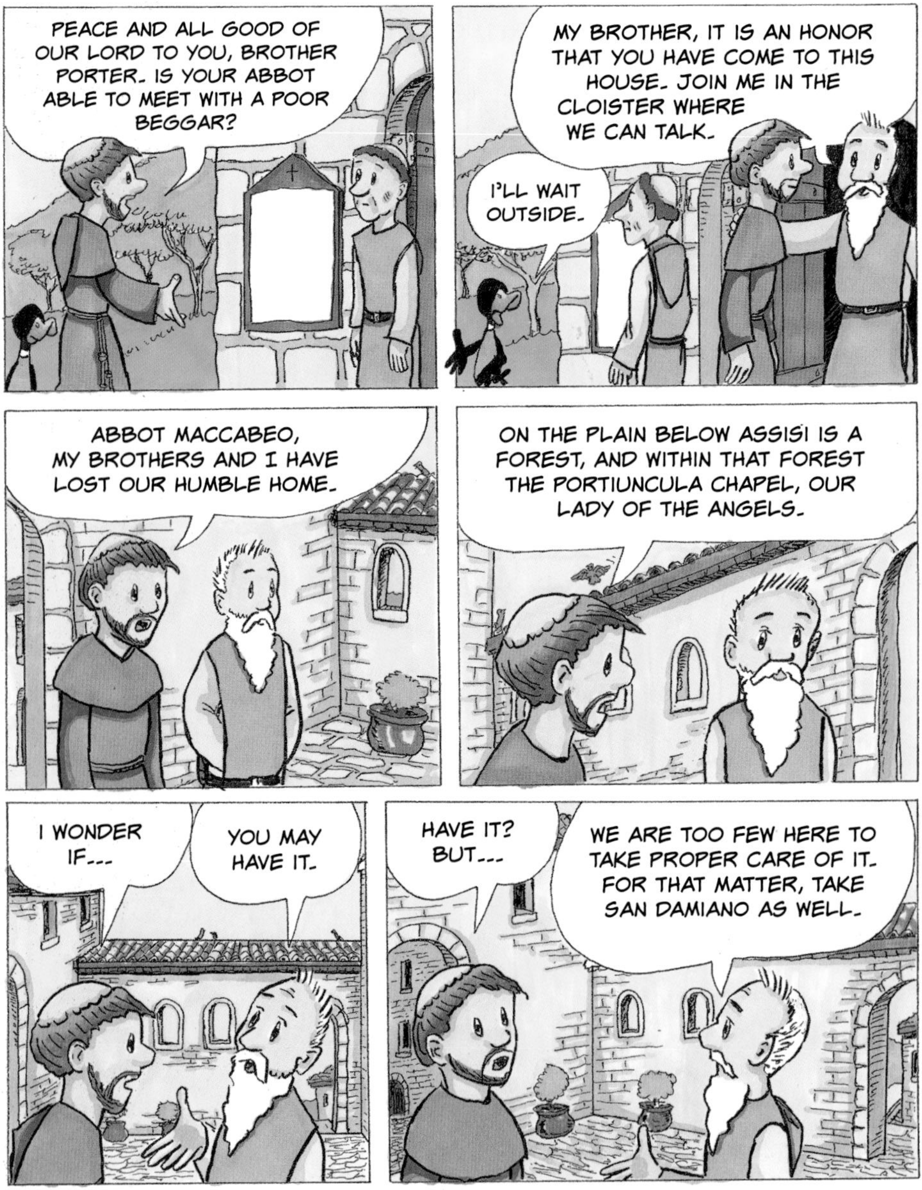
PEACE AND ALL GOOD OF OUR LORD TO YOU, BROTHER PORTER. IS YOUR ABBOT ABLE TO MEET WITH A POOR BEGGAR?
MY BROTHER, IT IS AN HONOR THAT YOU HAVE COME TO THIS HOUSE. JOIN ME IN THE CLOISTER WHERE WE CAN TALK.
I'LL WAIT OUTSIDE.
ABBOT MACCABEO, MY BROTHERS AND I HAVE LOST OUR HUMBLE HOME.
ON THE PLAIN BELOW ASSISI IS A FOREST, AND WITHIN THAT FOREST THE PORTIUNCULA CHAPEL, OUR LADY OF THE ANGELS.
I WONDER IF...
YOU MAY HAVE IT.
HAVE IT? BUT...
WE ARE TOO FEW HERE TO TAKE PROPER CARE OF IT. FOR THAT MATTER, TAKE SAN DAMIANO AS WELL.

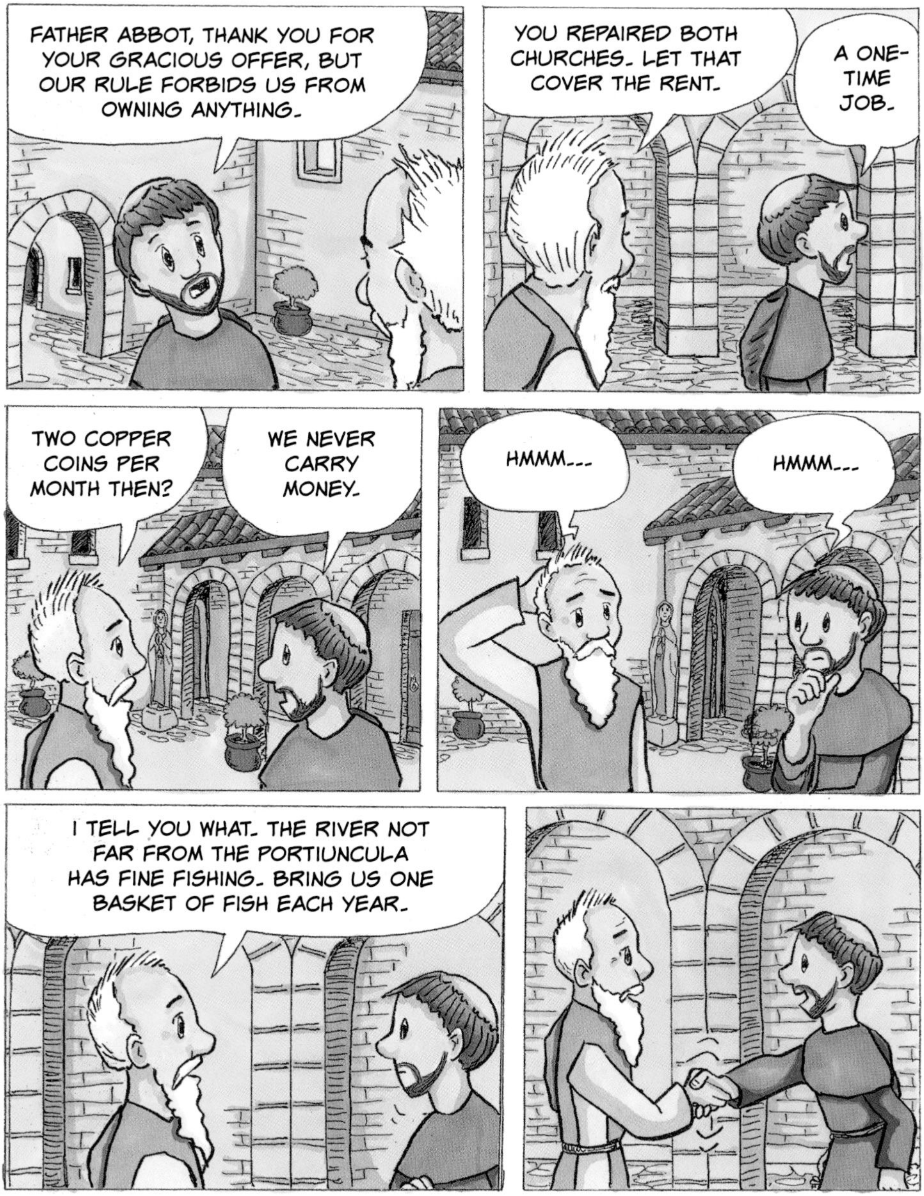
FATHER ABBOT, THANK YOU FOR YOUR GRACIOUS OFFER, BUT OUR RULE FORBIDS US FROM OWNING ANYTHING.
YOU REPAIRED BOTH CHURCHES. LET THAT COVER THE RENT.
A ONE-TIME JOB.
TWO COPPER COINS PER MONTH THEN?
WE NEVER CARRY MONEY.
HMMM...
HMMM...
I TELL YOU WHAT. THE RIVER NOT FAR FROM THE PORTIUNCULA HAS FINE FISHING. BRING US ONE BASKET OF FISH EACH YEAR.

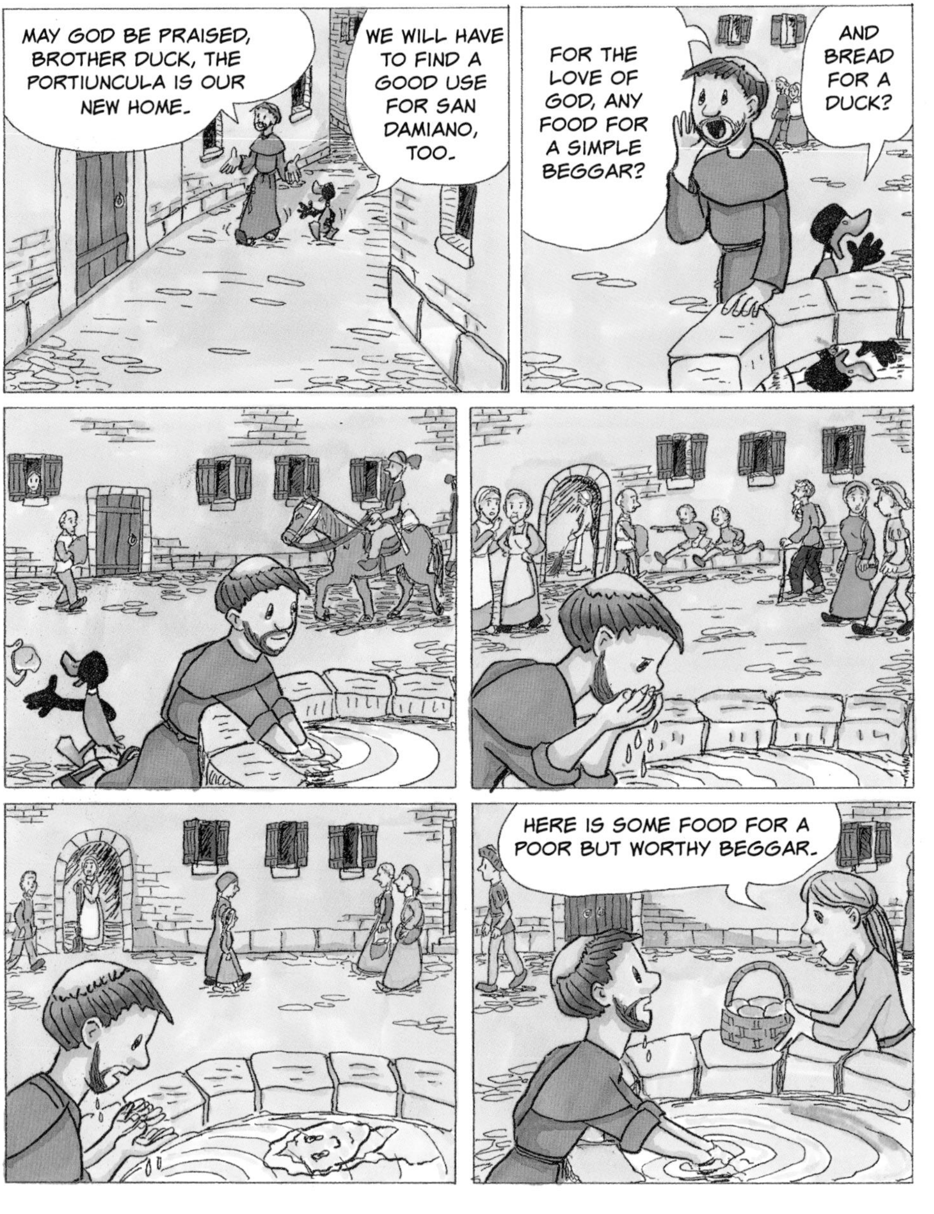
MAY GOD BE PRAISED, BROTHER DUCK, THE PORTIUNCULA IS OUR NEW HOME.
WE WILL HAVE TO FIND A GOOD USE FOR SAN DAMIANO, TOO.
FOR THE LOVE OF GOD, ANY FOOD FOR A SIMPLE BEGGAR?
AND BREAD FOR A DUCK?
HERE IS SOME FOOD FOR A POOR BUT WORTHY BEGGAR.

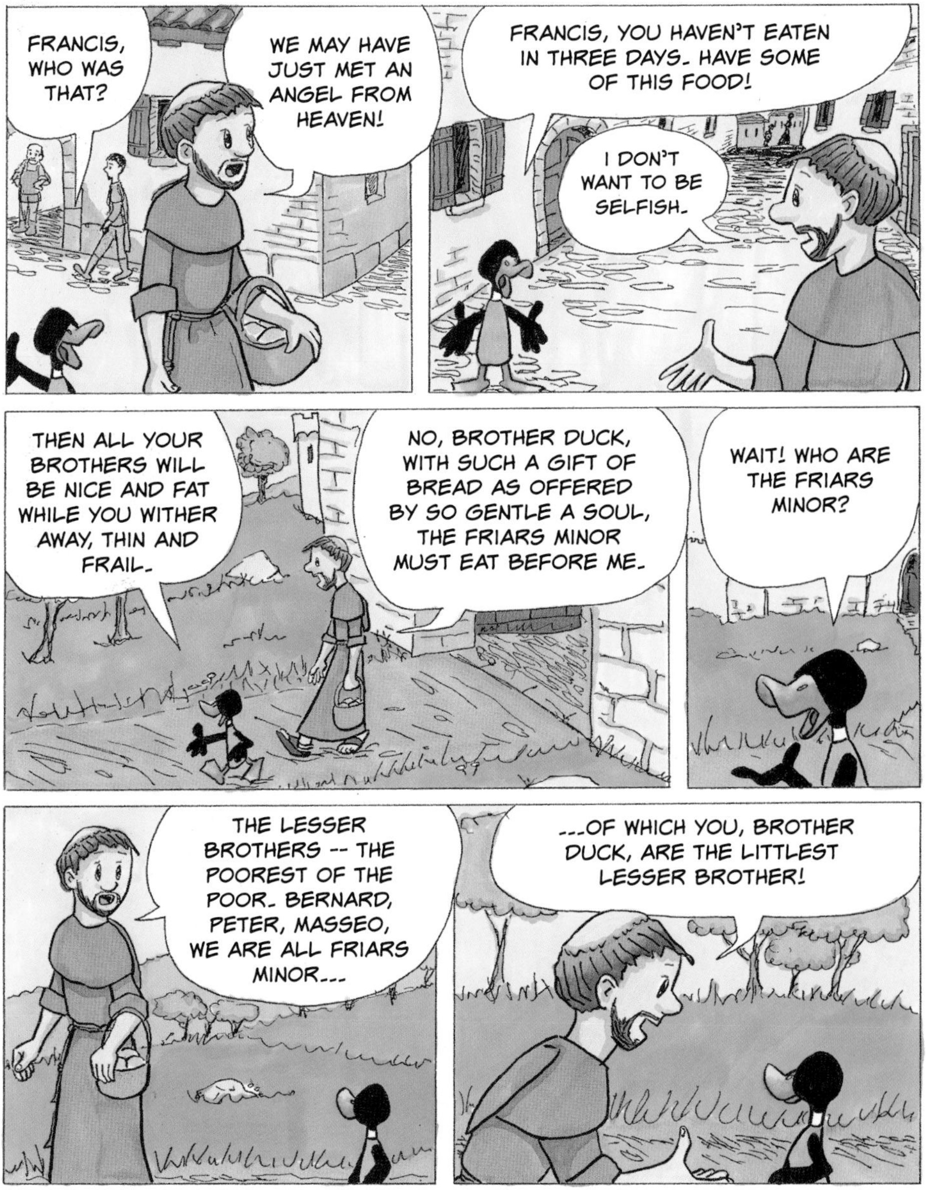
FRANCIS, WHO WAS THAT?
WE MAY HAVE JUST MET AN ANGEL FROM HEAVEN!
FRANCIS, YOU HAVEN'T EATEN IN THREE DAYS. HAVE SOME OF THIS FOOD!
I DON'T WANT TO BE SELFISH.
THEN ALL YOUR BROTHERS WILL BE NICE AND FAT WHILE YOU WITHER AWAY, THIN AND FRAIL.
NO, BROTHER DUCK, WITH SUCH A GIFT OF BREAD AS OFFERED BY SO GENTLE A SOUL, THE FRIARS MINOR MUST EAT BEFORE ME.
WAIT! WHO ARE THE FRIARS MINOR?
THE LESSER BROTHERS -- THE POOREST OF THE POOR. BERNARD, PETER, MASSEO, WE ARE ALL FRIARS MINOR...
...OF WHICH YOU, BROTHER DUCK, ARE THE LITTLEST LESSER BROTHER!

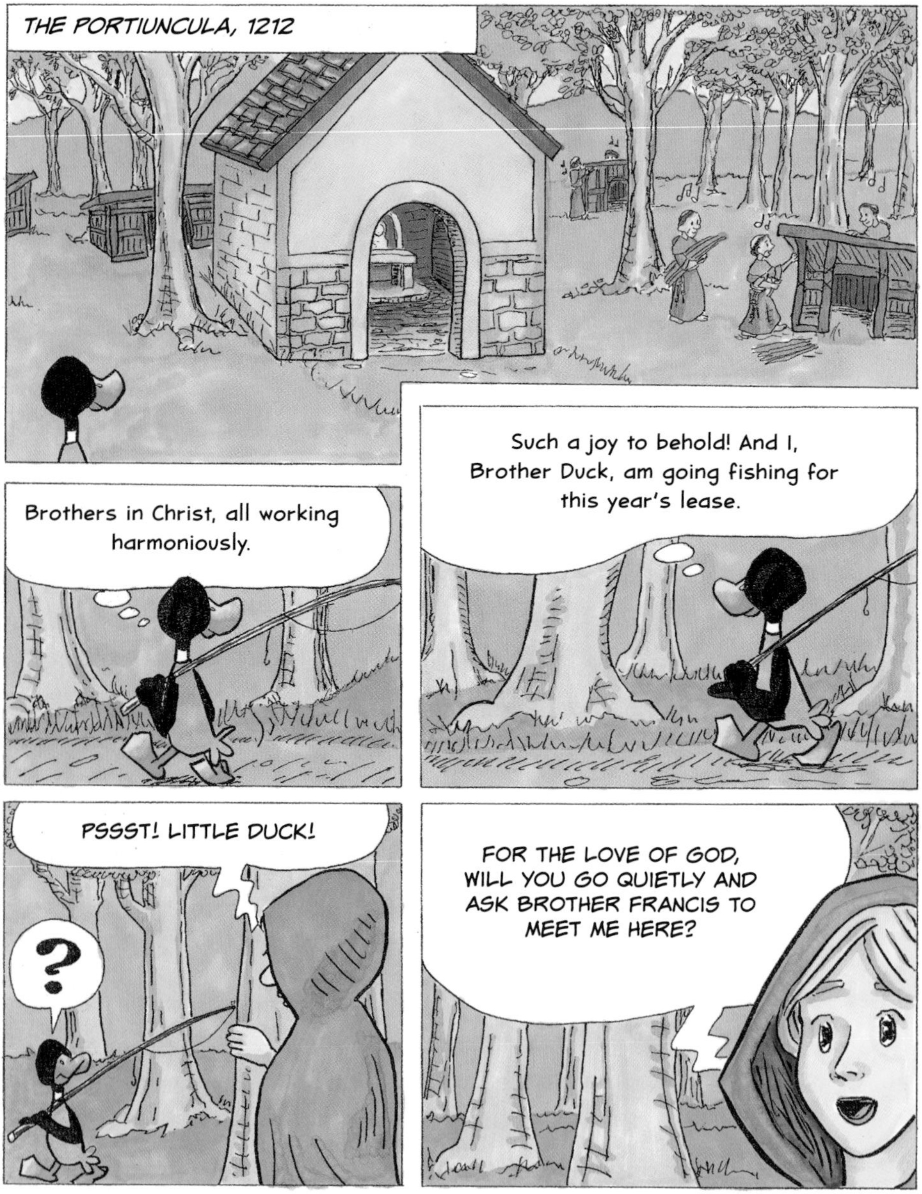
THE PORTIUNCULA, 1212
Brothers in Christ, all working harmoniously.
Such a joy to behold! And I, Brother Duck, am going fishing for this year's lease.
PSSST! LITTLE DUCK!
?
FOR THE LOVE OF GOD, WILL YOU GO QUIETLY AND ASK BROTHER FRANCIS TO MEET ME HERE?

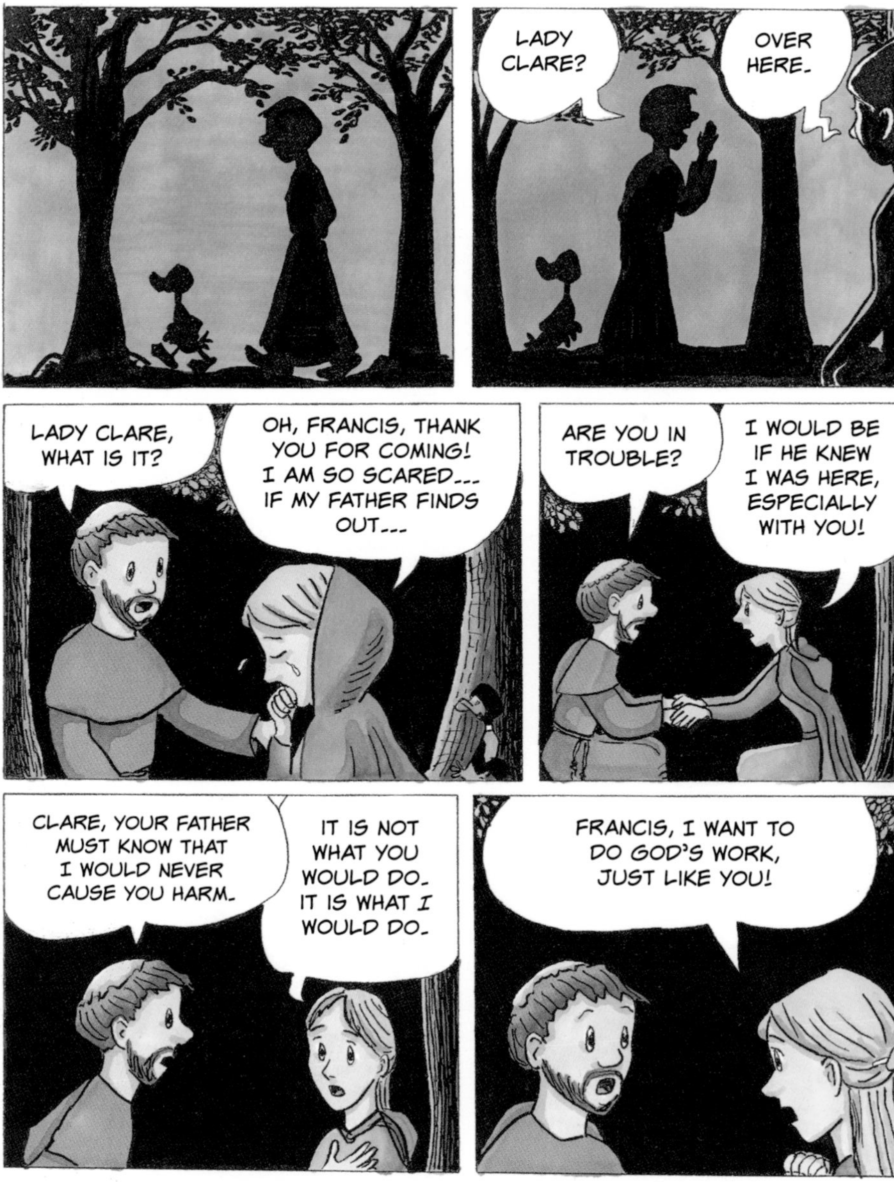
LADY CLARE?
OVER HERE.
LADY CLARE, WHAT IS IT?
OH, FRANCIS, THANK YOU FOR COMING! I AM SO SCARED... IF MY FATHER FINDS OUT...
ARE YOU IN TROUBLE?
I WOULD BE IF HE KNEW I WAS HERE, ESPECIALLY WITH YOU!
CLARE, YOUR FATHER MUST KNOW THAT I WOULD NEVER CAUSE YOU HARM.
IT IS NOT WHAT YOU WOULD DO. IT IS WHAT I WOULD DO.
FRANCIS, I WANT TO DO GOD'S WORK, JUST LIKE YOU!

MY FAMILY, THE OFFREDUCCIO, AND YOUR FAMILY, THE BERNARDONE, MAY HAVE CONSIDERED US A GOOD MATCH BEFORE YOU TOOK UP A LIFE OF POVERTY.

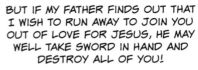

BUT IF MY FATHER FINDS OUT THAT I WISH TO RUN AWAY TO JOIN YOU OUT OF LOVE FOR JESUS, HE MAY WELL TAKE SWORD IN HAND AND DESTROY ALL OF YOU!

CLARE, IS THIS REALLY WHAT YOU DESIRE, TO GIVE UP WEALTH, STATUS, EVEN BEAUTY TO LIVE LIKE US?

OH, YES, WITH ALL MY HEART!

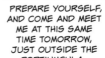

THEN DON'T BE AFRAID. WHEN GOD IS FOR US, WHO CAN PREVAIL AGAINST US?

AND EVEN IF BLESSED SISTER DEATH COMES TO GREET US, FOR THE LOVE OF GOD WE WILL WELCOME HER!

PREPARE YOURSELF, AND COME AND MEET ME AT THIS SAME TIME TOMORROW, JUST OUTSIDE THE PORTIUNCULA.

WITH ALL MY HEART I WILL BE THERE!!

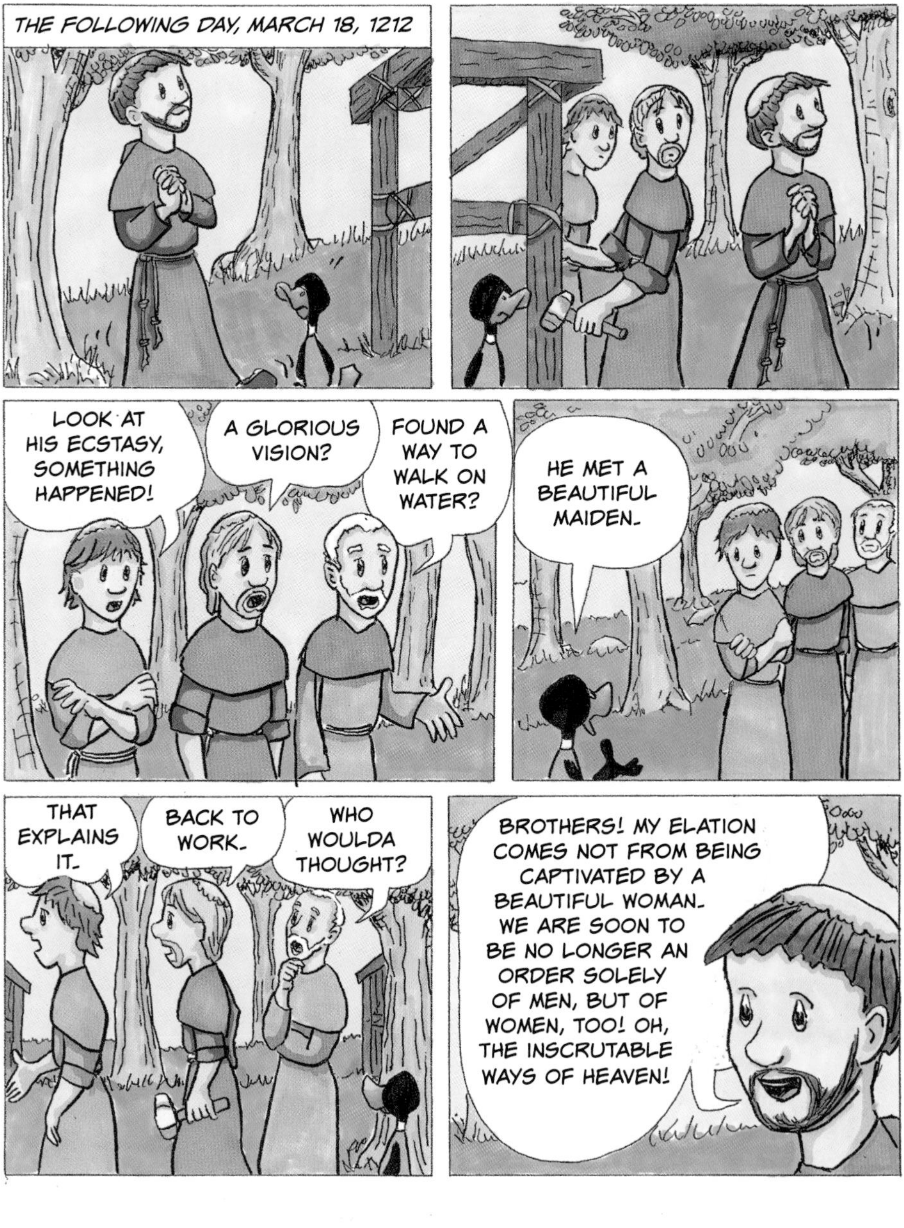
THE FOLLOWING DAY, MARCH 18, 1212
LOOK AT HIS ECSTASY, SOMETHING HAPPENED!
A GLORIOUS VISION?
FOUND A WAY TO WALK ON WATER?
HE MET A BEAUTIFUL MAIDEN.
THAT EXPLAINS IT.
BACK TO WORK.
WHO WOULDA THOUGHT?
BROTHERS! MY ELATION COMES NOT FROM BEING CAPTIVATED BY A BEAUTIFUL WOMAN. WE ARE SOON TO BE NO LONGER AN ORDER SOLELY OF MEN, BUT OF WOMEN, TOO! OH, THE INSCRUTABLE WAYS OF HEAVEN!

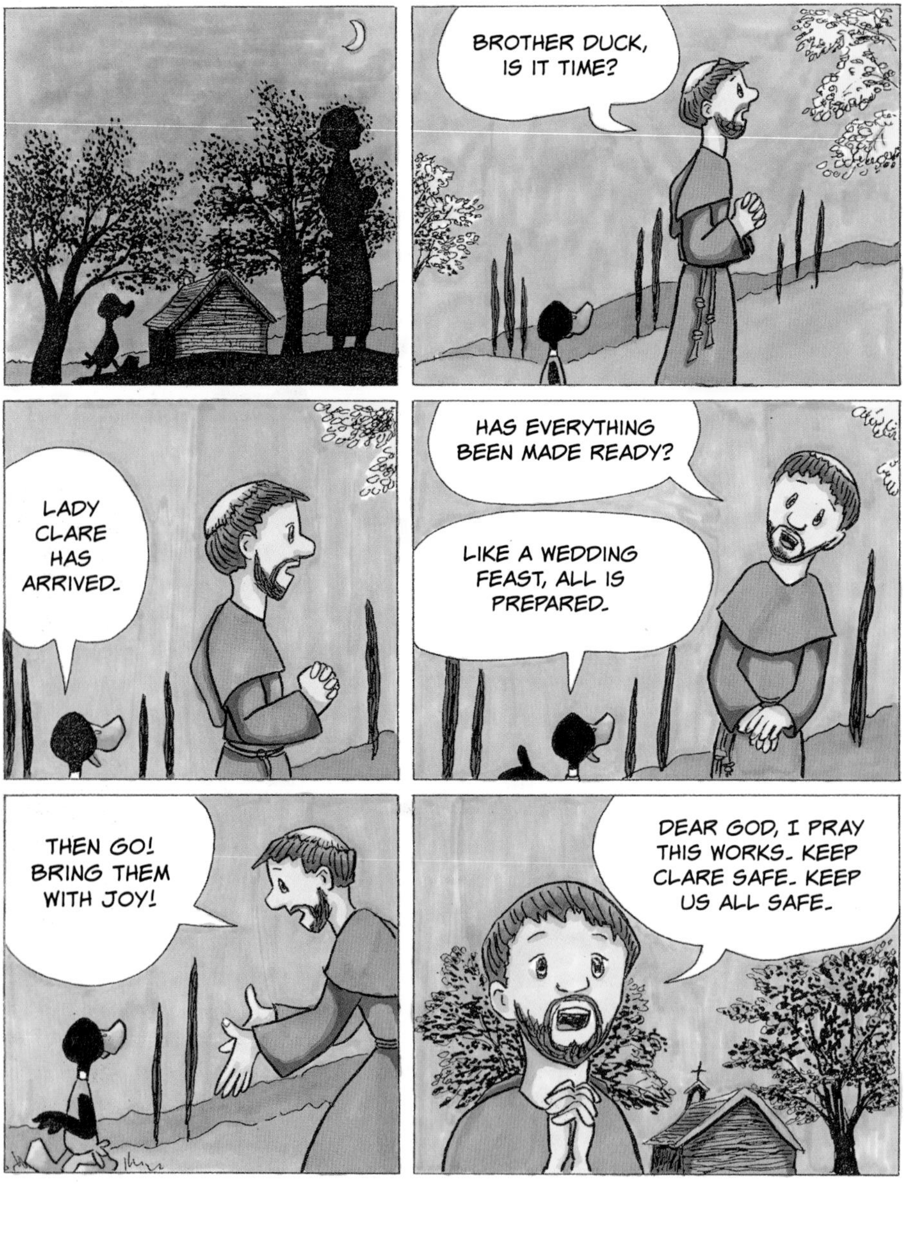
BROTHER DUCK, IS IT TIME?
LADY CLARE HAS ARRIVED.
HAS EVERYTHING BEEN MADE READY?
LIKE A WEDDING FEAST, ALL IS PREPARED.
THEN GO! BRING THEM WITH JOY!
DEAR GOD, I PRAY THIS WORKS. KEEP CLARE SAFE. KEEP US ALL SAFE.

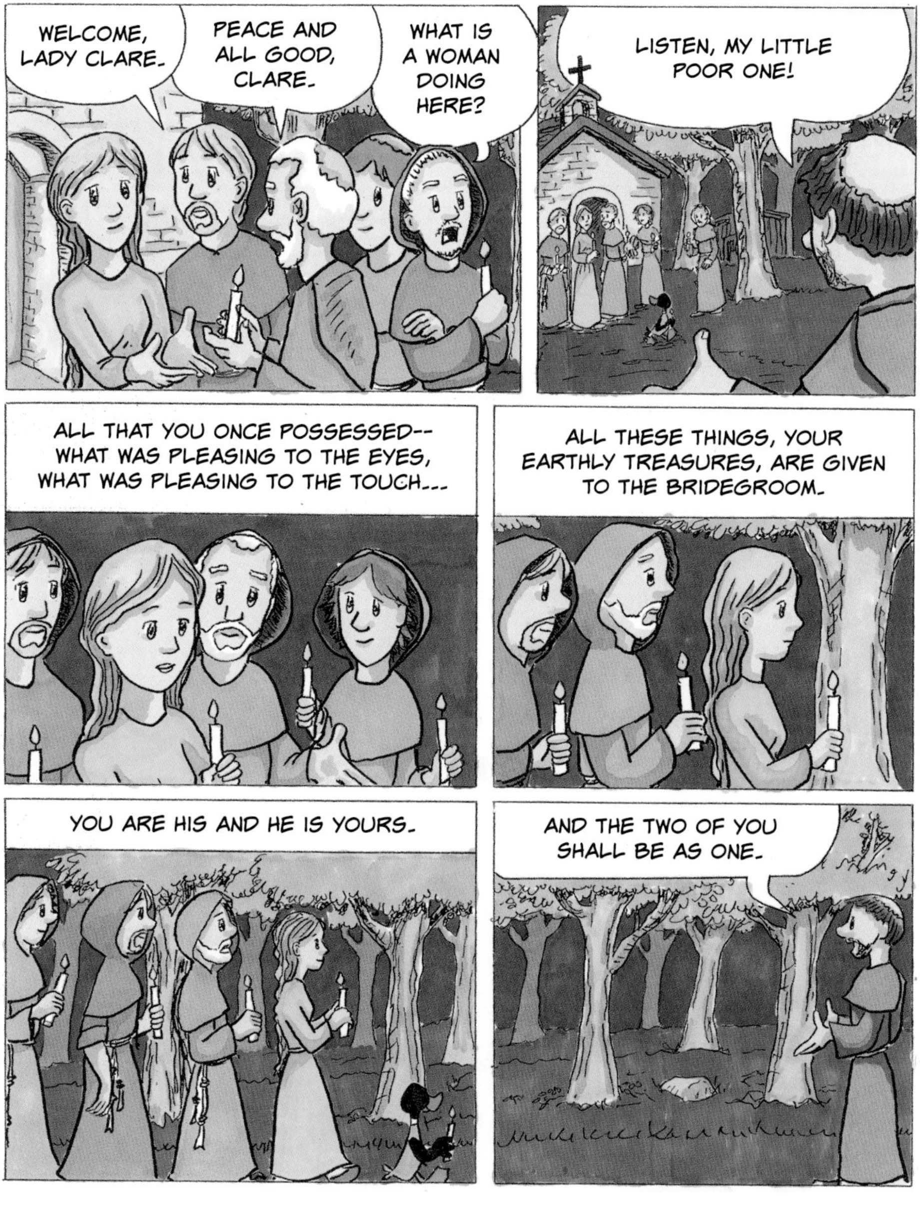
WELCOME, LADY CLARE.
PEACE AND ALL GOOD, CLARE.
WHAT IS A WOMAN DOING HERE?
LISTEN, MY LITTLE POOR ONE!
ALL THAT YOU ONCE POSSESSED-- WHAT WAS PLEASING TO THE EYES, WHAT WAS PLEASING TO THE TOUCH...
ALL THESE THINGS, YOUR EARTHLY TREASURES, ARE GIVEN TO THE BRIDEGROOM.
YOU ARE HIS AND HE IS YOURS.
AND THE TWO OF YOU SHALL BE AS ONE.

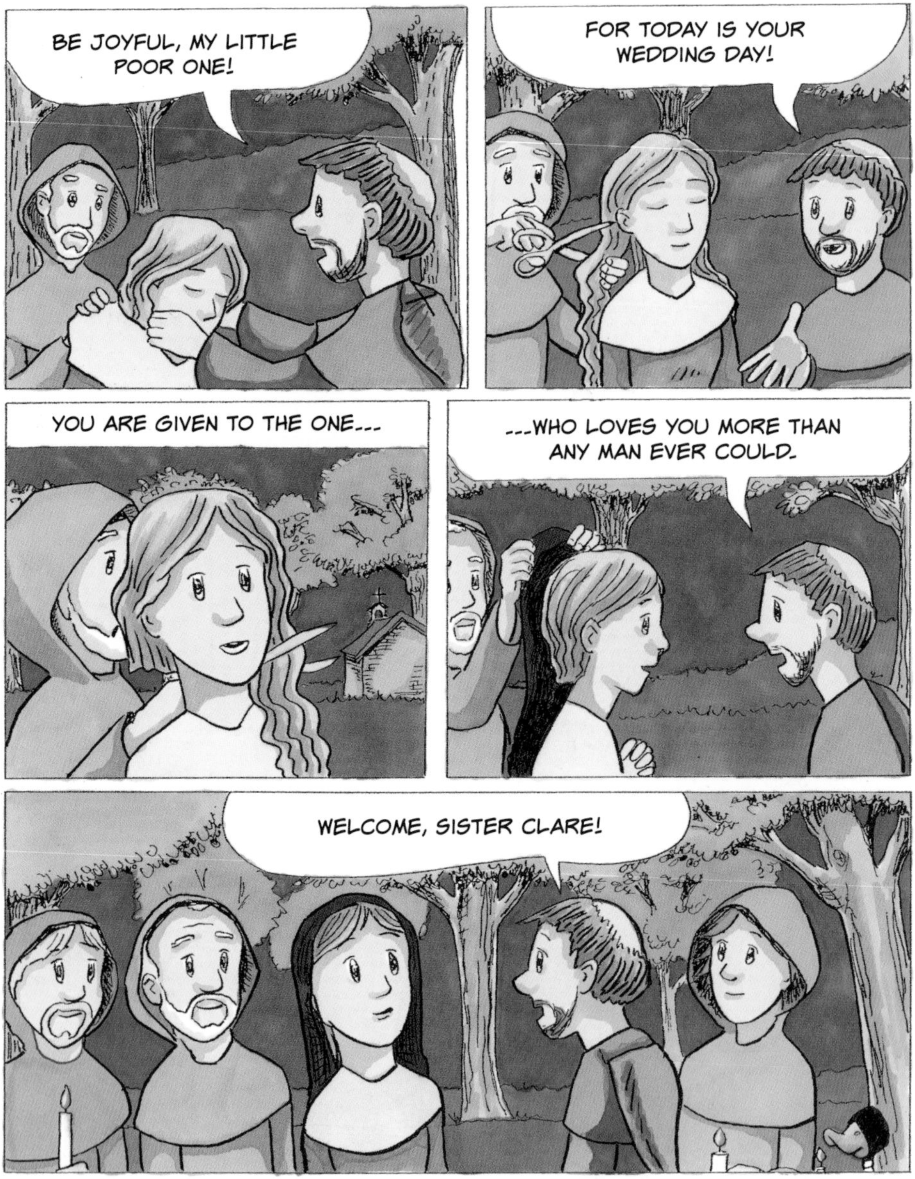
BE JOYFUL, MY LITTLE POOR ONE!
FOR TODAY IS YOUR WEDDING DAY!
YOU ARE GIVEN TO THE ONE...
...WHO LOVES YOU MORE THAN ANY MAN EVER COULD.
WELCOME, SISTER CLARE!

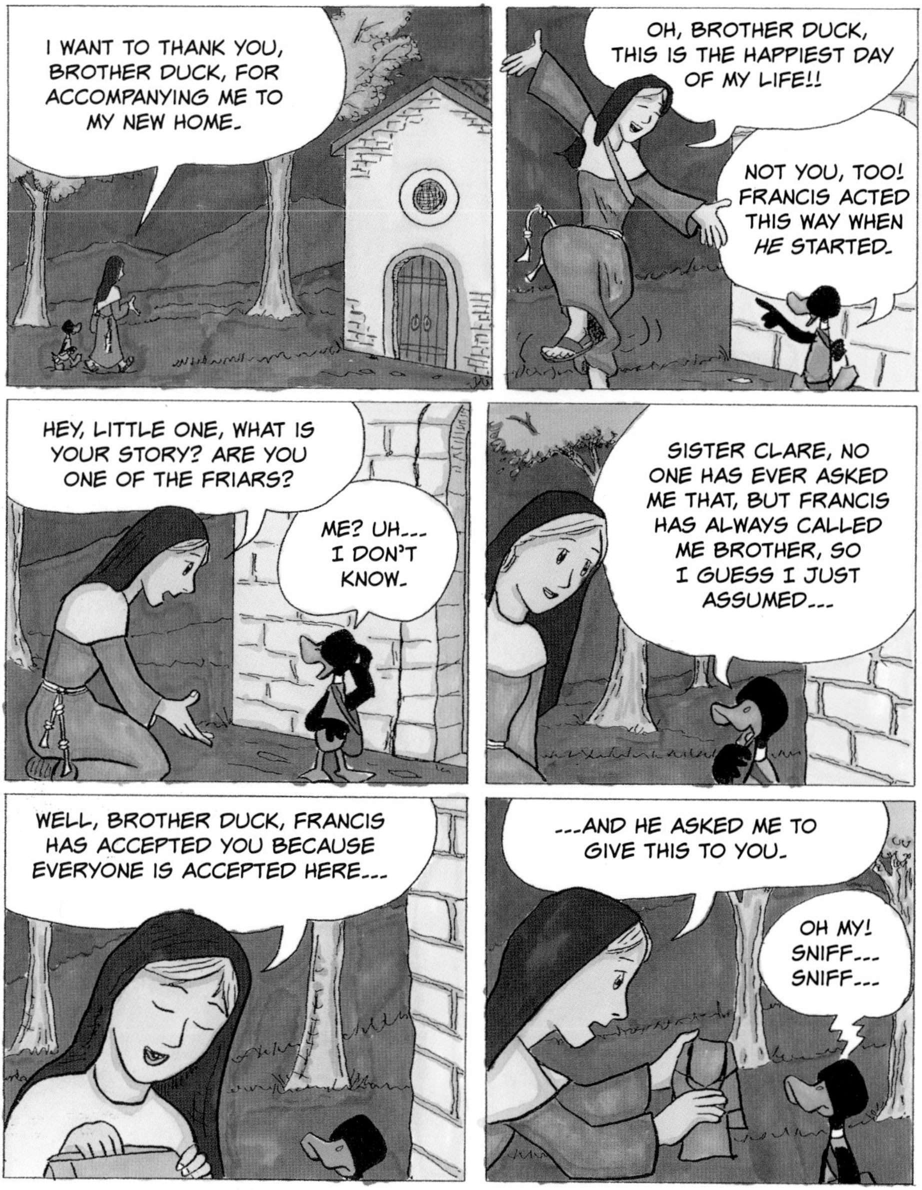
I WANT TO THANK YOU, BROTHER DUCK, FOR ACCOMPANYING ME TO MY NEW HOME.
OH, BROTHER DUCK, THIS IS THE HAPPIEST DAY OF MY LIFE!!
NOT YOU, TOO! FRANCIS ACTED THIS WAY WHEN *HE* STARTED.
HEY, LITTLE ONE, WHAT IS YOUR STORY? ARE YOU ONE OF THE FRIARS?
ME? UH... I DON'T KNOW.
SISTER CLARE, NO ONE HAS EVER ASKED ME THAT, BUT FRANCIS HAS ALWAYS CALLED ME BROTHER, SO I GUESS I JUST ASSUMED...
WELL, BROTHER DUCK, FRANCIS HAS ACCEPTED YOU BECAUSE EVERYONE IS ACCEPTED HERE...
...AND HE ASKED ME TO GIVE THIS TO YOU.
OH MY! SNIFF... SNIFF...

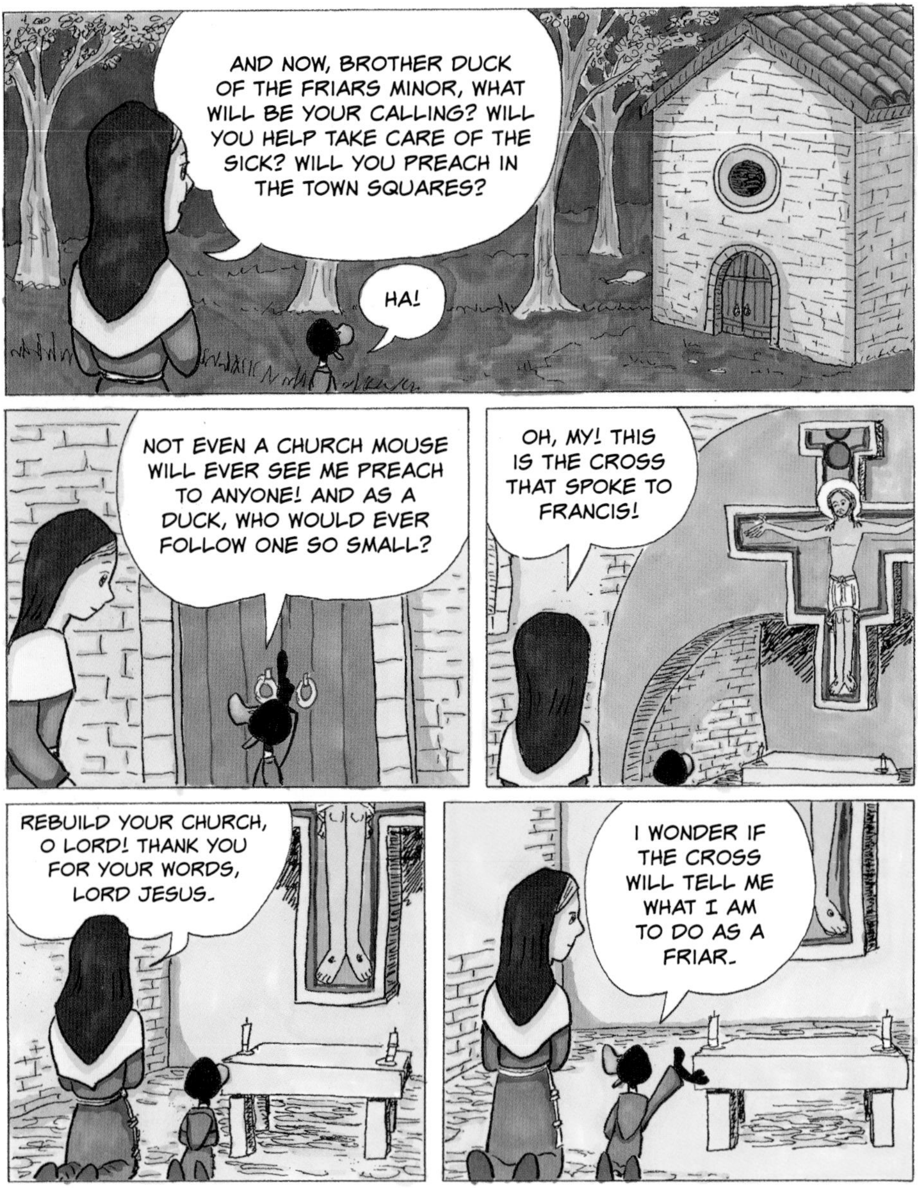
AND NOW, BROTHER DUCK OF THE FRIARS MINOR, WHAT WILL BE YOUR CALLING? WILL YOU HELP TAKE CARE OF THE SICK? WILL YOU PREACH IN THE TOWN SQUARES?
HA!
NOT EVEN A CHURCH MOUSE WILL EVER SEE ME PREACH TO ANYONE! AND AS A DUCK, WHO WOULD EVER FOLLOW ONE SO SMALL?
OH, MY! THIS IS THE CROSS THAT SPOKE TO FRANCIS!
REBUILD YOUR CHURCH, O LORD! THANK YOU FOR YOUR WORDS, LORD JESUS.
I WONDER IF THE CROSS WILL TELL ME WHAT I AM TO DO AS A FRIAR.

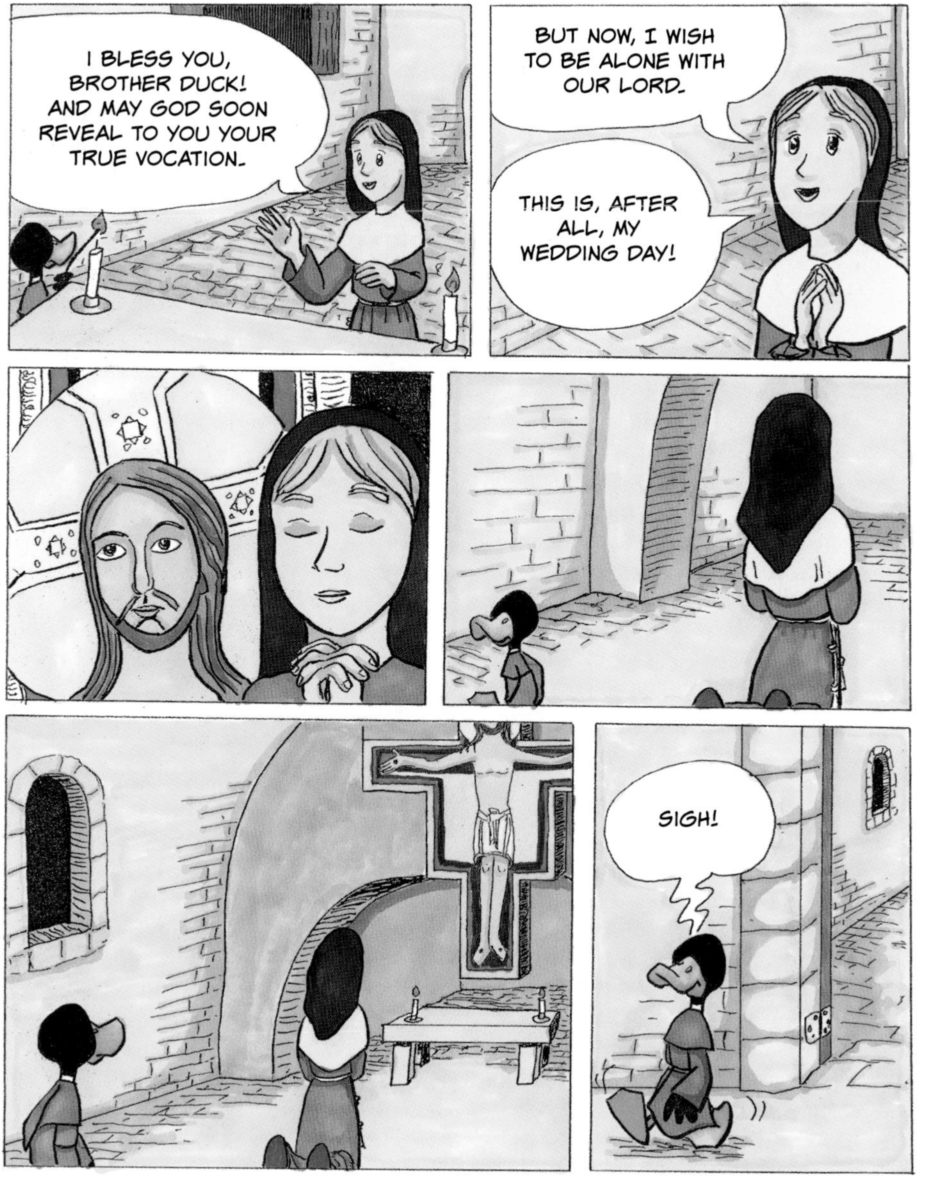
I BLESS YOU, BROTHER DUCK! AND MAY GOD SOON REVEAL TO YOU YOUR TRUE VOCATION.
BUT NOW, I WISH TO BE ALONE WITH OUR LORD.
THIS IS, AFTER ALL, MY WEDDING DAY!
SIGH!

CHAPTER 5
SAINT FRANCIS AND THE ANIMALS

"There is only one tragedy,
NOT to be a saint."
—*LÉON BLOY, FRENCH NOVELIST*

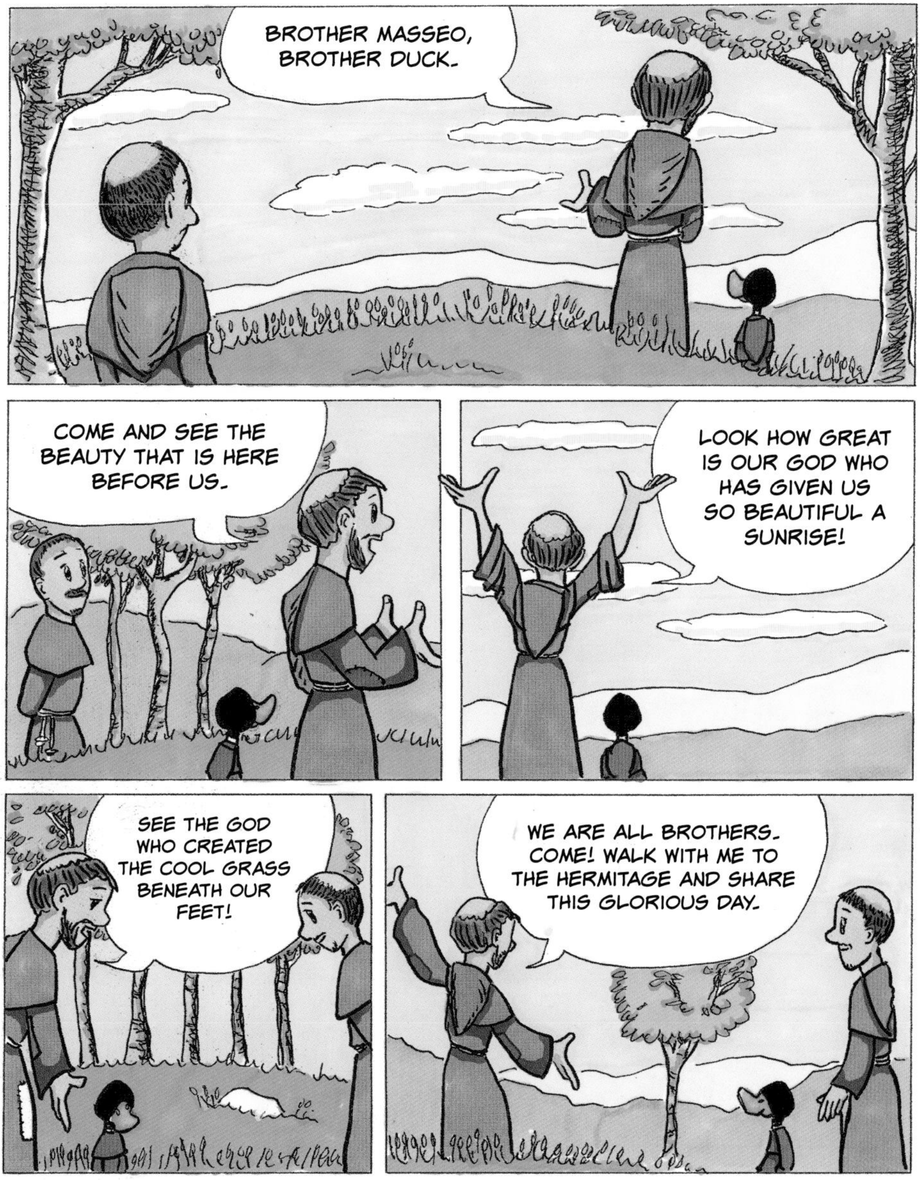
BROTHER MASSEO, BROTHER DUCK.
COME AND SEE THE BEAUTY THAT IS HERE BEFORE US.
LOOK HOW GREAT IS OUR GOD WHO HAS GIVEN US SO BEAUTIFUL A SUNRISE!
SEE THE GOD WHO CREATED THE COOL GRASS BENEATH OUR FEET!
WE ARE ALL BROTHERS. COME! WALK WITH ME TO THE HERMITAGE AND SHARE THIS GLORIOUS DAY.

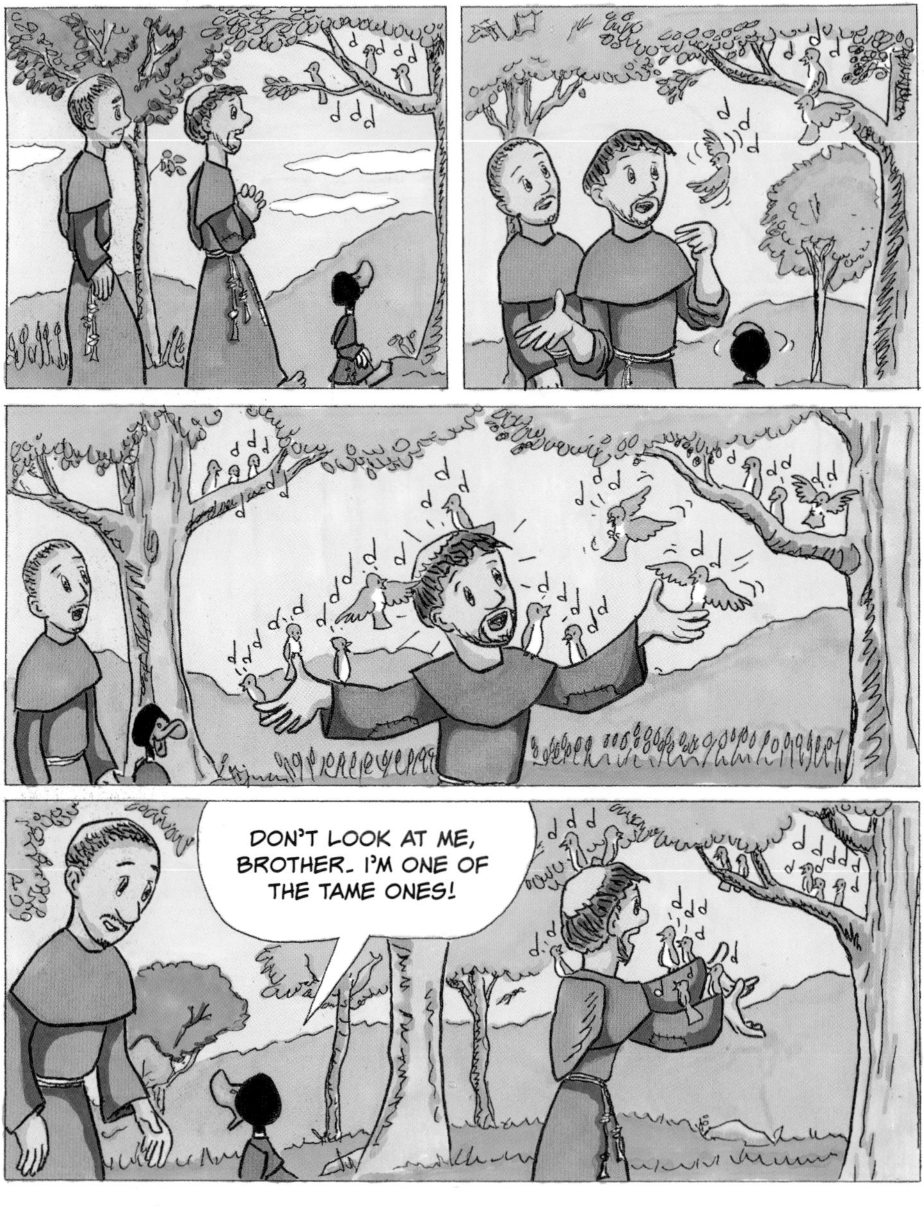
DON'T LOOK AT ME, BROTHER. I'M ONE OF THE TAME ONES!

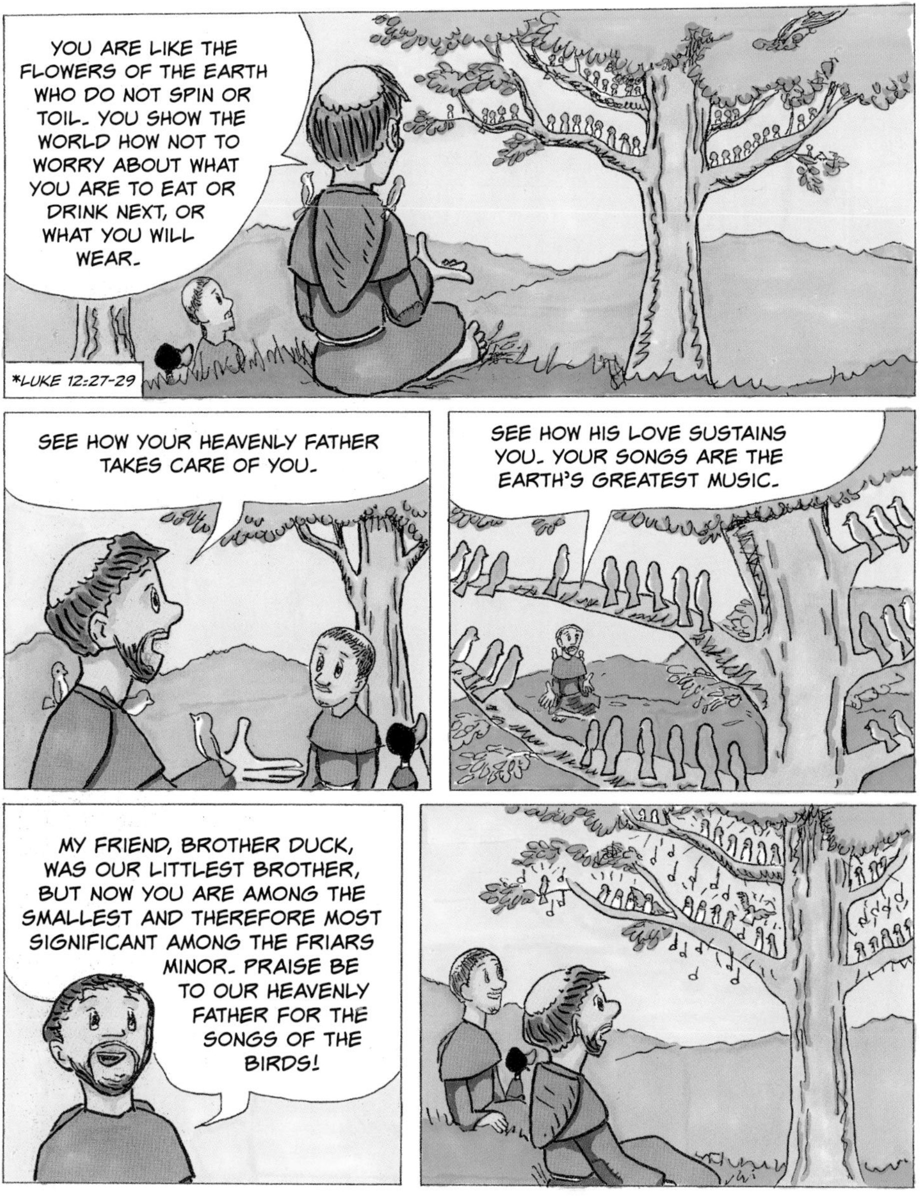
YOU ARE LIKE THE FLOWERS OF THE EARTH WHO DO NOT SPIN OR TOIL. YOU SHOW THE WORLD HOW NOT TO WORRY ABOUT WHAT YOU ARE TO EAT OR DRINK NEXT, OR WHAT YOU WILL WEAR.
*LUKE 12:27-29
SEE HOW YOUR HEAVENLY FATHER TAKES CARE OF YOU.
SEE HOW HIS LOVE SUSTAINS YOU. YOUR SONGS ARE THE EARTH'S GREATEST MUSIC.
MY FRIEND, BROTHER DUCK, WAS OUR LITTLEST BROTHER, BUT NOW YOU ARE AMONG THE SMALLEST AND THEREFORE MOST SIGNIFICANT AMONG THE FRIARS MINOR. PRAISE BE TO OUR HEAVENLY FATHER FOR THE SONGS OF THE BIRDS!

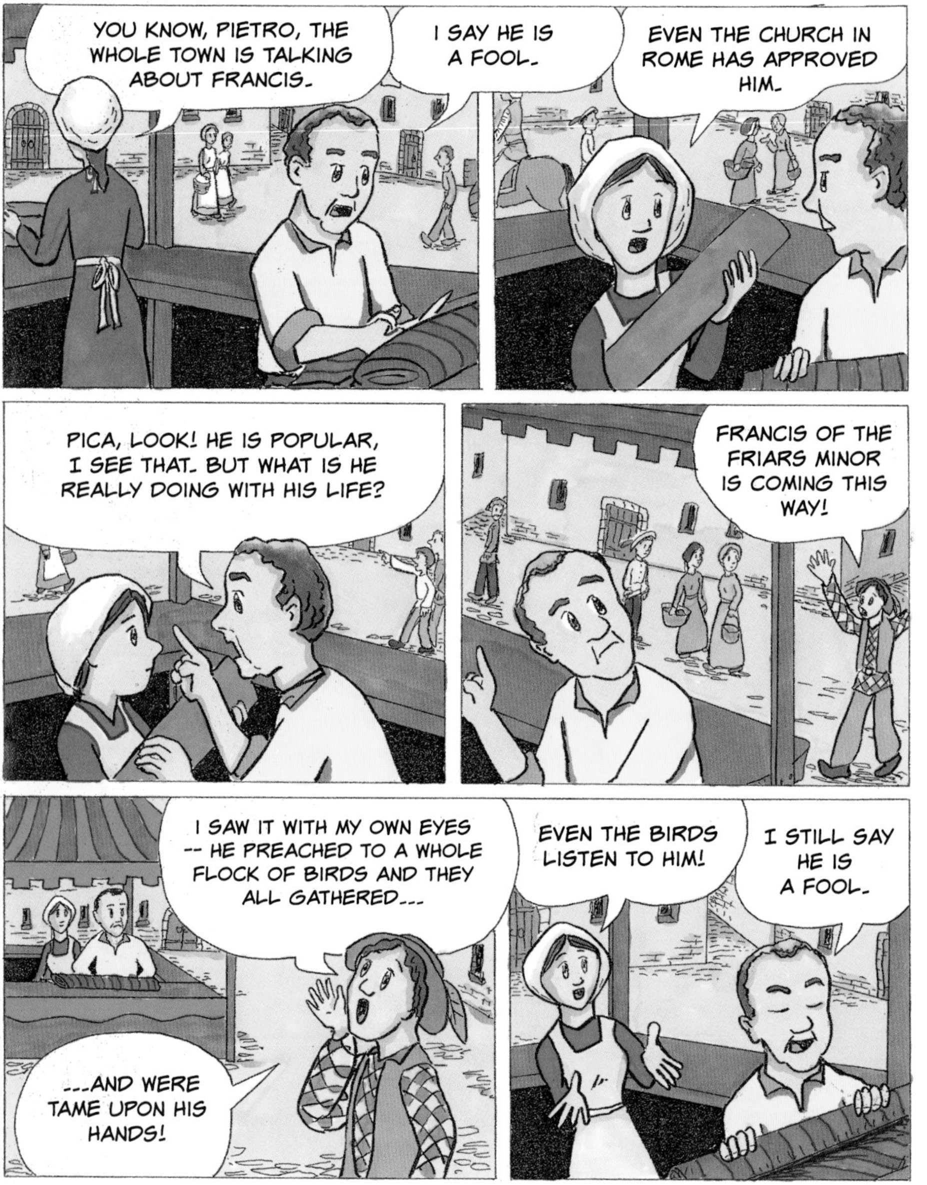
YOU KNOW, PIETRO, THE WHOLE TOWN IS TALKING ABOUT FRANCIS.
I SAY HE IS A FOOL.
EVEN THE CHURCH IN ROME HAS APPROVED HIM.
PICA, LOOK! HE IS POPULAR, I SEE THAT. BUT WHAT IS HE REALLY DOING WITH HIS LIFE?
FRANCIS OF THE FRIARS MINOR IS COMING THIS WAY!
I SAW IT WITH MY OWN EYES -- HE PREACHED TO A WHOLE FLOCK OF BIRDS AND THEY ALL GATHERED...
...AND WERE TAME UPON HIS HANDS!
EVEN THE BIRDS LISTEN TO HIM!
I STILL SAY HE IS A FOOL.

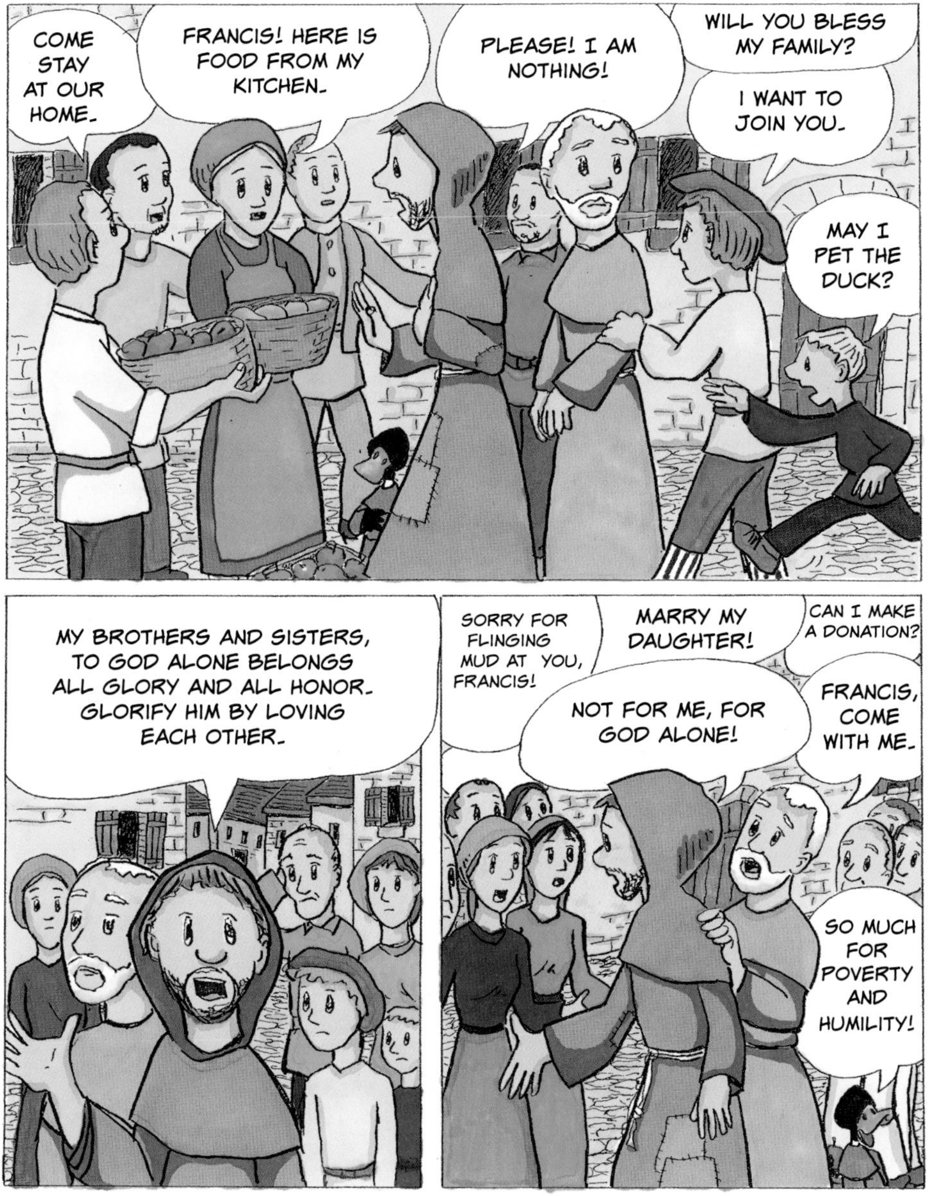
COME STAY AT OUR HOME.
FRANCIS! HERE IS FOOD FROM MY KITCHEN.
PLEASE! I AM NOTHING!
WILL YOU BLESS MY FAMILY?
I WANT TO JOIN YOU.
MAY I PET THE DUCK?
MY BROTHERS AND SISTERS, TO GOD ALONE BELONGS ALL GLORY AND ALL HONOR. GLORIFY HIM BY LOVING EACH OTHER.
SORRY FOR FLINGING MUD AT YOU, FRANCIS!
MARRY MY DAUGHTER!
CAN I MAKE A DONATION?
NOT FOR ME, FOR GOD ALONE!
FRANCIS, COME WITH ME.
SO MUCH FOR POVERTY AND HUMILITY!

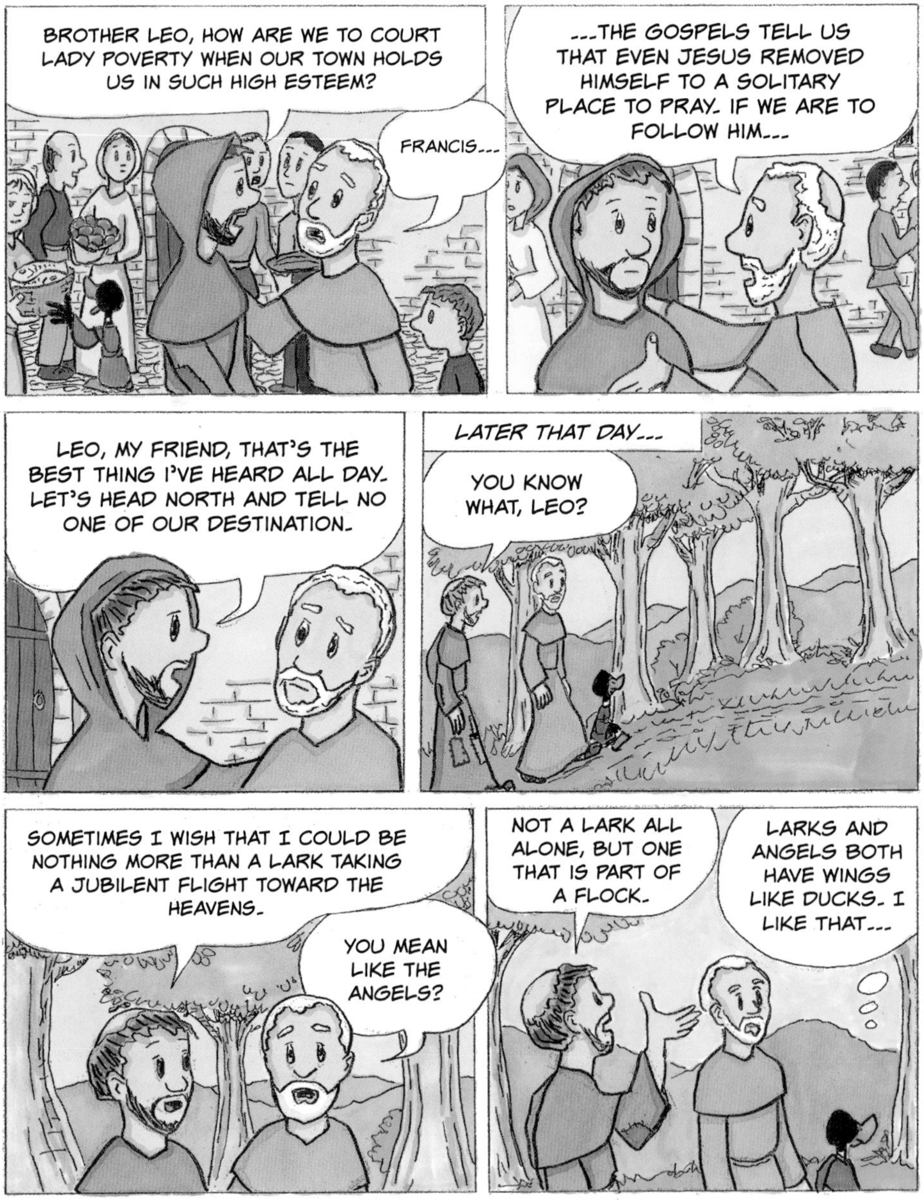
BROTHER LEO, HOW ARE WE TO COURT LADY POVERTY WHEN OUR TOWN HOLDS US IN SUCH HIGH ESTEEM?
FRANCIS...
...THE GOSPELS TELL US THAT EVEN JESUS REMOVED HIMSELF TO A SOLITARY PLACE TO PRAY. IF WE ARE TO FOLLOW HIM...
LEO, MY FRIEND, THAT'S THE BEST THING I'VE HEARD ALL DAY. LET'S HEAD NORTH AND TELL NO ONE OF OUR DESTINATION.
LATER THAT DAY...
YOU KNOW WHAT, LEO?
SOMETIMES I WISH THAT I COULD BE NOTHING MORE THAN A LARK TAKING A JUBILENT FLIGHT TOWARD THE HEAVENS.
YOU MEAN LIKE THE ANGELS?
NOT A LARK ALL ALONE, BUT ONE THAT IS PART OF A FLOCK.
LARKS AND ANGELS BOTH HAVE WINGS LIKE DUCKS. I LIKE THAT...

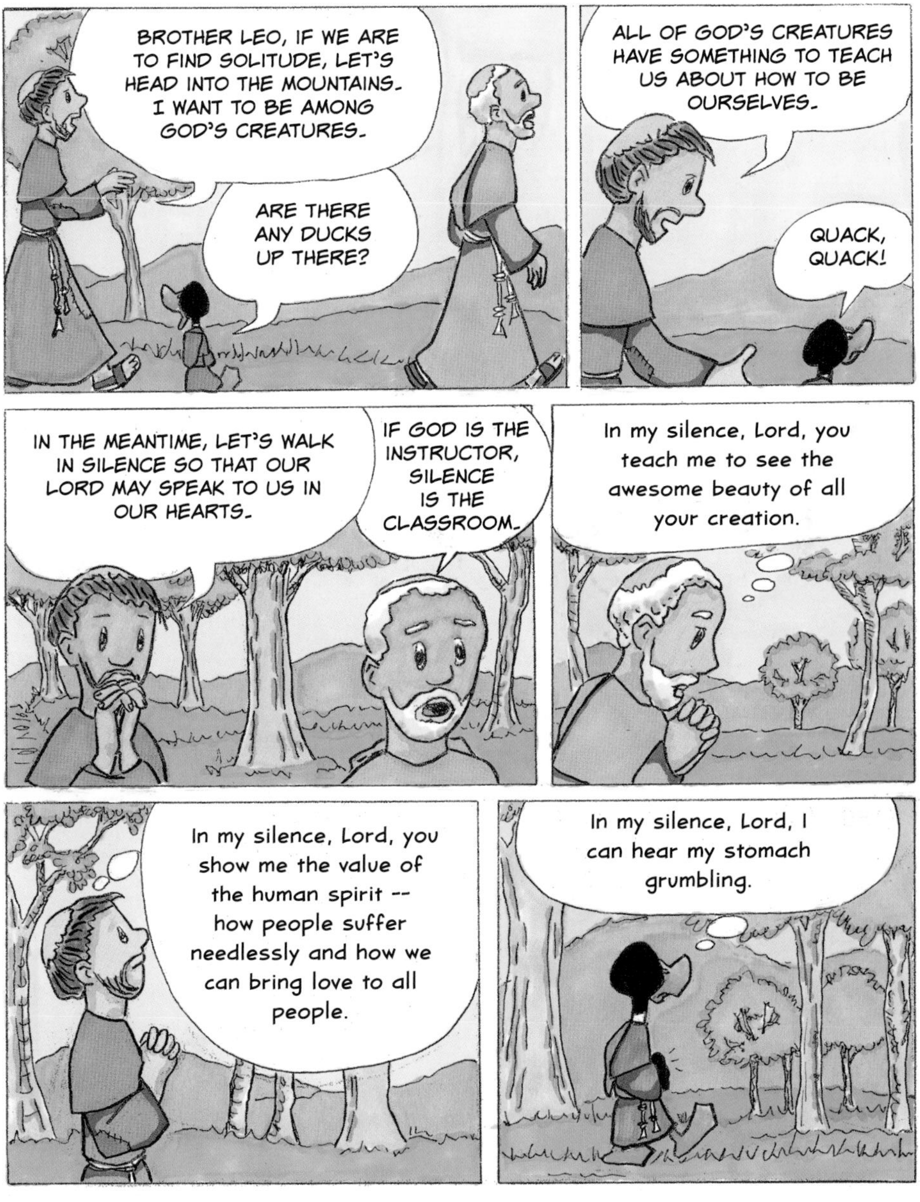
BROTHER LEO, IF WE ARE TO FIND SOLITUDE, LET'S HEAD INTO THE MOUNTAINS. I WANT TO BE AMONG GOD'S CREATURES.
ARE THERE ANY DUCKS UP THERE?
ALL OF GOD'S CREATURES HAVE SOMETHING TO TEACH US ABOUT HOW TO BE OURSELVES.
QUACK, QUACK!
IN THE MEANTIME, LET'S WALK IN SILENCE SO THAT OUR LORD MAY SPEAK TO US IN OUR HEARTS.
IF GOD IS THE INSTRUCTOR, SILENCE IS THE CLASSROOM.
In my silence, Lord, you teach me to see the awesome beauty of all your creation.
In my silence, Lord, you show me the value of the human spirit -- how people suffer needlessly and how we can bring love to all people.
In my silence, Lord, I can hear my stomach grumbling.

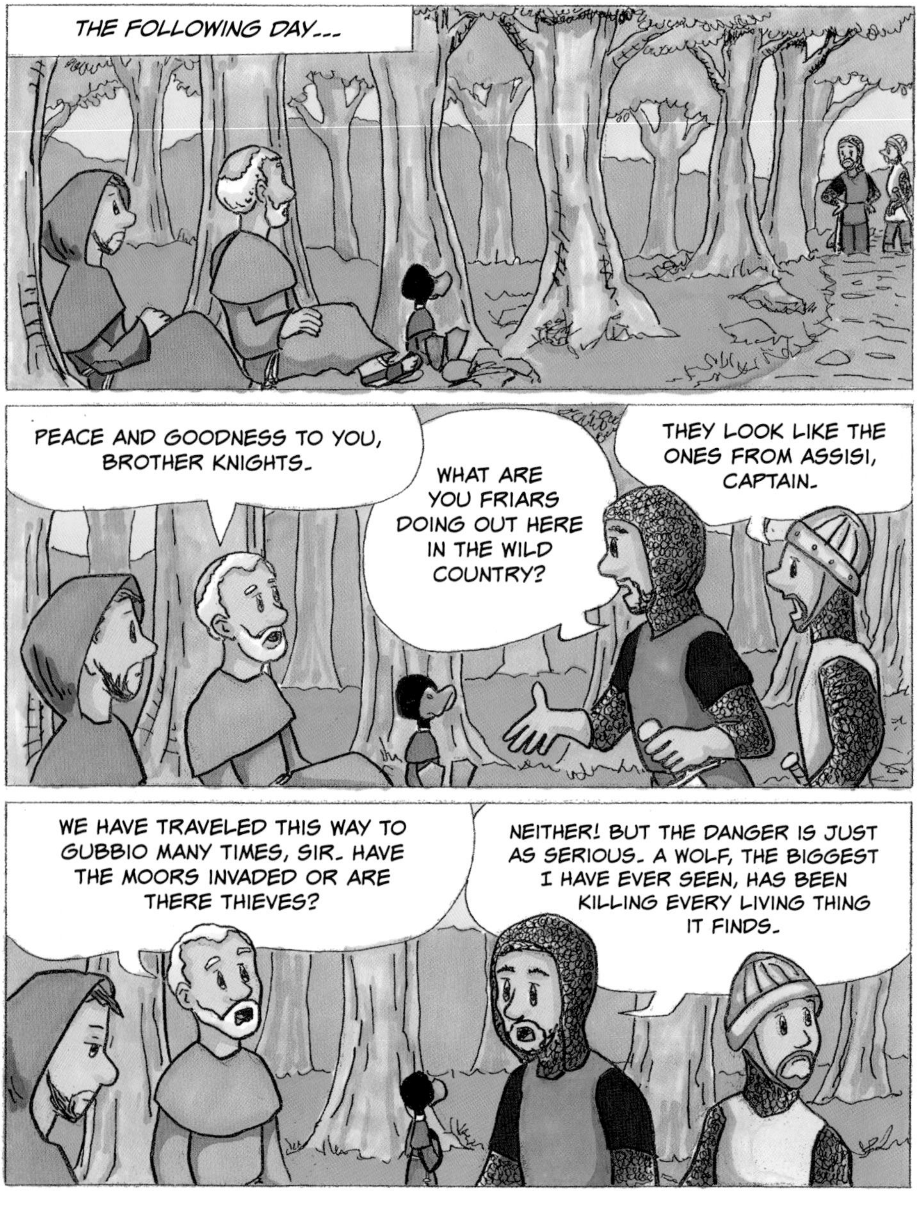
THE FOLLOWING DAY...
PEACE AND GOODNESS TO YOU, BROTHER KNIGHTS.
WHAT ARE YOU FRIARS DOING OUT HERE IN THE WILD COUNTRY?
THEY LOOK LIKE THE ONES FROM ASSISI, CAPTAIN.
WE HAVE TRAVELED THIS WAY TO GUBBIO MANY TIMES, SIR. HAVE THE MOORS INVADED OR ARE THERE THIEVES?
NEITHER! BUT THE DANGER IS JUST AS SERIOUS. A WOLF, THE BIGGEST I HAVE EVER SEEN, HAS BEEN KILLING EVERY LIVING THING IT FINDS.

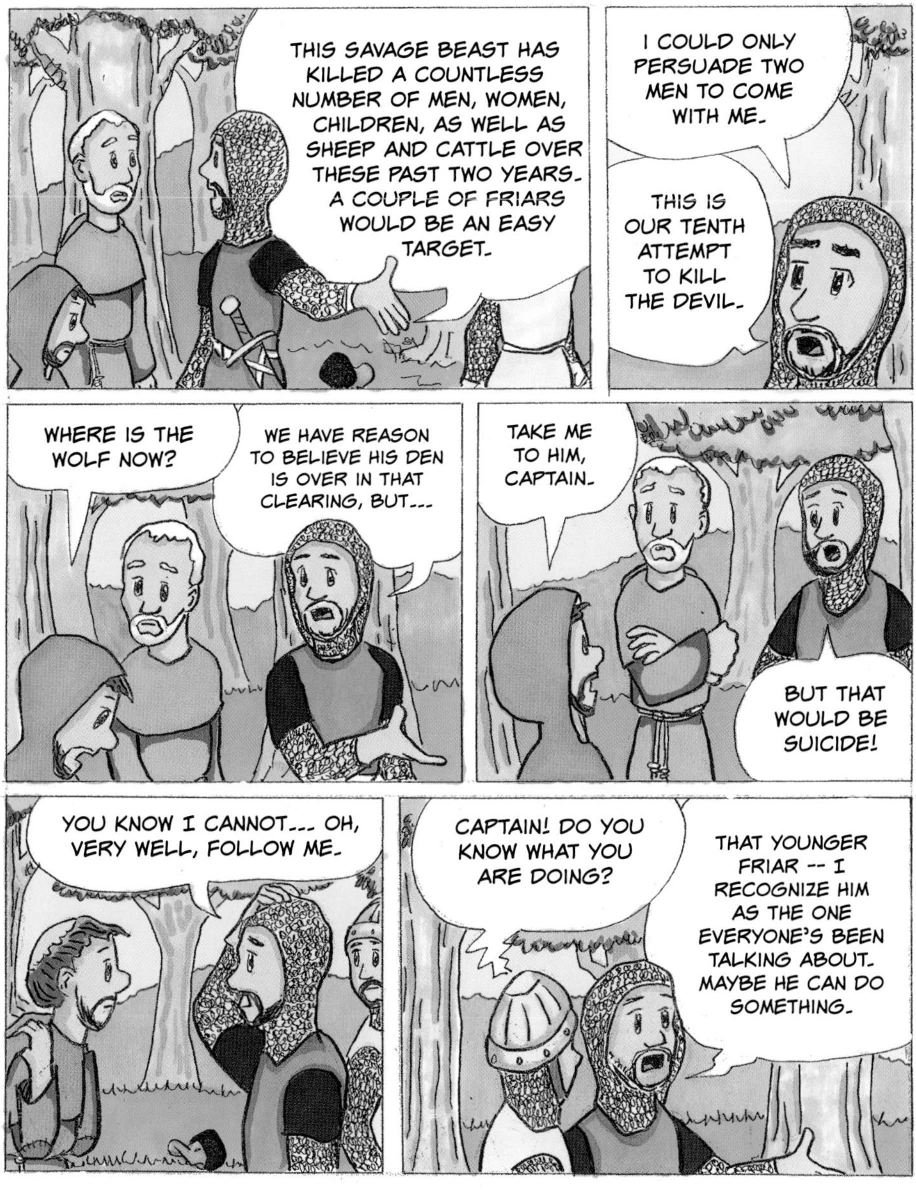
THIS SAVAGE BEAST HAS KILLED A COUNTLESS NUMBER OF MEN, WOMEN, CHILDREN, AS WELL AS SHEEP AND CATTLE OVER THESE PAST TWO YEARS. A COUPLE OF FRIARS WOULD BE AN EASY TARGET.
I COULD ONLY PERSUADE TWO MEN TO COME WITH ME.
THIS IS OUR TENTH ATTEMPT TO KILL THE DEVIL.
WHERE IS THE WOLF NOW?
WE HAVE REASON TO BELIEVE HIS DEN IS OVER IN THAT CLEARING, BUT...
TAKE ME TO HIM, CAPTAIN.
BUT THAT WOULD BE SUICIDE!
YOU KNOW I CANNOT... OH, VERY WELL, FOLLOW ME.
CAPTAIN! DO YOU KNOW WHAT YOU ARE DOING?
THAT YOUNGER FRIAR -- I RECOGNIZE HIM AS THE ONE EVERYONE'S BEEN TALKING ABOUT. MAYBE HE CAN DO SOMETHING.

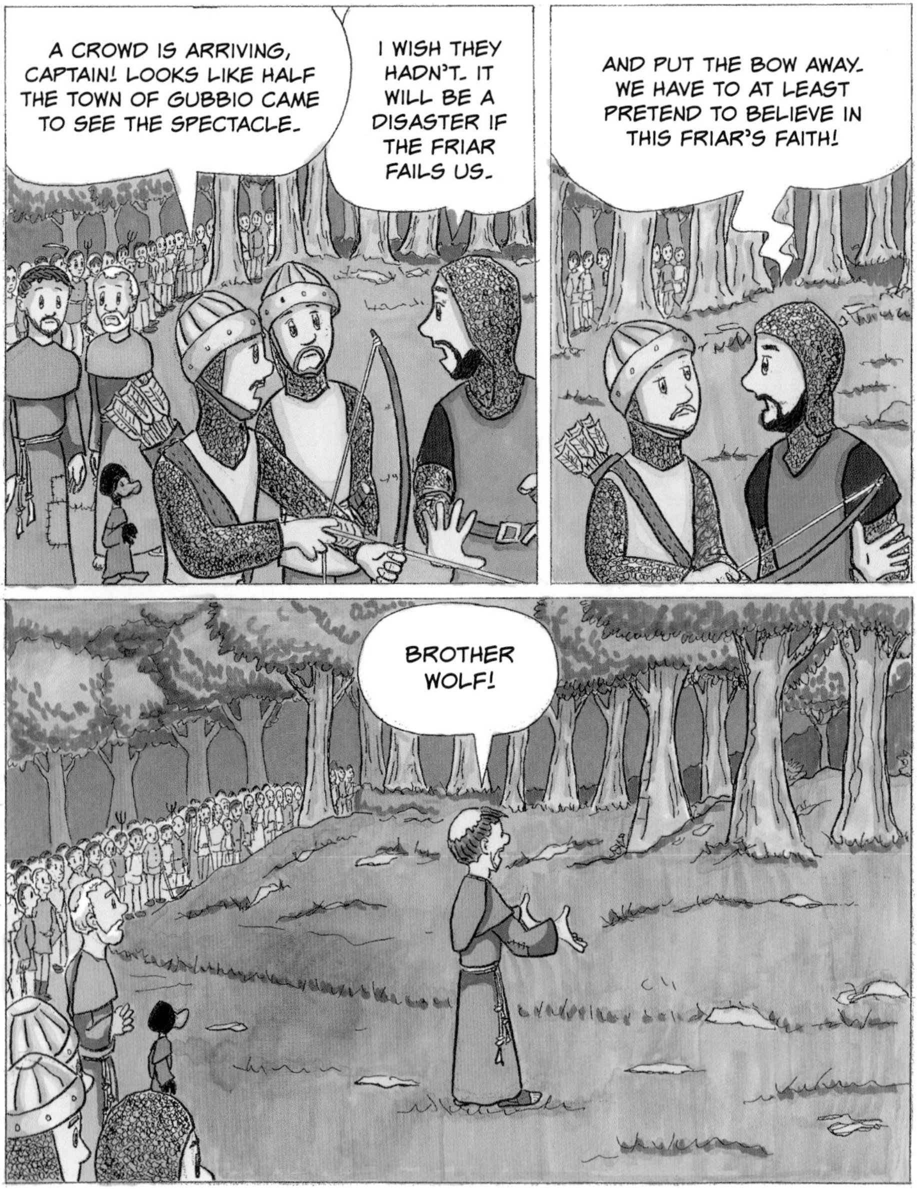
A CROWD IS ARRIVING, CAPTAIN! LOOKS LIKE HALF THE TOWN OF GUBBIO CAME TO SEE THE SPECTACLE.
I WISH THEY HADN'T. IT WILL BE A DISASTER IF THE FRIAR FAILS US.
AND PUT THE BOW AWAY. WE HAVE TO AT LEAST PRETEND TO BELIEVE IN THIS FRIAR'S FAITH!
BROTHER WOLF!

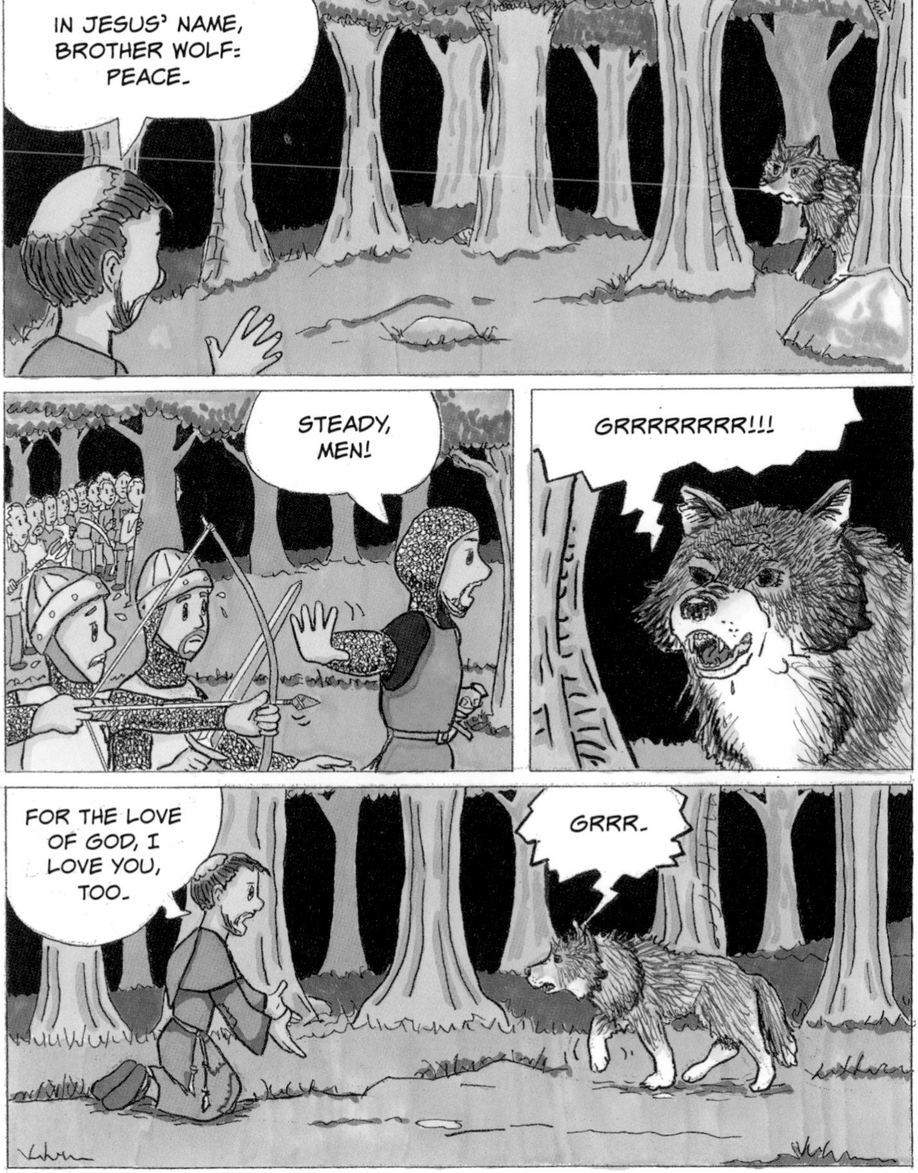

IN JESUS' NAME, BROTHER WOLF: PEACE.
STEADY, MEN!
GRRRRRRRR!!!
FOR THE LOVE OF GOD, I LOVE YOU, TOO.
GRRR.

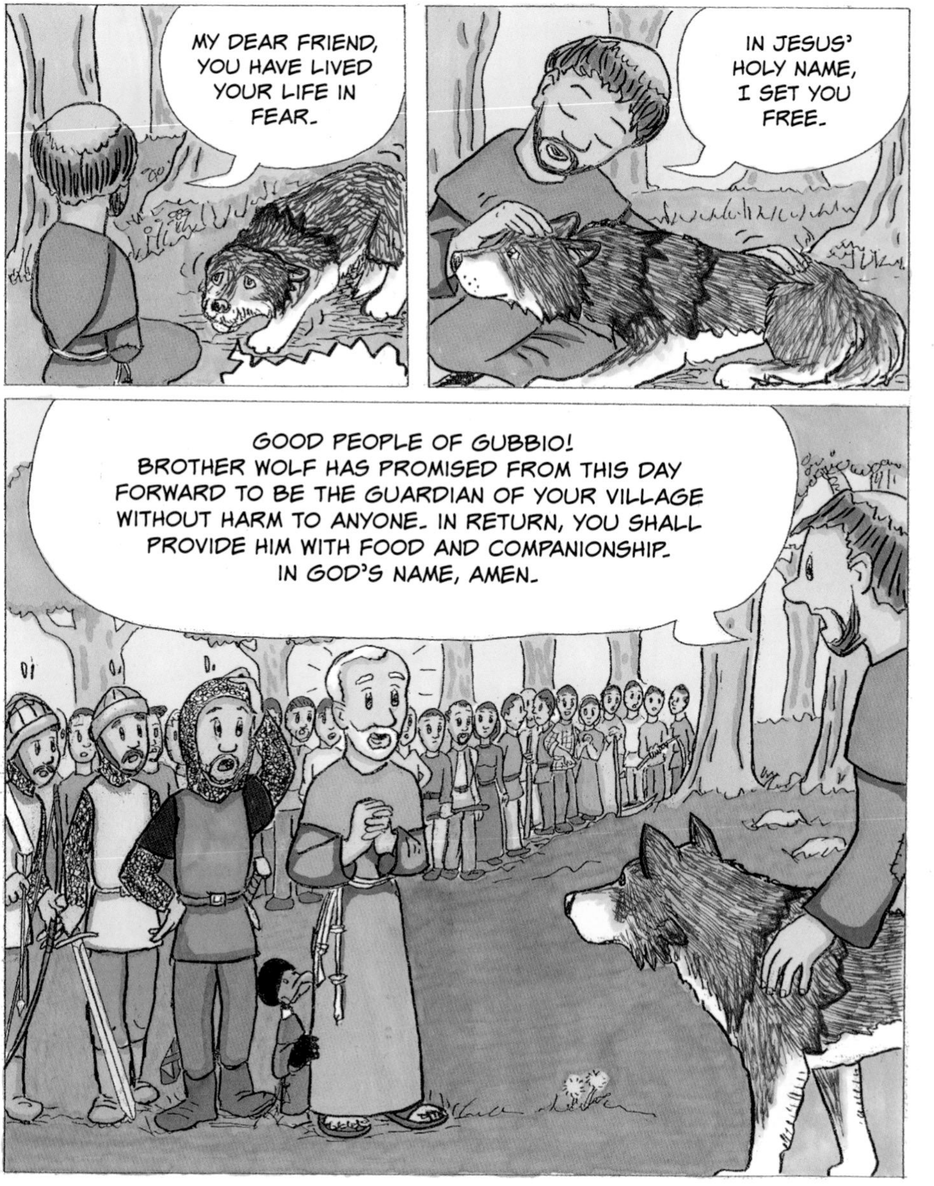
MY DEAR FRIEND, YOU HAVE LIVED YOUR LIFE IN FEAR.
IN JESUS' HOLY NAME, I SET YOU FREE.
GOOD PEOPLE OF GUBBIO! BROTHER WOLF HAS PROMISED FROM THIS DAY FORWARD TO BE THE GUARDIAN OF YOUR VILLAGE WITHOUT HARM TO ANYONE. IN RETURN, YOU SHALL PROVIDE HIM WITH FOOD AND COMPANIONSHIP. IN GOD'S NAME, AMEN.

CHAPTER 6
FRIARS
UPON A MOUNTAIN

To contemplate
Is to be separated
From all and to be
United with God alone.
—*BROTHER GILES OF ASSISI*

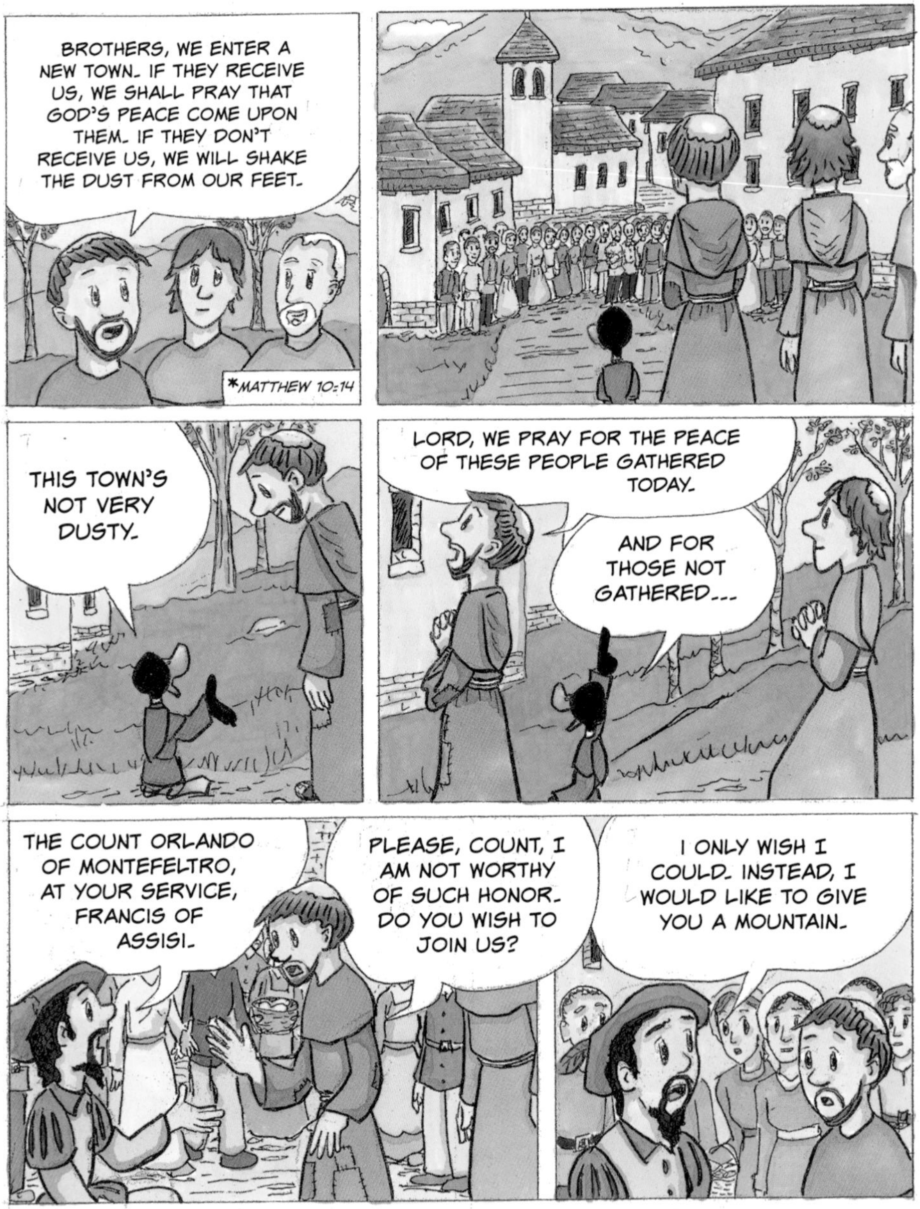
BROTHERS, WE ENTER A NEW TOWN. IF THEY RECEIVE US, WE SHALL PRAY THAT GOD'S PEACE COME UPON THEM. IF THEY DON'T RECEIVE US, WE WILL SHAKE THE DUST FROM OUR FEET.
*MATTHEW 10:14
THIS TOWN'S NOT VERY DUSTY.
LORD, WE PRAY FOR THE PEACE OF THESE PEOPLE GATHERED TODAY.
AND FOR THOSE NOT GATHERED...
THE COUNT ORLANDO OF MONTEFELTRO, AT YOUR SERVICE, FRANCIS OF ASSISI.
PLEASE, COUNT, I AM NOT WORTHY OF SUCH HONOR. DO YOU WISH TO JOIN US?
I ONLY WISH I COULD. INSTEAD, I WOULD LIKE TO GIVE YOU A MOUNTAIN.

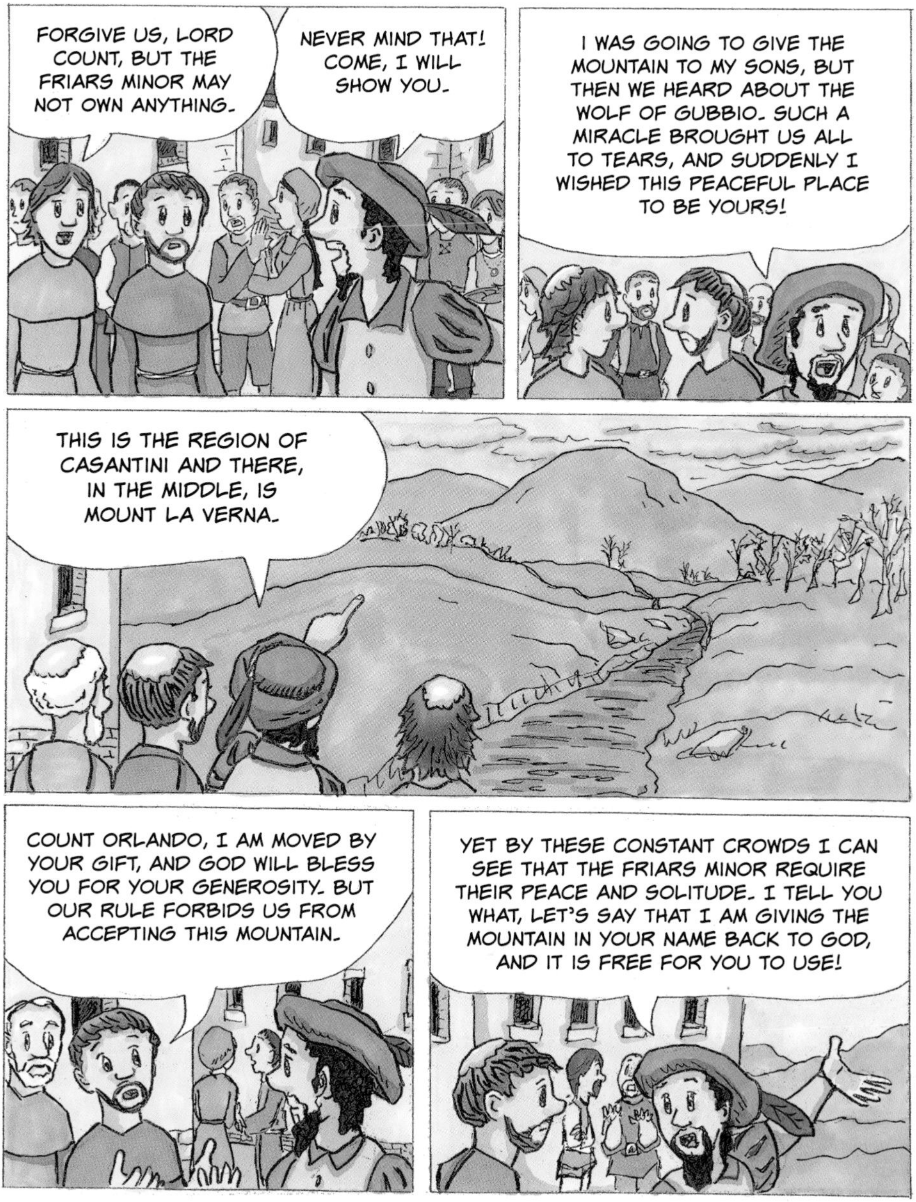
FORGIVE US, LORD COUNT, BUT THE FRIARS MINOR MAY NOT OWN ANYTHING.
NEVER MIND THAT! COME, I WILL SHOW YOU.
I WAS GOING TO GIVE THE MOUNTAIN TO MY SONS, BUT THEN WE HEARD ABOUT THE WOLF OF GUBBIO. SUCH A MIRACLE BROUGHT US ALL TO TEARS, AND SUDDENLY I WISHED THIS PEACEFUL PLACE TO BE YOURS!
THIS IS THE REGION OF CASANTINI AND THERE, IN THE MIDDLE, IS MOUNT LA VERNA.
COUNT ORLANDO, I AM MOVED BY YOUR GIFT, AND GOD WILL BLESS YOU FOR YOUR GENEROSITY. BUT OUR RULE FORBIDS US FROM ACCEPTING THIS MOUNTAIN.
YET BY THESE CONSTANT CROWDS I CAN SEE THAT THE FRIARS MINOR REQUIRE THEIR PEACE AND SOLITUDE. I TELL YOU WHAT, LET'S SAY THAT I AM GIVING THE MOUNTAIN IN YOUR NAME BACK TO GOD, AND IT IS FREE FOR YOU TO USE!

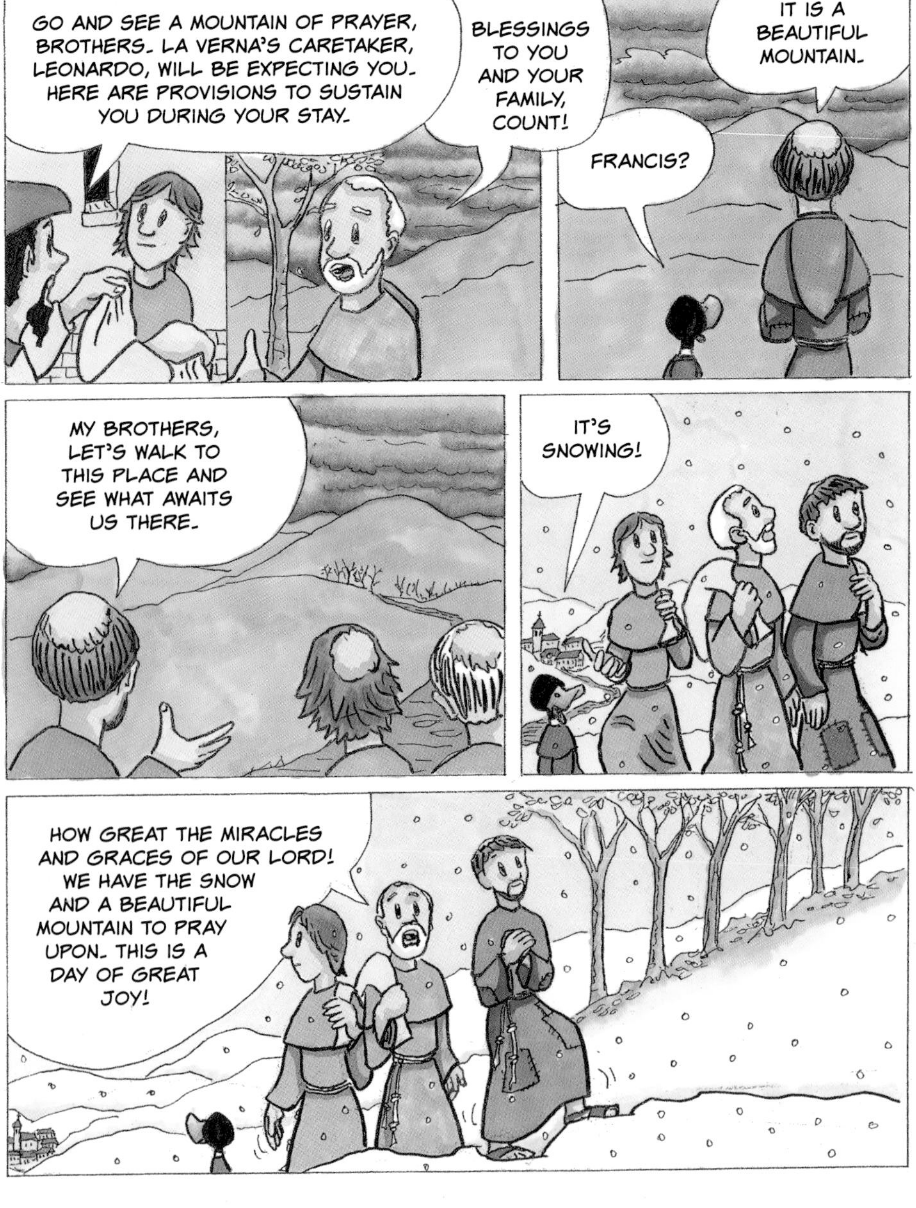
GO AND SEE A MOUNTAIN OF PRAYER, BROTHERS. LA VERNA'S CARETAKER, LEONARDO, WILL BE EXPECTING YOU. HERE ARE PROVISIONS TO SUSTAIN YOU DURING YOUR STAY.
BLESSINGS TO YOU AND YOUR FAMILY, COUNT!
IT IS A BEAUTIFUL MOUNTAIN.
FRANCIS?
MY BROTHERS, LET'S WALK TO THIS PLACE AND SEE WHAT AWAITS US THERE.
IT'S SNOWING!
HOW GREAT THE MIRACLES AND GRACES OF OUR LORD! WE HAVE THE SNOW AND A BEAUTIFUL MOUNTAIN TO PRAY UPON. THIS IS A DAY OF GREAT JOY!

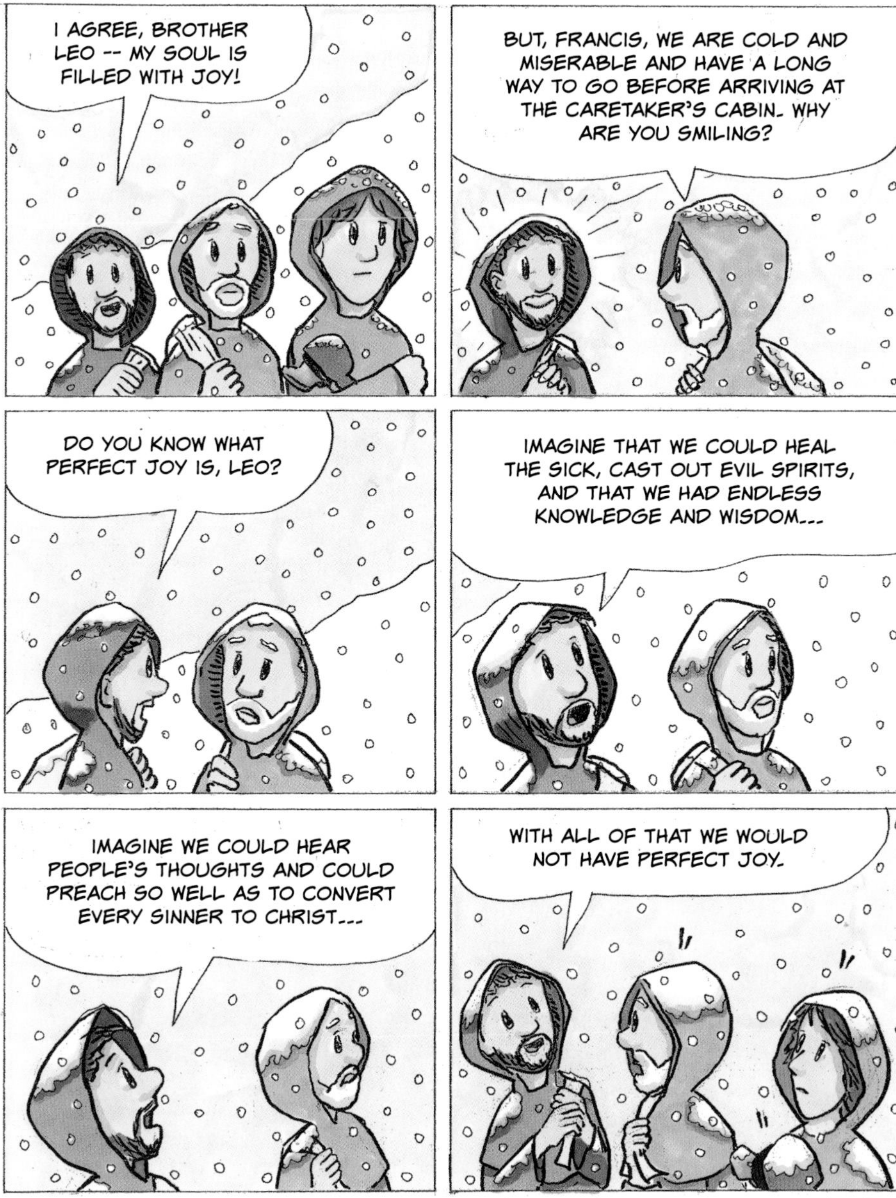
I AGREE, BROTHER LEO -- MY SOUL IS FILLED WITH JOY!
BUT, FRANCIS, WE ARE COLD AND MISERABLE AND HAVE A LONG WAY TO GO BEFORE ARRIVING AT THE CARETAKER'S CABIN. WHY ARE YOU SMILING?
DO YOU KNOW WHAT PERFECT JOY IS, LEO?
IMAGINE THAT WE COULD HEAL THE SICK, CAST OUT EVIL SPIRITS, AND THAT WE HAD ENDLESS KNOWLEDGE AND WISDOM...
IMAGINE WE COULD HEAR PEOPLE'S THOUGHTS AND COULD PREACH SO WELL AS TO CONVERT EVERY SINNER TO CHRIST...
WITH ALL OF THAT WE WOULD NOT HAVE PERFECT JOY.

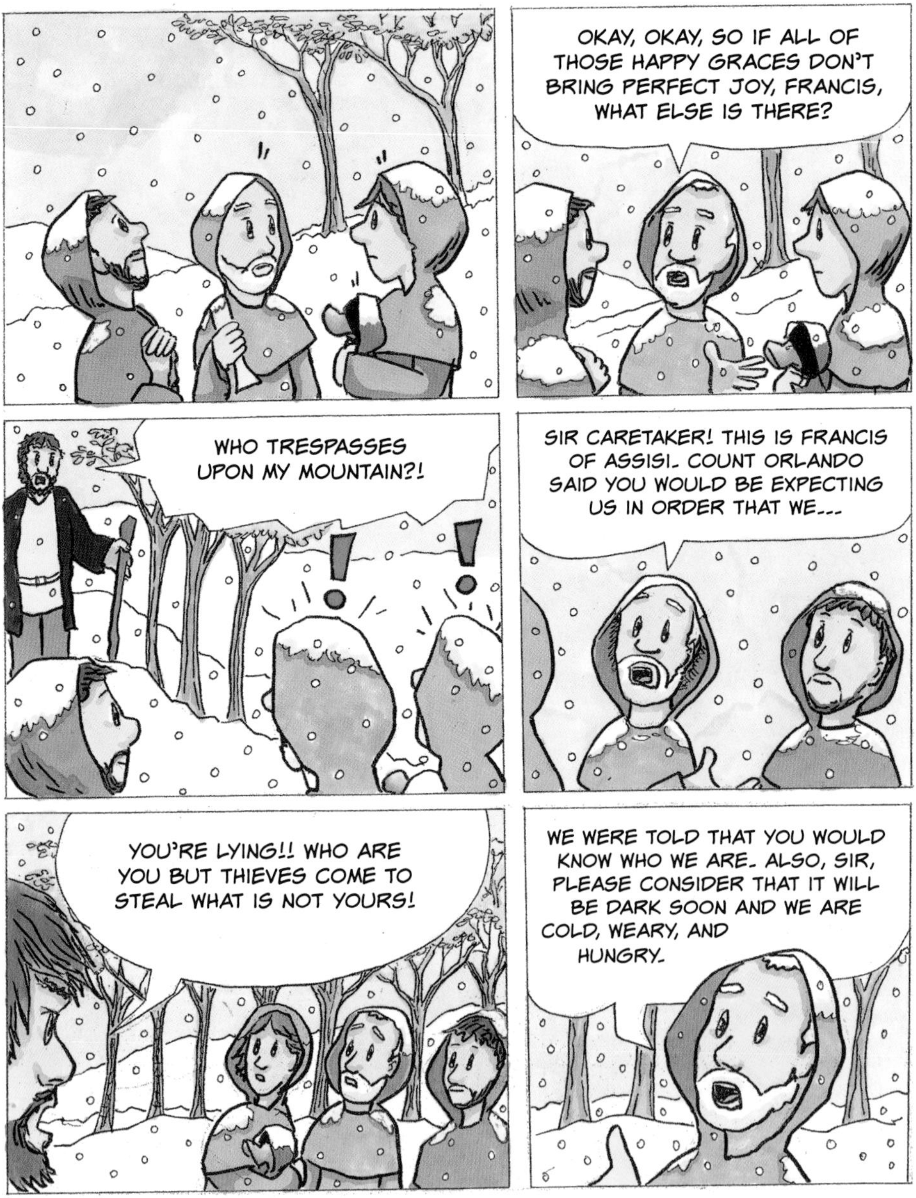

OKAY, OKAY, SO IF ALL OF THOSE HAPPY GRACES DON'T BRING PERFECT JOY, FRANCIS, WHAT ELSE IS THERE?
WHO TRESPASSES UPON MY MOUNTAIN?!
SIR CARETAKER! THIS IS FRANCIS OF ASSISI. COUNT ORLANDO SAID YOU WOULD BE EXPECTING US IN ORDER THAT WE...
YOU'RE LYING!! WHO ARE YOU BUT THIEVES COME TO STEAL WHAT IS NOT YOURS!
WE WERE TOLD THAT YOU WOULD KNOW WHO WE ARE. ALSO, SIR, PLEASE CONSIDER THAT IT WILL BE DARK SOON AND WE ARE COLD, WEARY, AND HUNGRY.

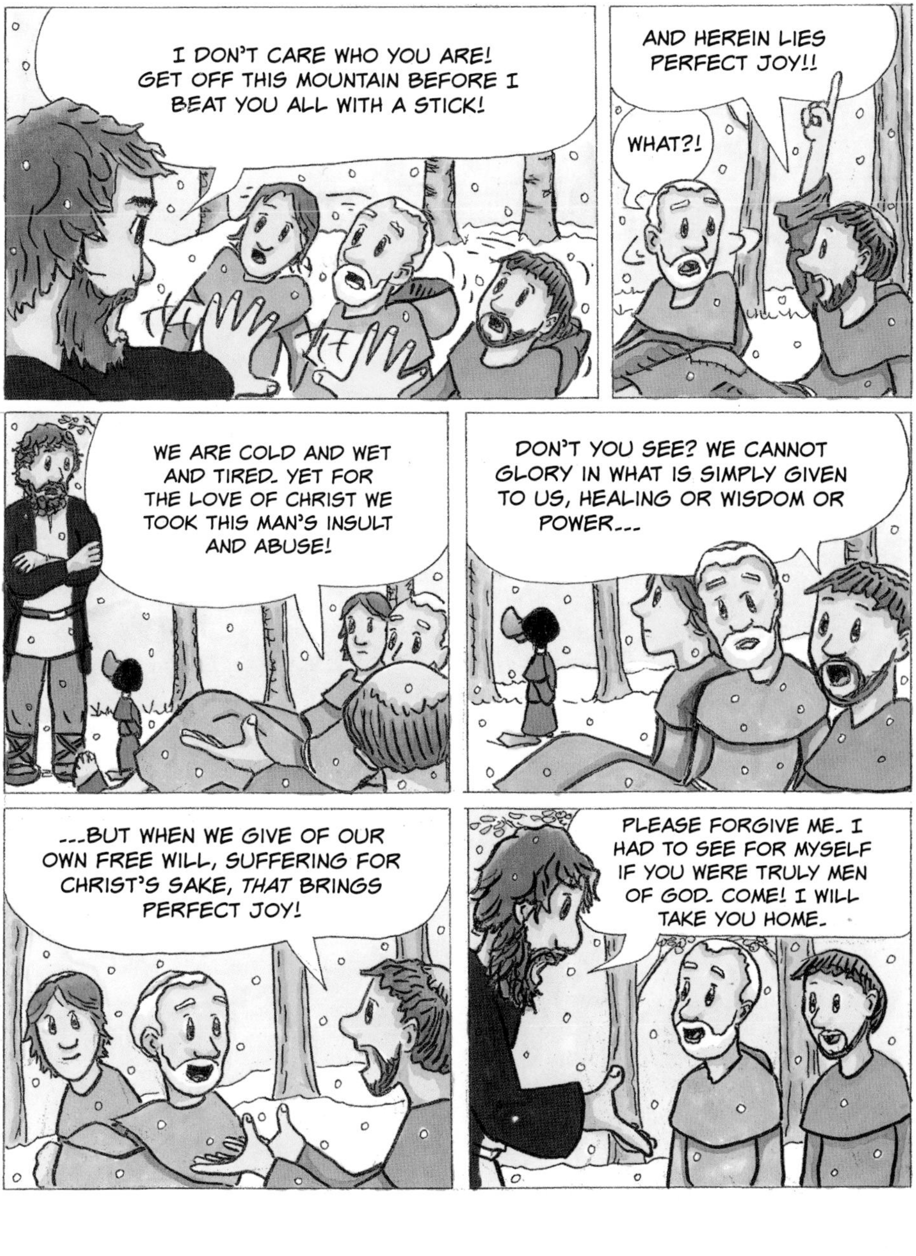
I DON'T CARE WHO YOU ARE! GET OFF THIS MOUNTAIN BEFORE I BEAT YOU ALL WITH A STICK!
AND HEREIN LIES PERFECT JOY!!
WHAT?!
WE ARE COLD AND WET AND TIRED. YET FOR THE LOVE OF CHRIST WE TOOK THIS MAN'S INSULT AND ABUSE!
DON'T YOU SEE? WE CANNOT GLORY IN WHAT IS SIMPLY GIVEN TO US, HEALING OR WISDOM OR POWER...
...BUT WHEN WE GIVE OF OUR OWN FREE WILL, SUFFERING FOR CHRIST'S SAKE, *THAT* BRINGS PERFECT JOY!
PLEASE FORGIVE ME. I HAD TO SEE FOR MYSELF IF YOU WERE TRULY MEN OF GOD. COME! I WILL TAKE YOU HOME.

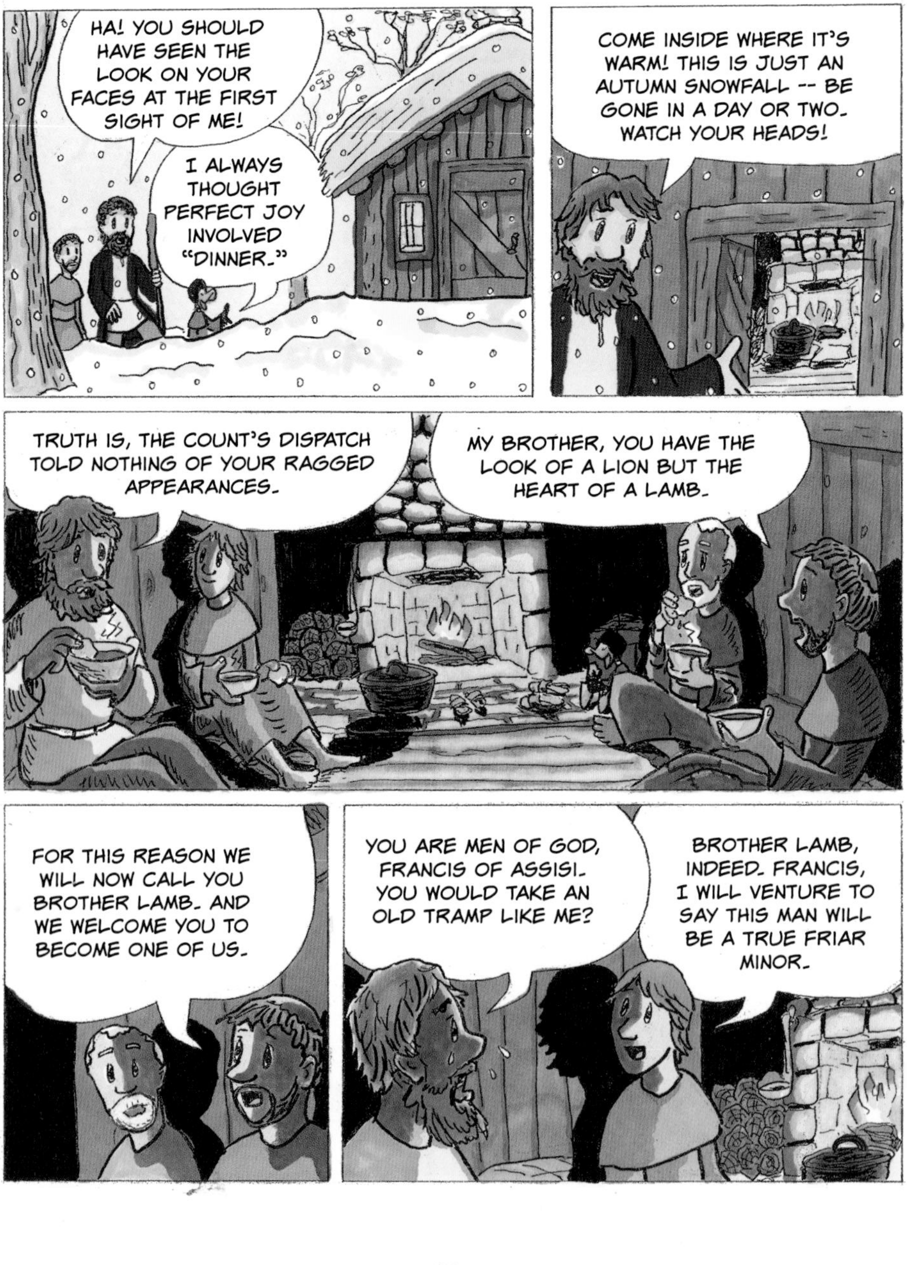
HA! YOU SHOULD HAVE SEEN THE LOOK ON YOUR FACES AT THE FIRST SIGHT OF ME!
I ALWAYS THOUGHT PERFECT JOY INVOLVED "DINNER."
COME INSIDE WHERE IT'S WARM! THIS IS JUST AN AUTUMN SNOWFALL -- BE GONE IN A DAY OR TWO. WATCH YOUR HEADS!
TRUTH IS, THE COUNT'S DISPATCH TOLD NOTHING OF YOUR RAGGED APPEARANCES.
MY BROTHER, YOU HAVE THE LOOK OF A LION BUT THE HEART OF A LAMB.
FOR THIS REASON WE WILL NOW CALL YOU BROTHER LAMB. AND WE WELCOME YOU TO BECOME ONE OF US.
YOU ARE MEN OF GOD, FRANCIS OF ASSISI. YOU WOULD TAKE AN OLD TRAMP LIKE ME?
BROTHER LAMB, INDEED. FRANCIS, I WILL VENTURE TO SAY THIS MAN WILL BE A TRUE FRIAR MINOR.

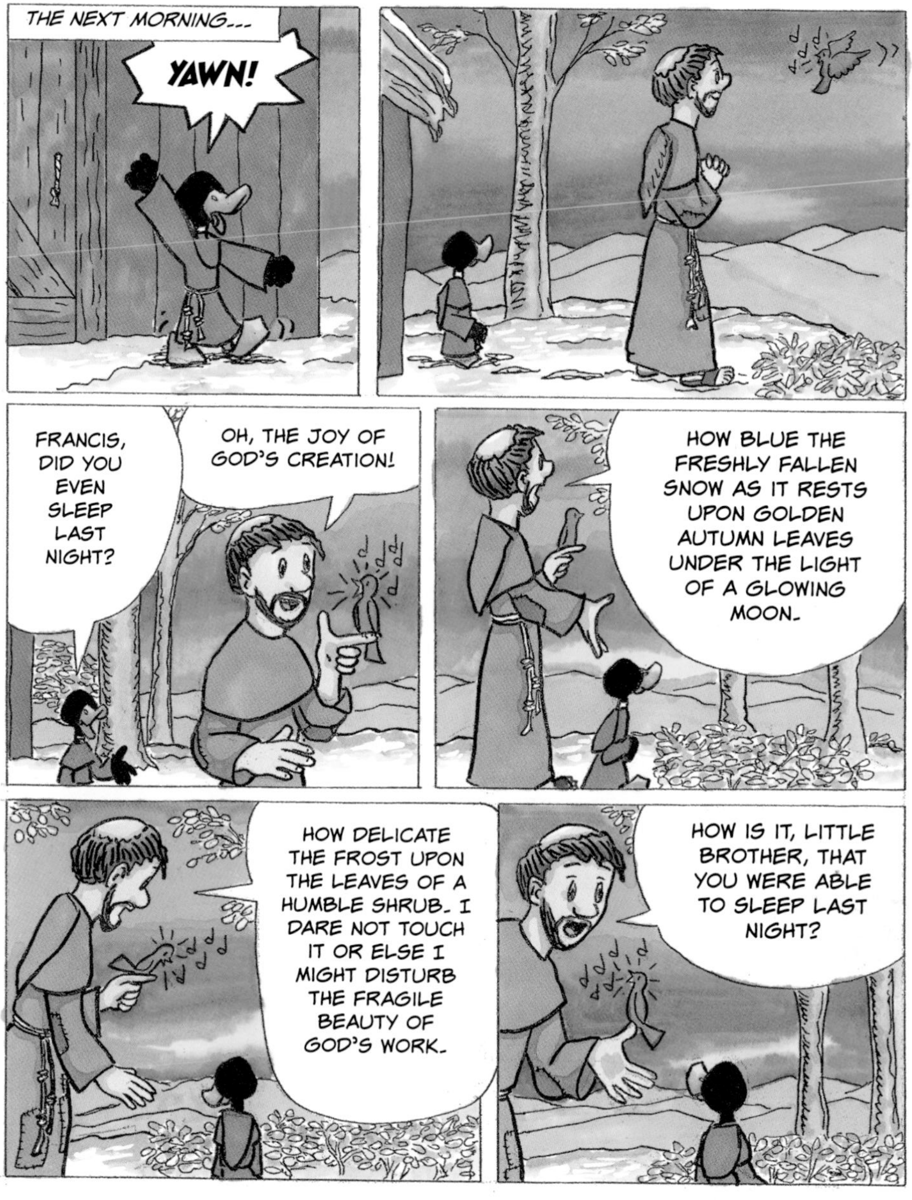
THE NEXT MORNING...
YAWN!
FRANCIS, DID YOU EVEN SLEEP LAST NIGHT?
OH, THE JOY OF GOD'S CREATION!
HOW BLUE THE FRESHLY FALLEN SNOW AS IT RESTS UPON GOLDEN AUTUMN LEAVES UNDER THE LIGHT OF A GLOWING MOON.
HOW DELICATE THE FROST UPON THE LEAVES OF A HUMBLE SHRUB. I DARE NOT TOUCH IT OR ELSE I MIGHT DISTURB THE FRAGILE BEAUTY OF GOD'S WORK.
HOW IS IT, LITTLE BROTHER, THAT YOU WERE ABLE TO SLEEP LAST NIGHT?

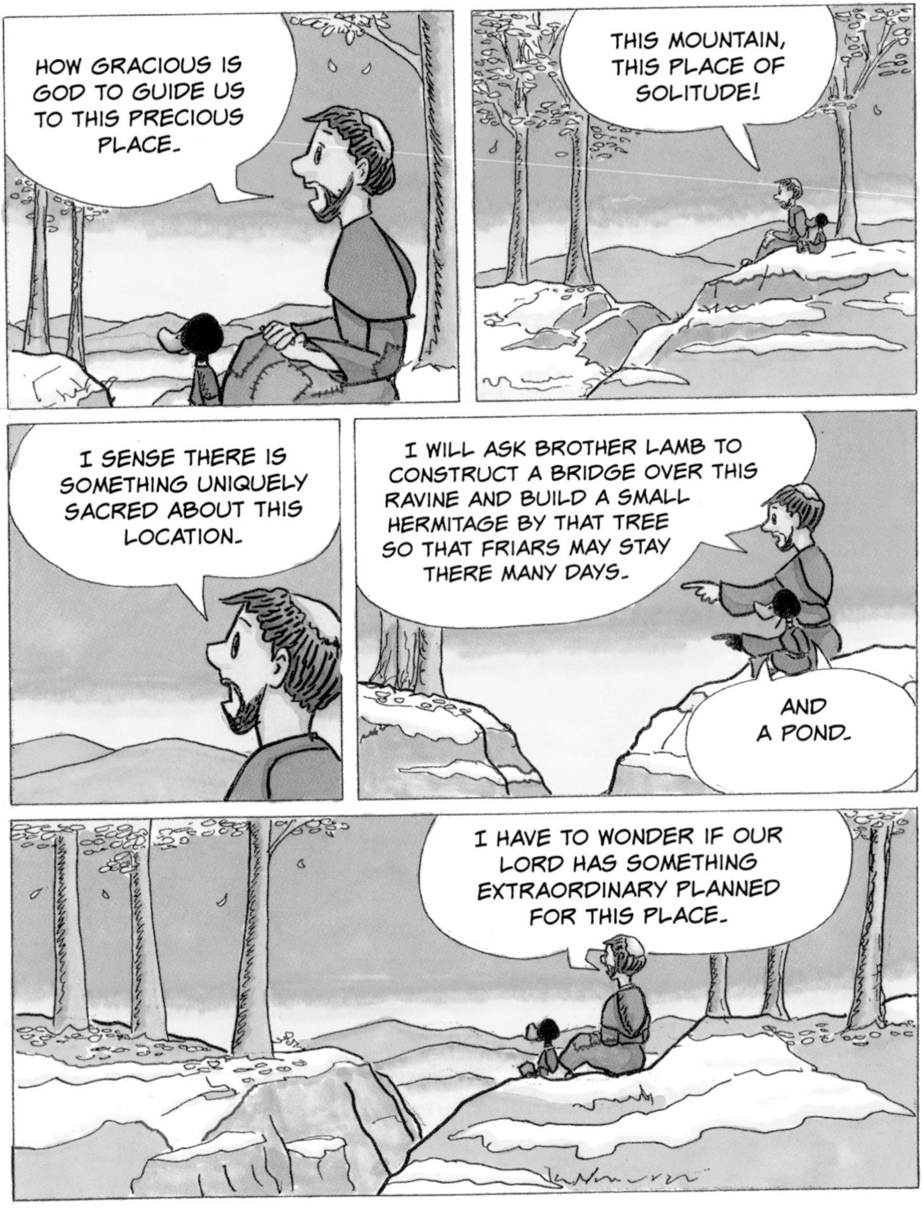
HOW GRACIOUS IS GOD TO GUIDE US TO THIS PRECIOUS PLACE.
THIS MOUNTAIN, THIS PLACE OF SOLITUDE!
I SENSE THERE IS SOMETHING UNIQUELY SACRED ABOUT THIS LOCATION.
I WILL ASK BROTHER LAMB TO CONSTRUCT A BRIDGE OVER THIS RAVINE AND BUILD A SMALL HERMITAGE BY THAT TREE SO THAT FRIARS MAY STAY THERE MANY DAYS.
AND A POND.
I HAVE TO WONDER IF OUR LORD HAS SOMETHING EXTRAORDINARY PLANNED FOR THIS PLACE.

CHAPTER 7
SAINT FRANCIS AND THE SULTAN

If the world hates you
Realize that it hated me first.
If you belonged to the world
The world would love its own;
But because you do not belong to the world
And I have chosen you out of the world
The world hates you.
—JOHN 15:18-19

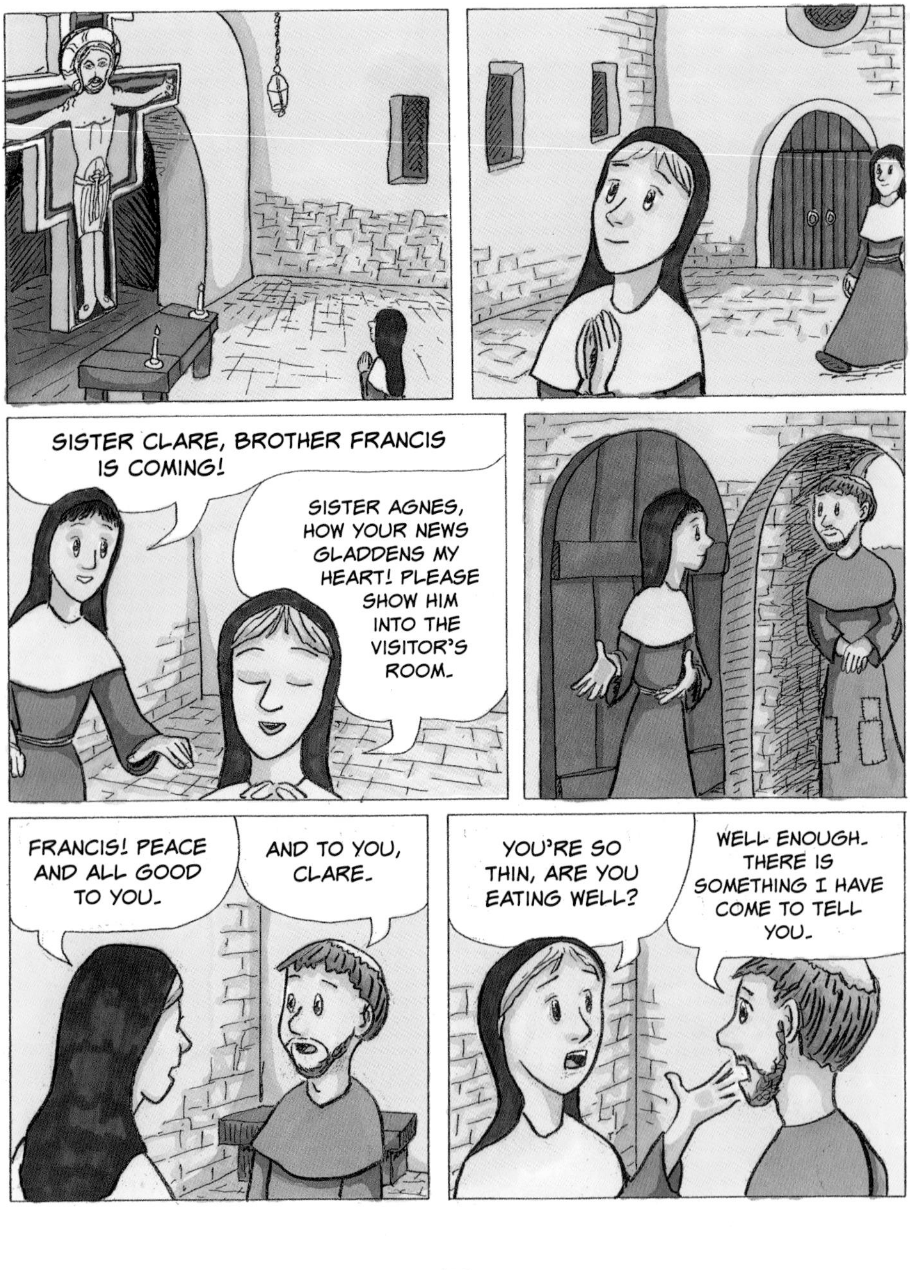
SISTER CLARE, BROTHER FRANCIS IS COMING!
SISTER AGNES, HOW YOUR NEWS GLADDENS MY HEART! PLEASE SHOW HIM INTO THE VISITOR'S ROOM.
FRANCIS! PEACE AND ALL GOOD TO YOU.
AND TO YOU, CLARE.
YOU'RE SO THIN, ARE YOU EATING WELL?
WELL ENOUGH. THERE IS SOMETHING I HAVE COME TO TELL YOU.

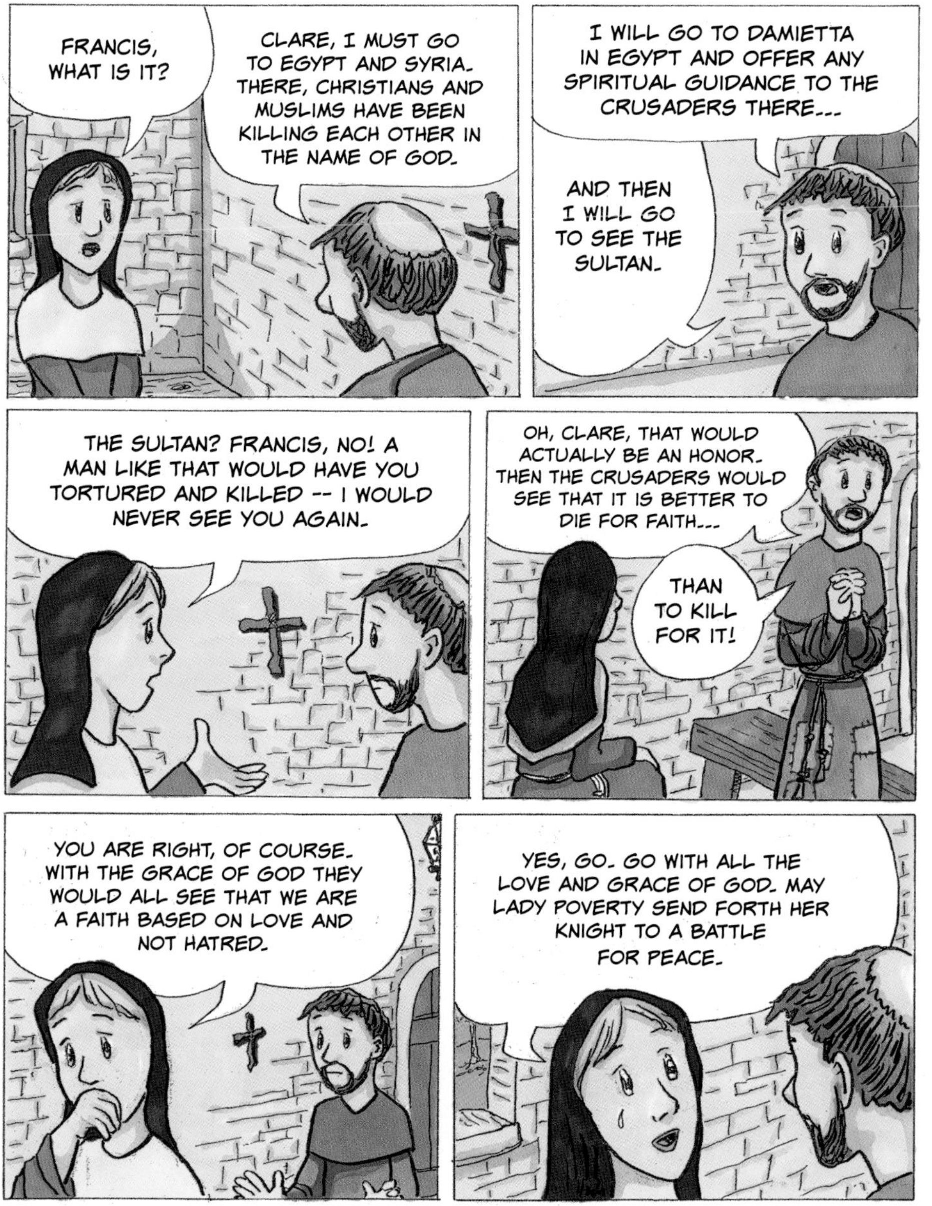
FRANCIS, WHAT IS IT?
CLARE, I MUST GO TO EGYPT AND SYRIA. THERE, CHRISTIANS AND MUSLIMS HAVE BEEN KILLING EACH OTHER IN THE NAME OF GOD.
I WILL GO TO DAMIETTA IN EGYPT AND OFFER ANY SPIRITUAL GUIDANCE TO THE CRUSADERS THERE...
AND THEN I WILL GO TO SEE THE SULTAN.
THE SULTAN? FRANCIS, NO! A MAN LIKE THAT WOULD HAVE YOU TORTURED AND KILLED -- I WOULD NEVER SEE YOU AGAIN.
OH, CLARE, THAT WOULD ACTUALLY BE AN HONOR. THEN THE CRUSADERS WOULD SEE THAT IT IS BETTER TO DIE FOR FAITH...
THAN TO KILL FOR IT!
YOU ARE RIGHT, OF COURSE. WITH THE GRACE OF GOD THEY WOULD ALL SEE THAT WE ARE A FAITH BASED ON LOVE AND NOT HATRED.
YES, GO. GO WITH ALL THE LOVE AND GRACE OF GOD. MAY LADY POVERTY SEND FORTH HER KNIGHT TO A BATTLE FOR PEACE.

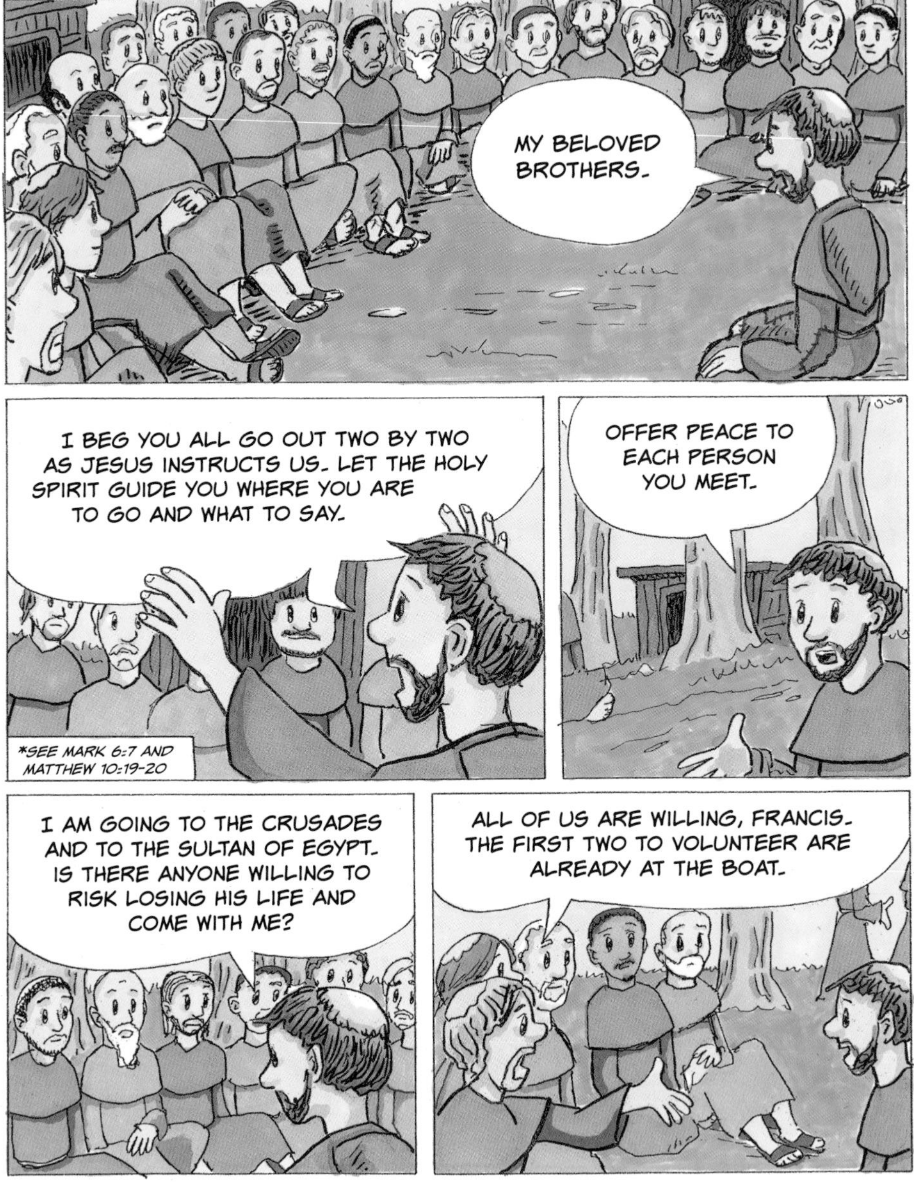
MY BELOVED BROTHERS.
I BEG YOU ALL GO OUT TWO BY TWO AS JESUS INSTRUCTS US. LET THE HOLY SPIRIT GUIDE YOU WHERE YOU ARE TO GO AND WHAT TO SAY.
*SEE MARK 6:7 AND MATTHEW 10:19-20
OFFER PEACE TO EACH PERSON YOU MEET.
I AM GOING TO THE CRUSADES AND TO THE SULTAN OF EGYPT. IS THERE ANYONE WILLING TO RISK LOSING HIS LIFE AND COME WITH ME?
ALL OF US ARE WILLING, FRANCIS. THE FIRST TWO TO VOLUNTEER ARE ALREADY AT THE BOAT.

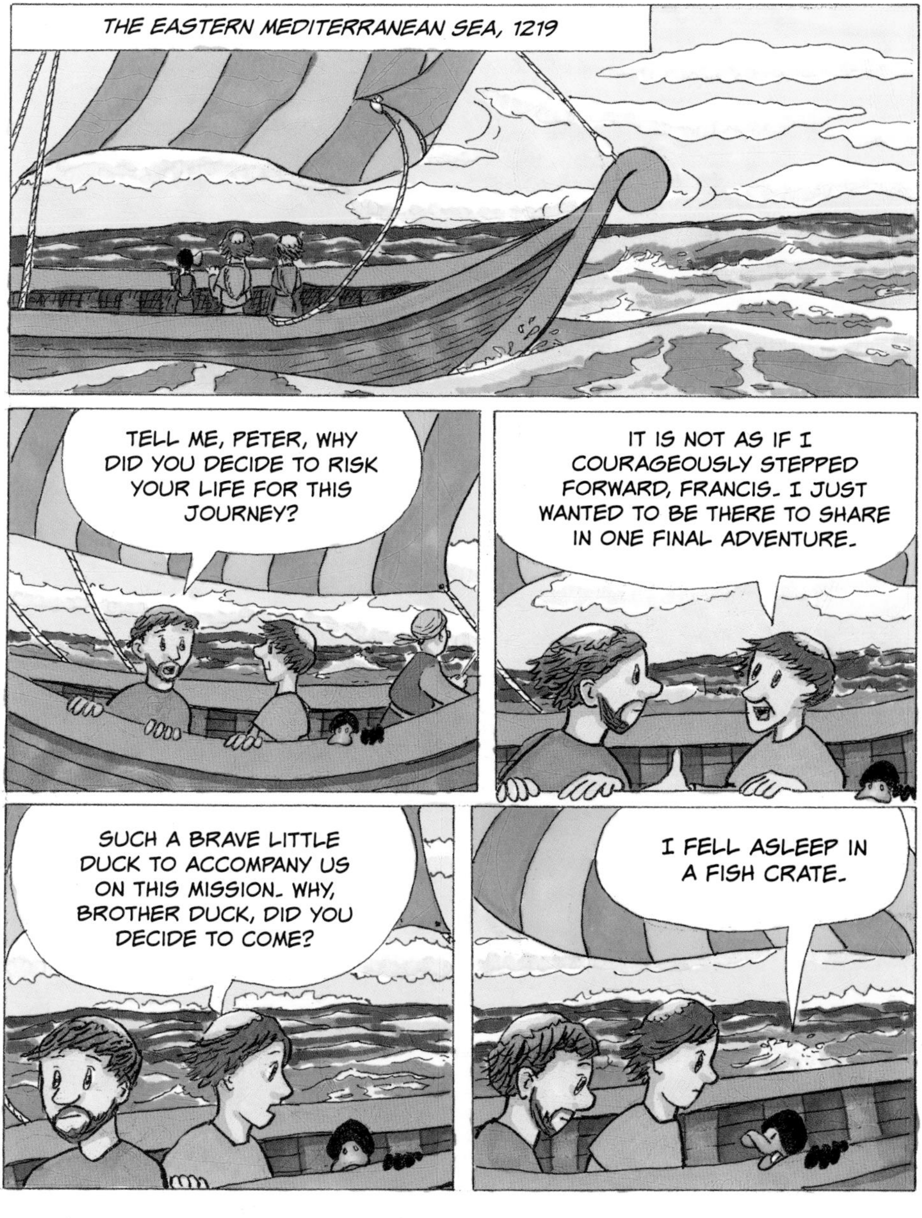
THE EASTERN MEDITERRANEAN SEA, 1219
TELL ME, PETER, WHY DID YOU DECIDE TO RISK YOUR LIFE FOR THIS JOURNEY?
IT IS NOT AS IF I COURAGEOUSLY STEPPED FORWARD, FRANCIS. I JUST WANTED TO BE THERE TO SHARE IN ONE FINAL ADVENTURE.
SUCH A BRAVE LITTLE DUCK TO ACCOMPANY US ON THIS MISSION. WHY, BROTHER DUCK, DID YOU DECIDE TO COME?
I FELL ASLEEP IN A FISH CRATE.

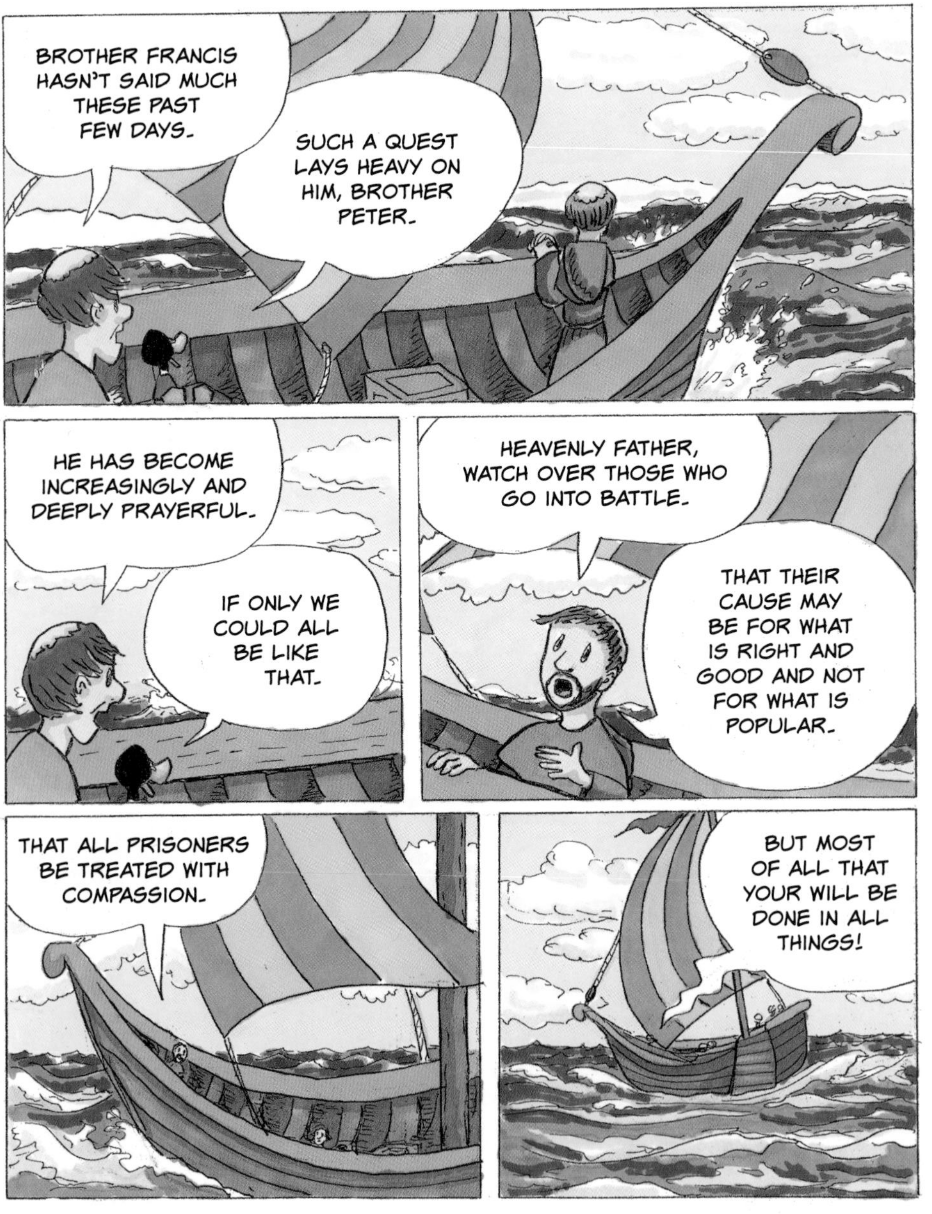
BROTHER FRANCIS HASN'T SAID MUCH THESE PAST FEW DAYS.
SUCH A QUEST LAYS HEAVY ON HIM, BROTHER PETER.
HE HAS BECOME INCREASINGLY AND DEEPLY PRAYERFUL.
IF ONLY WE COULD ALL BE LIKE THAT.
HEAVENLY FATHER, WATCH OVER THOSE WHO GO INTO BATTLE.
THAT THEIR CAUSE MAY BE FOR WHAT IS RIGHT AND GOOD AND NOT FOR WHAT IS POPULAR.
THAT ALL PRISONERS BE TREATED WITH COMPASSION.
BUT MOST OF ALL THAT YOUR WILL BE DONE IN ALL THINGS!

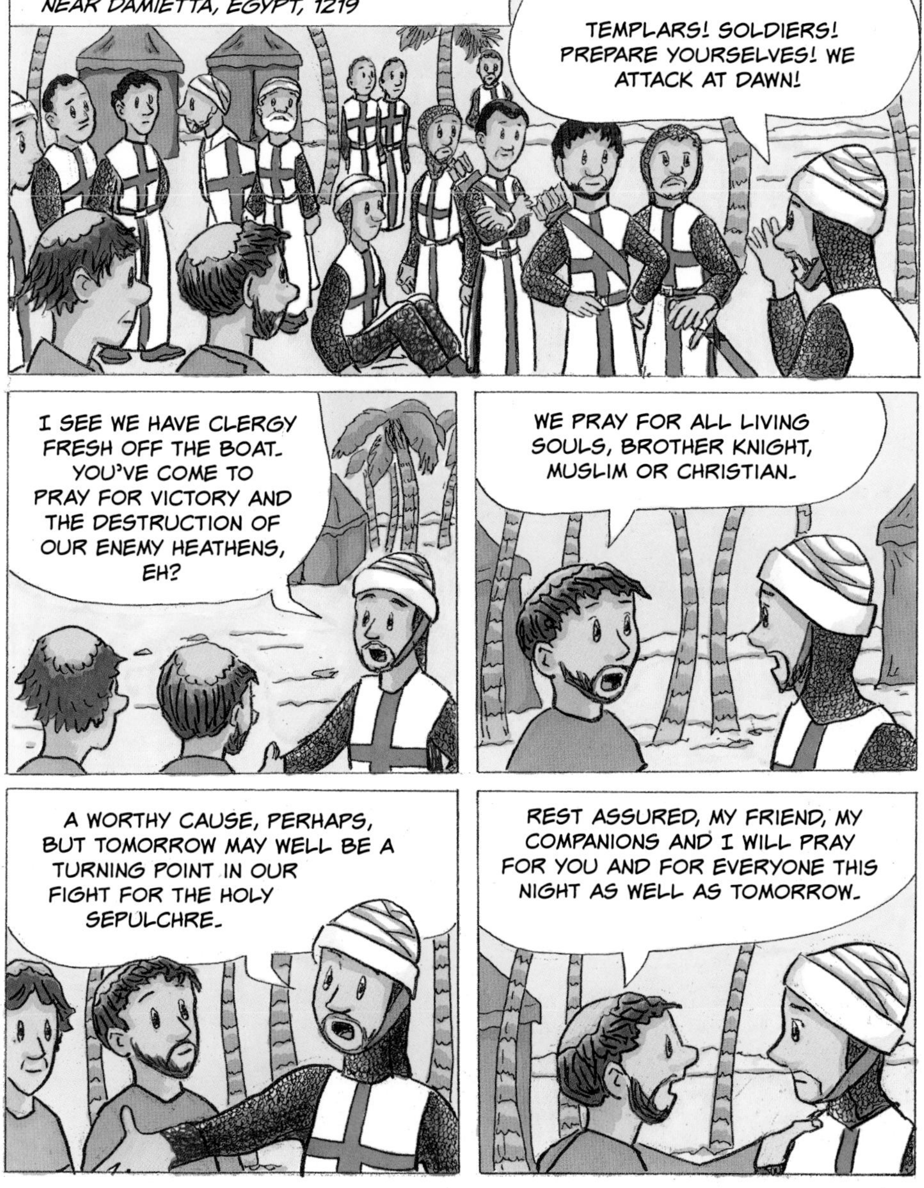
NEAR DAMIETTA, EGYPT, 1219
TEMPLARS! SOLDIERS! PREPARE YOURSELVES! WE ATTACK AT DAWN!
I SEE WE HAVE CLERGY FRESH OFF THE BOAT. YOU'VE COME TO PRAY FOR VICTORY AND THE DESTRUCTION OF OUR ENEMY HEATHENS, EH?
WE PRAY FOR ALL LIVING SOULS, BROTHER KNIGHT, MUSLIM OR CHRISTIAN.
A WORTHY CAUSE, PERHAPS, BUT TOMORROW MAY WELL BE A TURNING POINT IN OUR FIGHT FOR THE HOLY SEPULCHRE.
REST ASSURED, MY FRIEND, MY COMPANIONS AND I WILL PRAY FOR YOU AND FOR EVERYONE THIS NIGHT AS WELL AS TOMORROW.

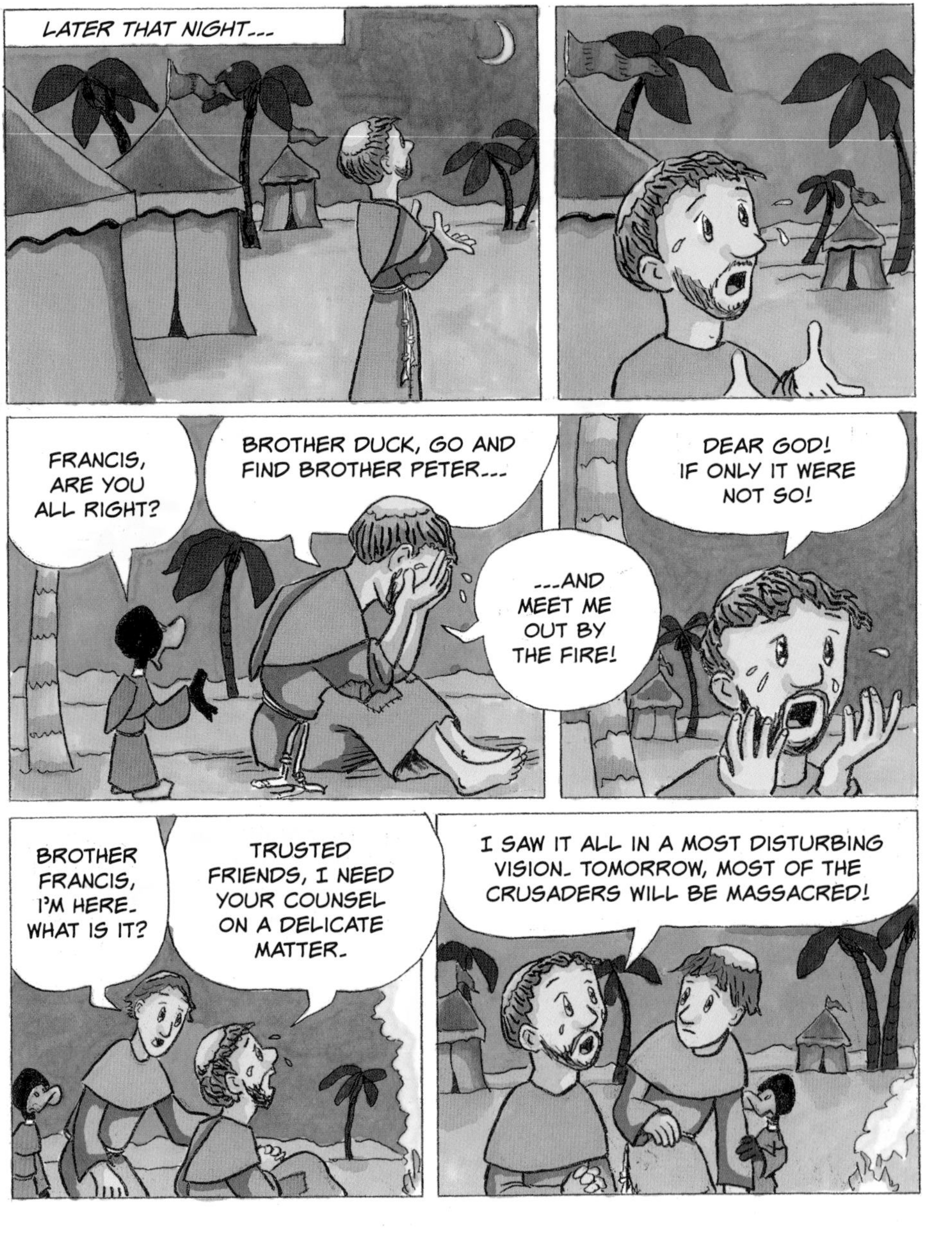
LATER THAT NIGHT...
FRANCIS, ARE YOU ALL RIGHT?
BROTHER DUCK, GO AND FIND BROTHER PETER...
...AND MEET ME OUT BY THE FIRE!
DEAR GOD! IF ONLY IT WERE NOT SO!
BROTHER FRANCIS, I'M HERE. WHAT IS IT?
TRUSTED FRIENDS, I NEED YOUR COUNSEL ON A DELICATE MATTER.
I SAW IT ALL IN A MOST DISTURBING VISION. TOMORROW, MOST OF THE CRUSADERS WILL BE MASSACRED!

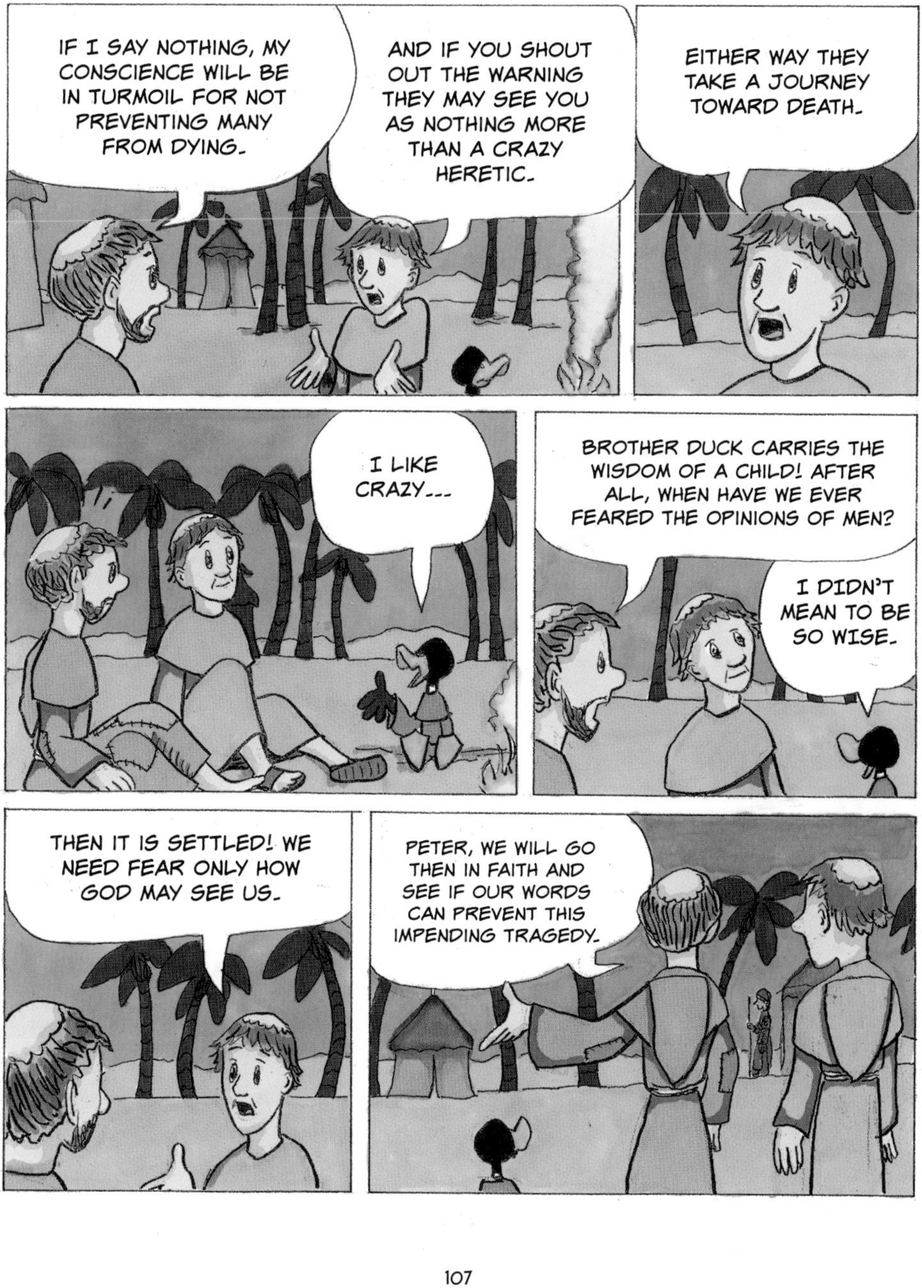
IF I SAY NOTHING, MY CONSCIENCE WILL BE IN TURMOIL FOR NOT PREVENTING MANY FROM DYING.
AND IF YOU SHOUT OUT THE WARNING THEY MAY SEE YOU AS NOTHING MORE THAN A CRAZY HERETIC.
EITHER WAY THEY TAKE A JOURNEY TOWARD DEATH.
I LIKE CRAZY...
BROTHER DUCK CARRIES THE WISDOM OF A CHILD! AFTER ALL, WHEN HAVE WE EVER FEARED THE OPINIONS OF MEN?
I DIDN'T MEAN TO BE SO WISE.
THEN IT IS SETTLED! WE NEED FEAR ONLY HOW GOD MAY SEE US.
PETER, WE WILL GO THEN IN FAITH AND SEE IF OUR WORDS CAN PREVENT THIS IMPENDING TRAGEDY.

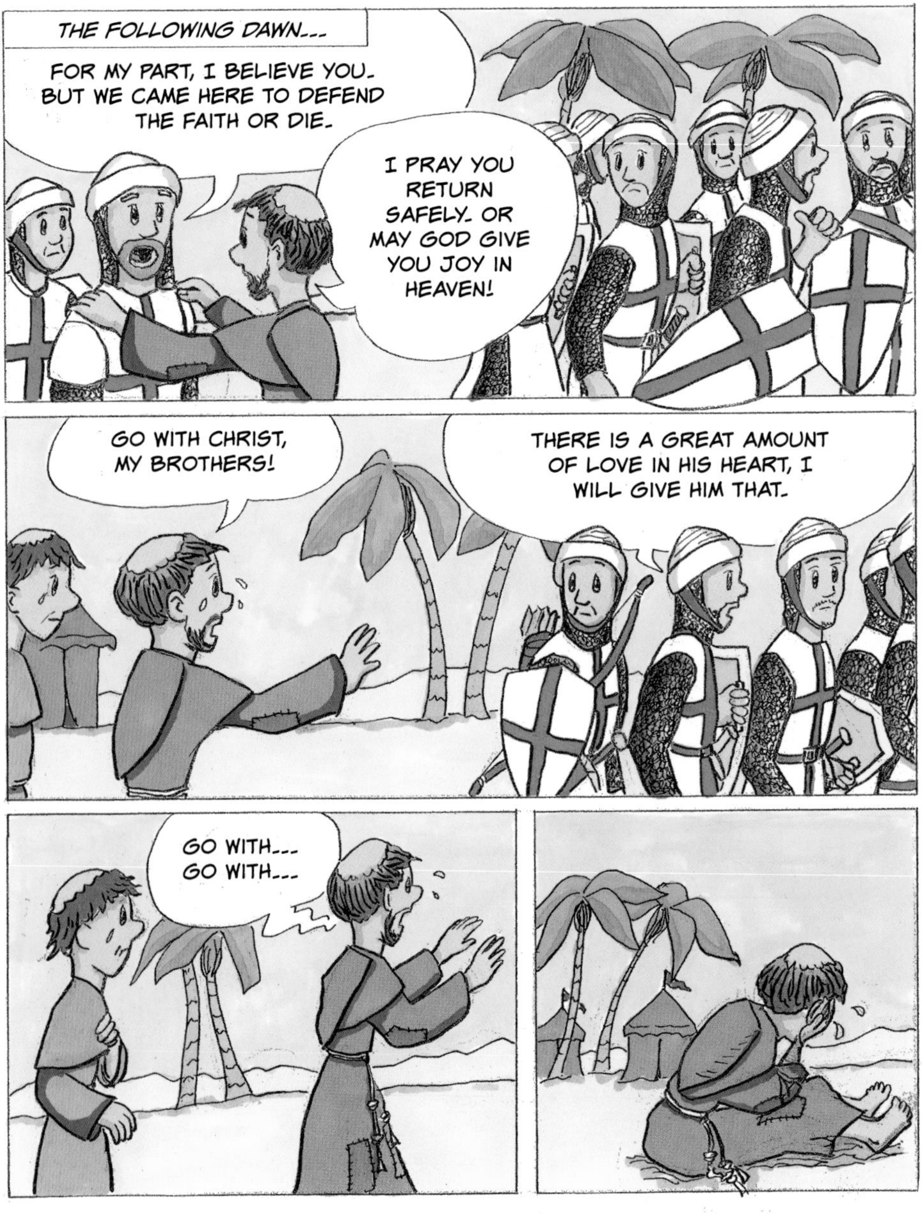

THE FOLLOWING DAWN...
FOR MY PART, I BELIEVE YOU. BUT WE CAME HERE TO DEFEND THE FAITH OR DIE.
I PRAY YOU RETURN SAFELY. OR MAY GOD GIVE YOU JOY IN HEAVEN!
GO WITH CHRIST, MY BROTHERS!
THERE IS A GREAT AMOUNT OF LOVE IN HIS HEART, I WILL GIVE HIM THAT.
GO WITH... GO WITH...

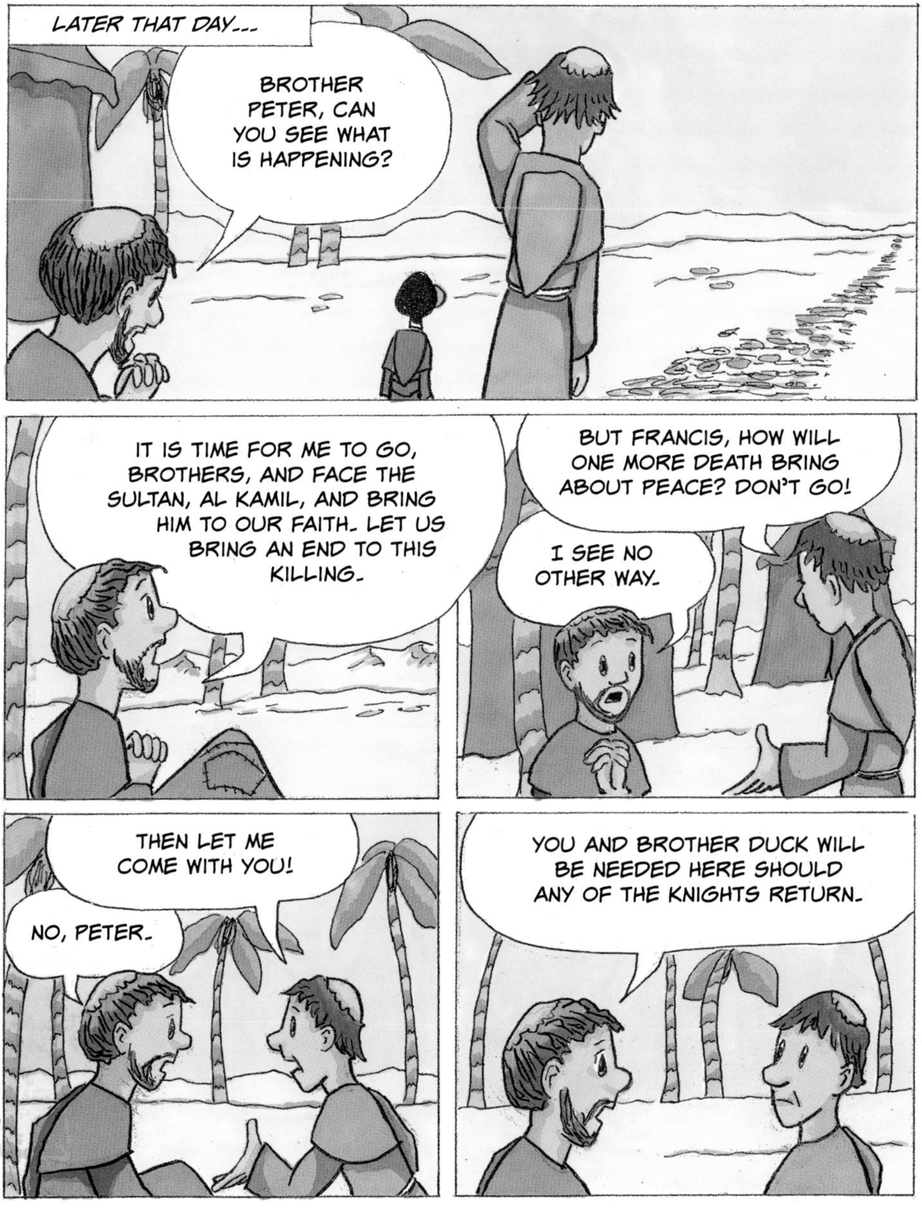
LATER THAT DAY...
BROTHER PETER, CAN YOU SEE WHAT IS HAPPENING?
IT IS TIME FOR ME TO GO, BROTHERS, AND FACE THE SULTAN, AL KAMIL, AND BRING HIM TO OUR FAITH. LET US BRING AN END TO THIS KILLING.
BUT FRANCIS, HOW WILL ONE MORE DEATH BRING ABOUT PEACE? DON'T GO!
I SEE NO OTHER WAY.
THEN LET ME COME WITH YOU!
NO, PETER.
YOU AND BROTHER DUCK WILL BE NEEDED HERE SHOULD ANY OF THE KNIGHTS RETURN.

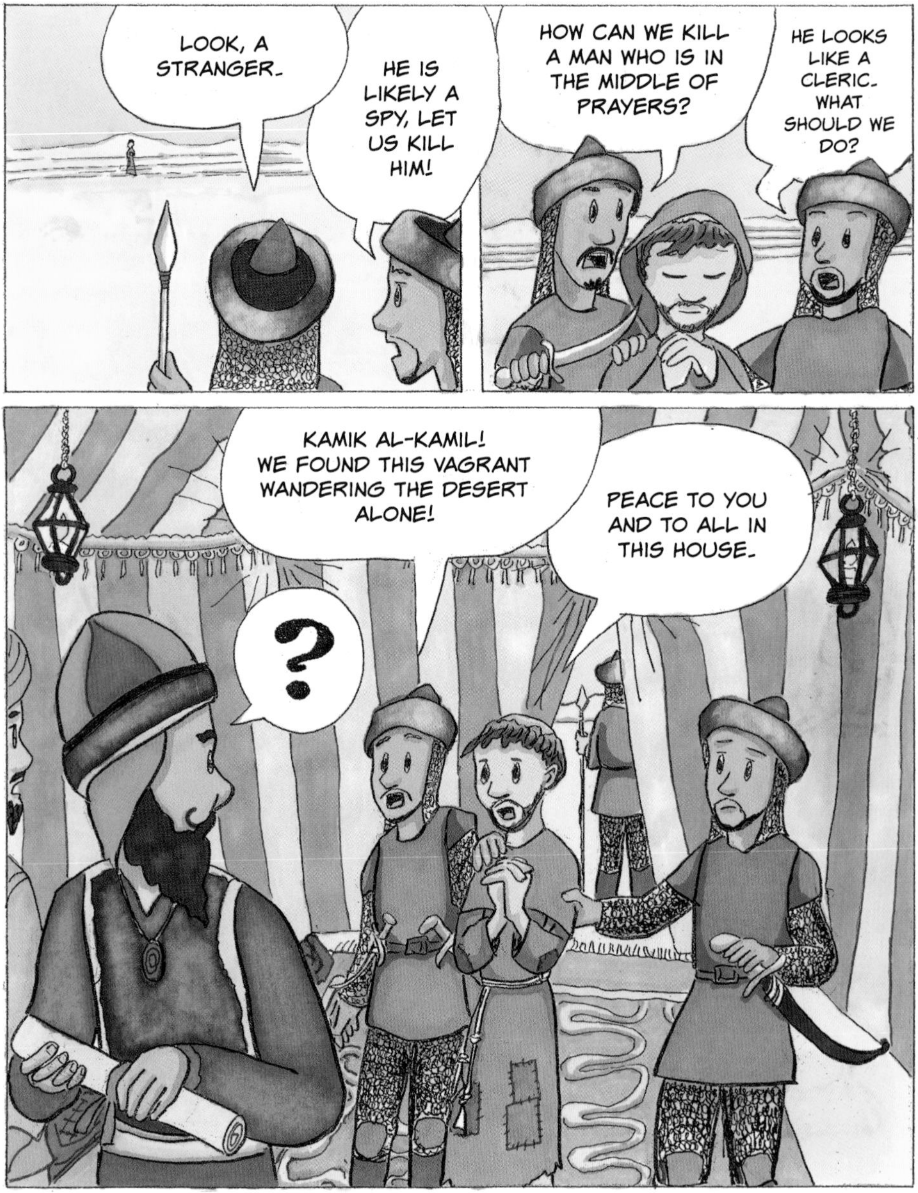
LOOK, A STRANGER.
HE IS LIKELY A SPY, LET US KILL HIM!
HOW CAN WE KILL A MAN WHO IS IN THE MIDDLE OF PRAYERS?
HE LOOKS LIKE A CLERIC. WHAT SHOULD WE DO?
KAMIK AL-KAMIL! WE FOUND THIS VAGRANT WANDERING THE DESERT ALONE!
?
PEACE TO YOU AND TO ALL IN THIS HOUSE.

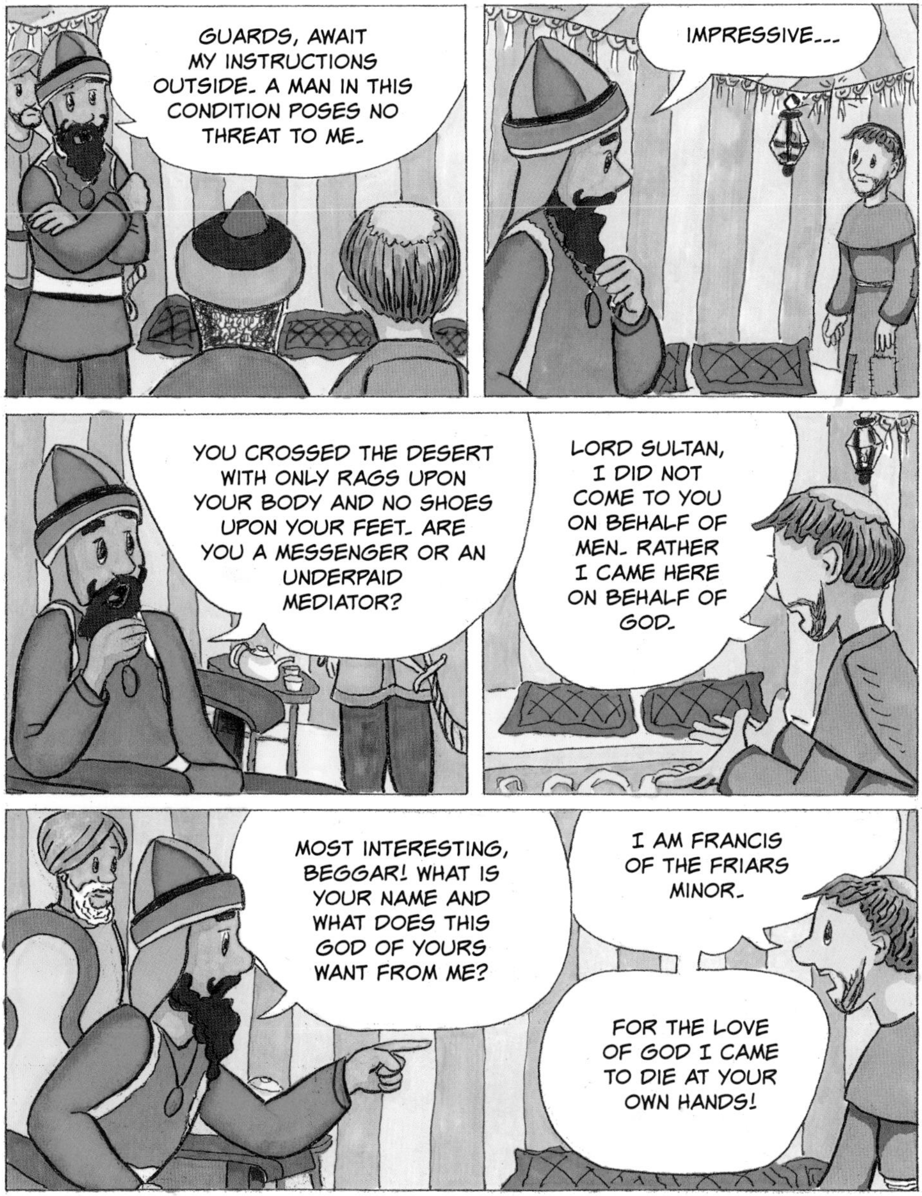
GUARDS, AWAIT MY INSTRUCTIONS OUTSIDE. A MAN IN THIS CONDITION POSES NO THREAT TO ME.
IMPRESSIVE...
YOU CROSSED THE DESERT WITH ONLY RAGS UPON YOUR BODY AND NO SHOES UPON YOUR FEET. ARE YOU A MESSENGER OR AN UNDERPAID MEDIATOR?
LORD SULTAN, I DID NOT COME TO YOU ON BEHALF OF MEN. RATHER I CAME HERE ON BEHALF OF GOD.
MOST INTERESTING, BEGGAR! WHAT IS YOUR NAME AND WHAT DOES THIS GOD OF YOURS WANT FROM ME?
I AM FRANCIS OF THE FRIARS MINOR.
FOR THE LOVE OF GOD I CAME TO DIE AT YOUR OWN HANDS!

FOR MANY DAYS I HAVE WITNESSED THIS WAR BETWEEN RELIGIONS -- EACH SIDE TORTURING AND KILLING ALL IN THE NAME OF GOD IN HEAVEN.

AND WHAT DOES OUR WAR HAVE TO DO WITH ME HAVING YOU PUT TO DEATH?

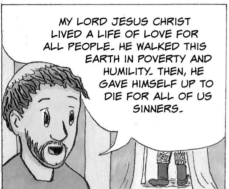

MY LORD JESUS CHRIST LIVED A LIFE OF LOVE FOR ALL PEOPLE. HE WALKED THIS EARTH IN POVERTY AND HUMILITY. THEN, HE GAVE HIMSELF UP TO DIE FOR ALL OF US SINNERS.

MY LIFE IS A FEEBLE ATTEMPT TO IMITATE THIS LOVE OF CHRIST FOR ALL HUMANITY. I WOULD GLADLY GIVE UP MY OWN LIFE IF IT WERE A MEANS OF BRINGING PEACE AND FORGIVENESS BETWEEN OUR PEOPLES.

HONORABLE SIR! HOW MAY I SHOW YOU THAT CHRIST WAS MORE THAN JUST A PROPHET? FOR WORDS PROVE NOTHING.

AND SO I OFFER YOU THIS. HAVE YOUR MEN PREPARE A LARGE FIRE. I WILL ENTER THE FIRE AS A CHALLENGE. IF I COME THROUGH UNHARMED BY THE FLAMES, THEN YOU WILL KNOW THAT WHAT I TELL YOU ABOUT JESUS IS REAL.

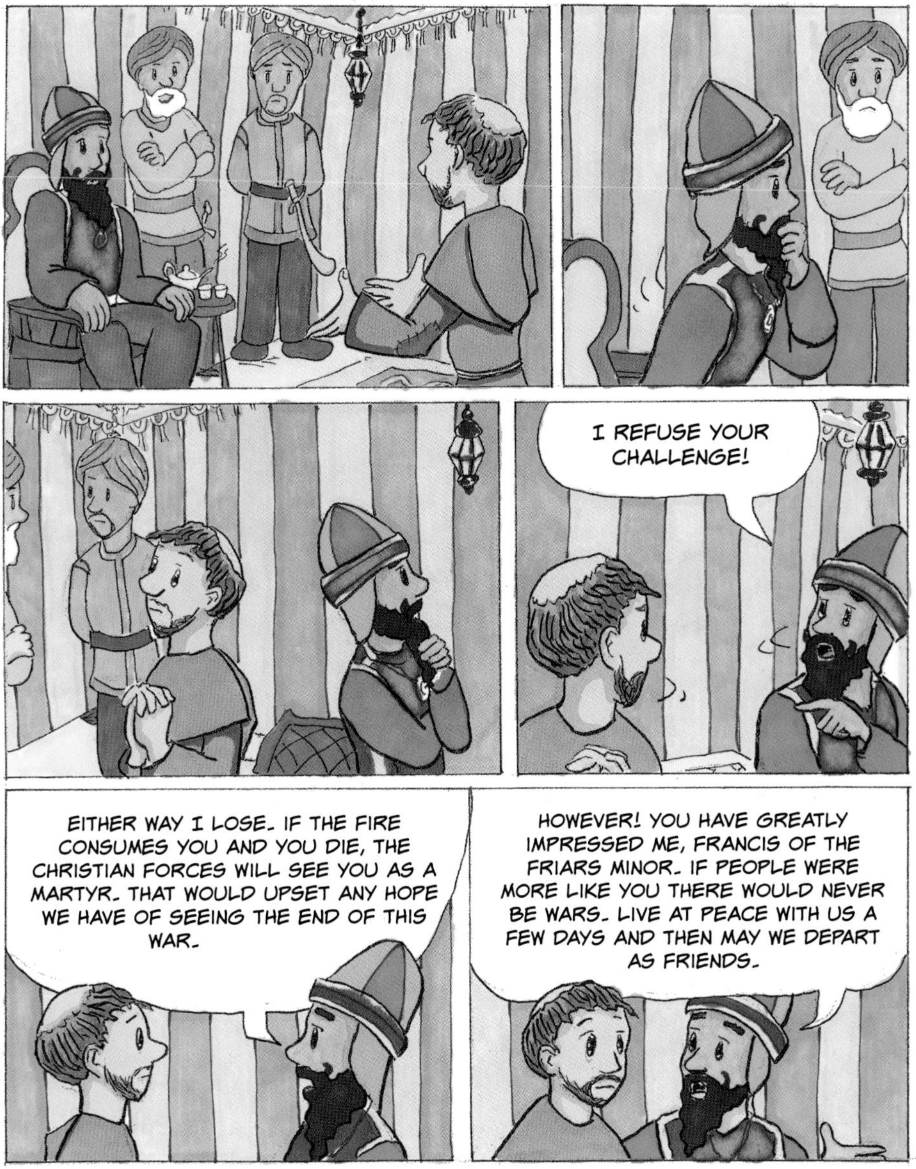
I REFUSE YOUR CHALLENGE!
EITHER WAY I LOSE. IF THE FIRE CONSUMES YOU AND YOU DIE, THE CHRISTIAN FORCES WILL SEE YOU AS A MARTYR. THAT WOULD UPSET ANY HOPE WE HAVE OF SEEING THE END OF THIS WAR.
HOWEVER! YOU HAVE GREATLY IMPRESSED ME, FRANCIS OF THE FRIARS MINOR. IF PEOPLE WERE MORE LIKE YOU THERE WOULD NEVER BE WARS. LIVE AT PEACE WITH US A FEW DAYS AND THEN MAY WE DEPART AS FRIENDS.

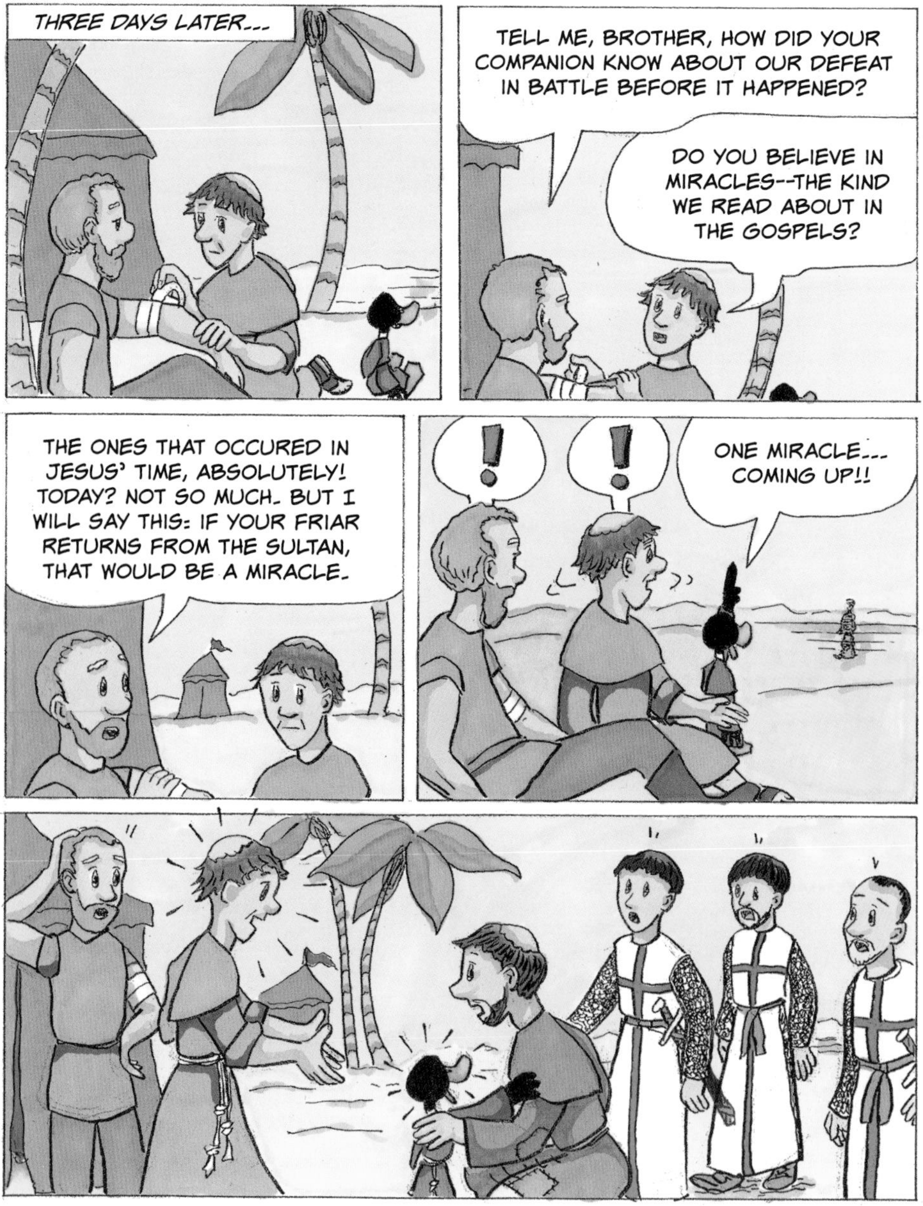
THREE DAYS LATER...
TELL ME, BROTHER, HOW DID YOUR COMPANION KNOW ABOUT OUR DEFEAT IN BATTLE BEFORE IT HAPPENED?
DO YOU BELIEVE IN MIRACLES--THE KIND WE READ ABOUT IN THE GOSPELS?
THE ONES THAT OCCURED IN JESUS' TIME, ABSOLUTELY! TODAY? NOT SO MUCH. BUT I WILL SAY THIS: IF YOUR FRIAR RETURNS FROM THE SULTAN, THAT WOULD BE A MIRACLE.
!
!
ONE MIRACLE... COMING UP!!

CHAPTER 8
BY WAY OF THE CROSS

Set on fire, therefore,
By that perfect charity
Which drives out fear
He longed to offer to the Lord
His own life as a living sacrifice.
—ST. BONAVENTURE

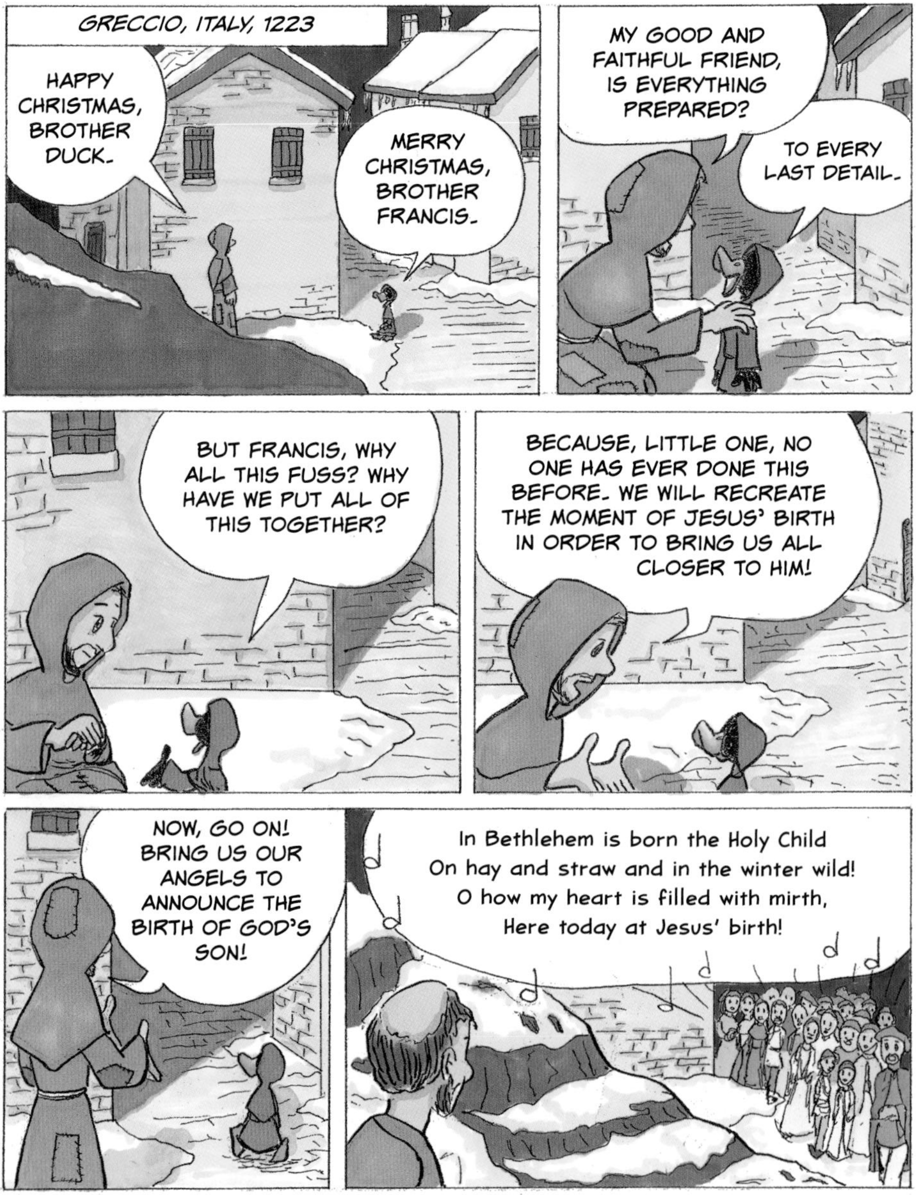
GRECCIO, ITALY, 1223
HAPPY CHRISTMAS, BROTHER DUCK.
MERRY CHRISTMAS, BROTHER FRANCIS.
MY GOOD AND FAITHFUL FRIEND, IS EVERYTHING PREPARED?
TO EVERY LAST DETAIL.
BUT FRANCIS, WHY ALL THIS FUSS? WHY HAVE WE PUT ALL OF THIS TOGETHER?
BECAUSE, LITTLE ONE, NO ONE HAS EVER DONE THIS BEFORE. WE WILL RECREATE THE MOMENT OF JESUS' BIRTH IN ORDER TO BRING US ALL CLOSER TO HIM!
NOW, GO ON! BRING US OUR ANGELS TO ANNOUNCE THE BIRTH OF GOD'S SON!
In Bethlehem is born the Holy Child
On hay and straw and in the winter wild!
O how my heart is filled with mirth,
Here today at Jesus' birth!

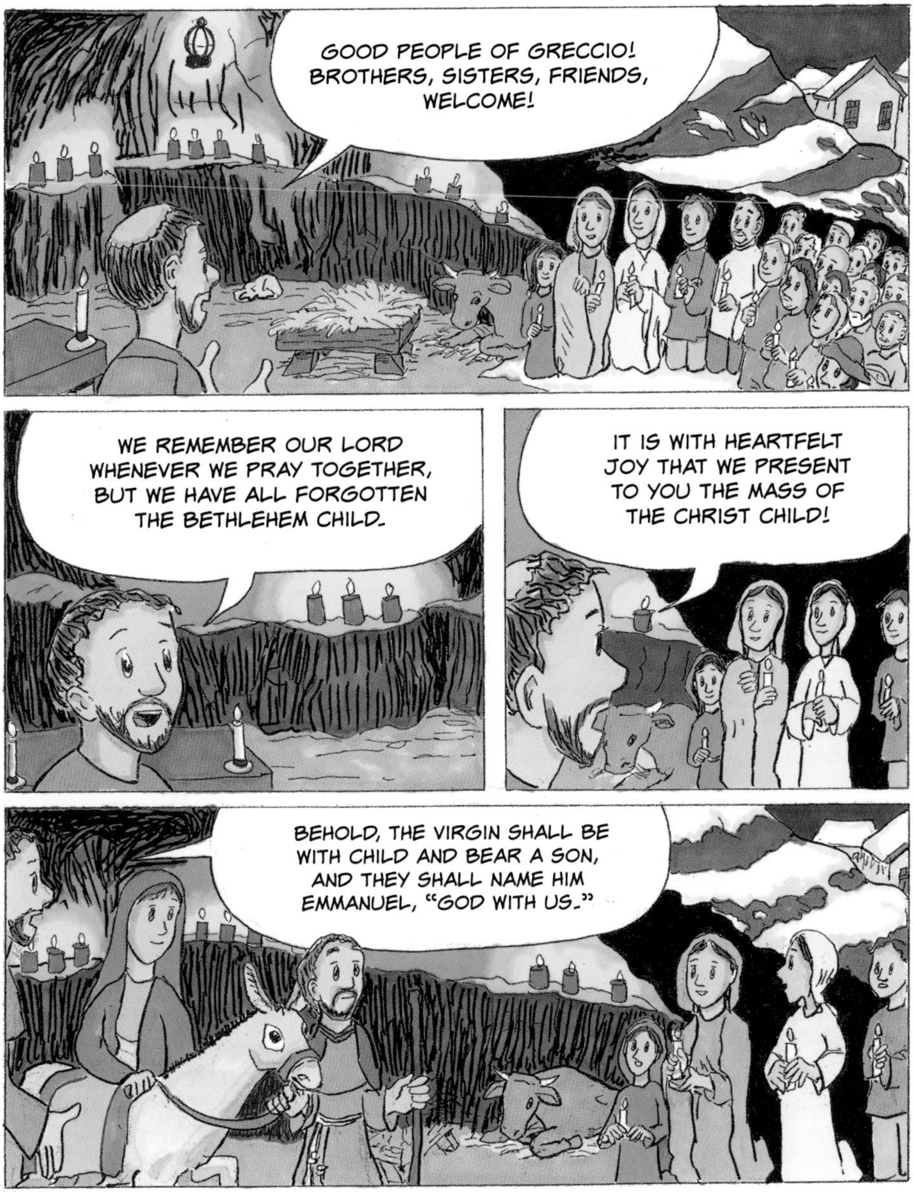
GOOD PEOPLE OF GRECCIO! BROTHERS, SISTERS, FRIENDS, WELCOME!
WE REMEMBER OUR LORD WHENEVER WE PRAY TOGETHER, BUT WE HAVE ALL FORGOTTEN THE BETHLEHEM CHILD.
IT IS WITH HEARTFELT JOY THAT WE PRESENT TO YOU THE MASS OF THE CHRIST CHILD!
BEHOLD, THE VIRGIN SHALL BE WITH CHILD AND BEAR A SON, AND THEY SHALL NAME HIM EMMANUEL, "GOD WITH US."

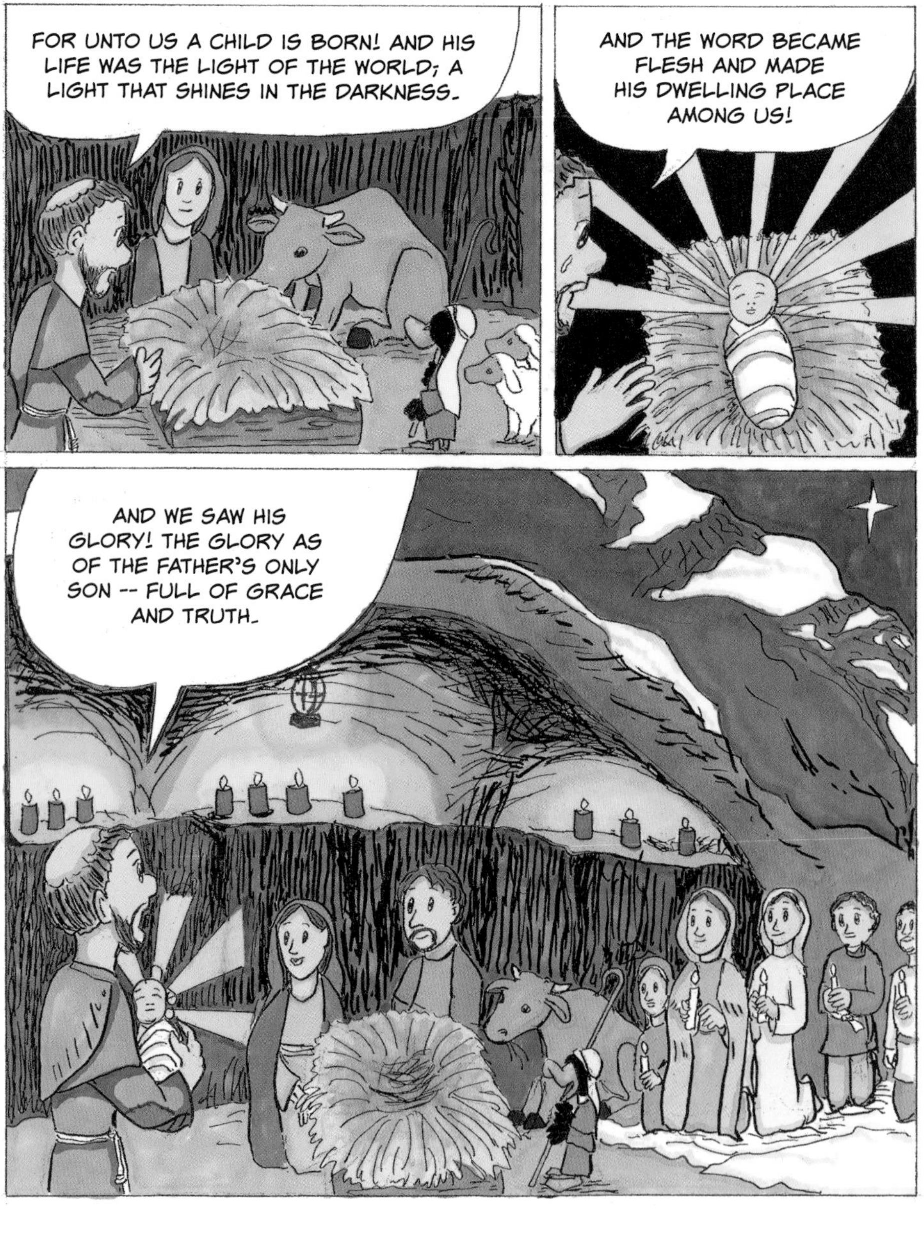
FOR UNTO US A CHILD IS BORN! AND HIS LIFE WAS THE LIGHT OF THE WORLD; A LIGHT THAT SHINES IN THE DARKNESS.
AND THE WORD BECAME FLESH AND MADE HIS DWELLING PLACE AMONG US!
AND WE SAW HIS GLORY! THE GLORY AS OF THE FATHER'S ONLY SON -- FULL OF GRACE AND TRUTH.

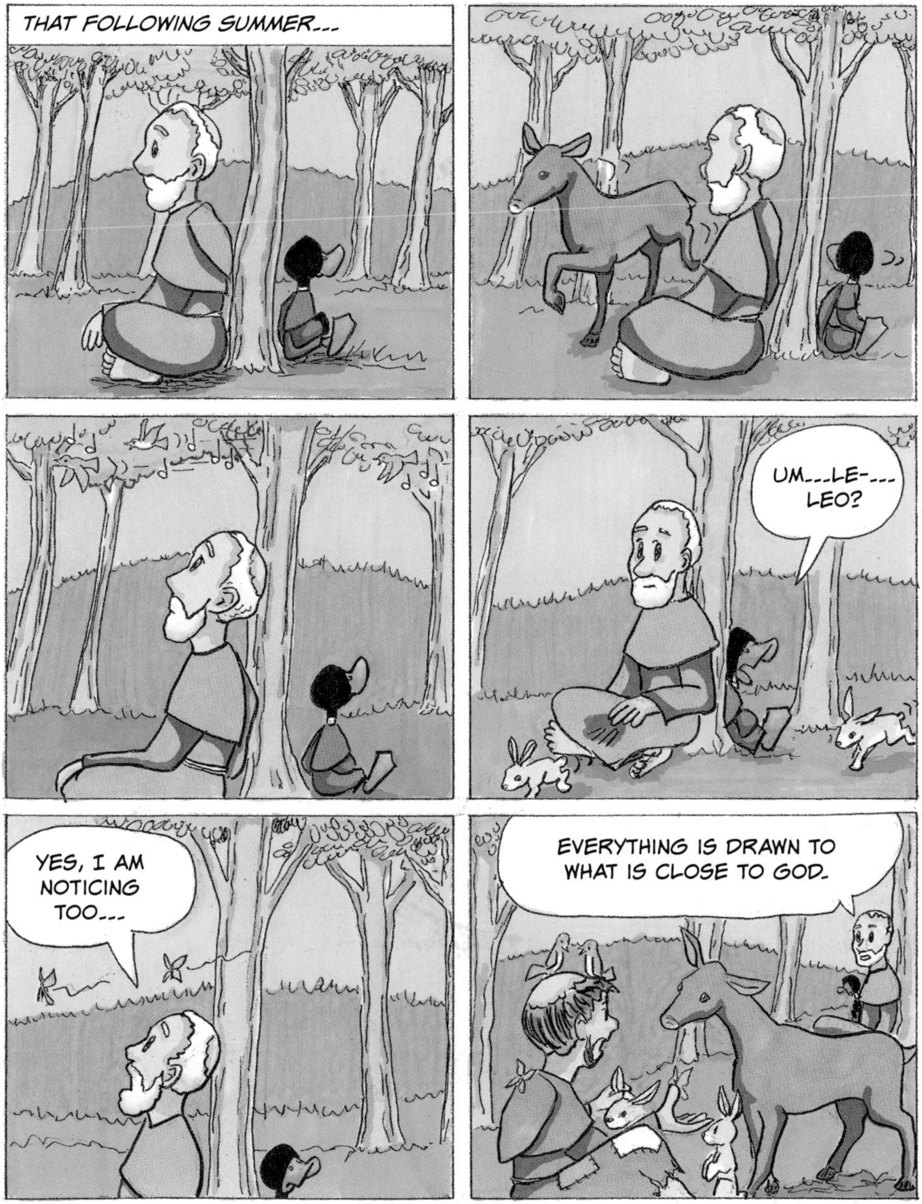
THAT FOLLOWING SUMMER...
UM...LE-...LEO?
YES, I AM NOTICING TOO...
EVERYTHING IS DRAWN TO WHAT IS CLOSE TO GOD.

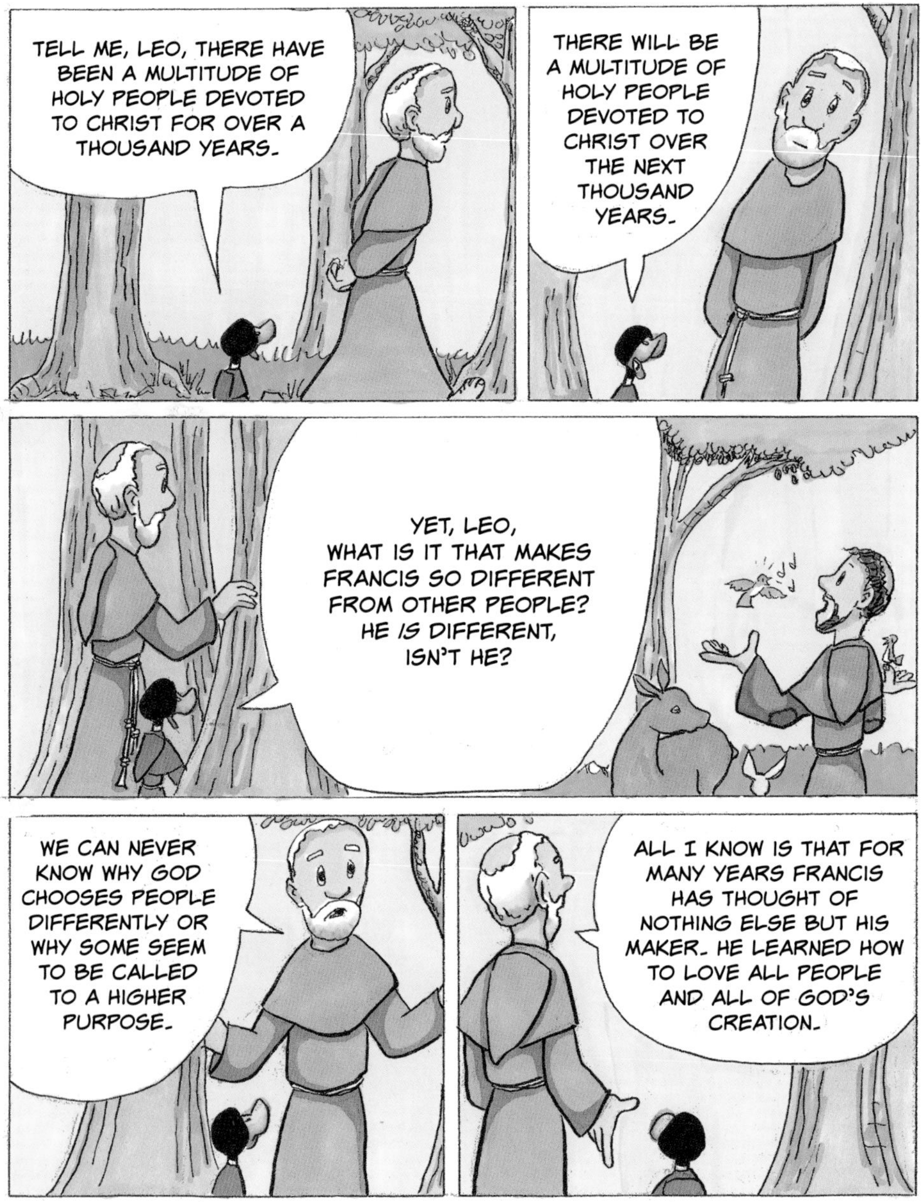
TELL ME, LEO, THERE HAVE BEEN A MULTITUDE OF HOLY PEOPLE DEVOTED TO CHRIST FOR OVER A THOUSAND YEARS.
THERE WILL BE A MULTITUDE OF HOLY PEOPLE DEVOTED TO CHRIST OVER THE NEXT THOUSAND YEARS.
YET, LEO, WHAT IS IT THAT MAKES FRANCIS SO DIFFERENT FROM OTHER PEOPLE? HE *IS* DIFFERENT, ISN'T HE?
WE CAN NEVER KNOW WHY GOD CHOOSES PEOPLE DIFFERENTLY OR WHY SOME SEEM TO BE CALLED TO A HIGHER PURPOSE.
ALL I KNOW IS THAT FOR MANY YEARS FRANCIS HAS THOUGHT OF NOTHING ELSE BUT HIS MAKER. HE LEARNED HOW TO LOVE ALL PEOPLE AND ALL OF GOD'S CREATION.

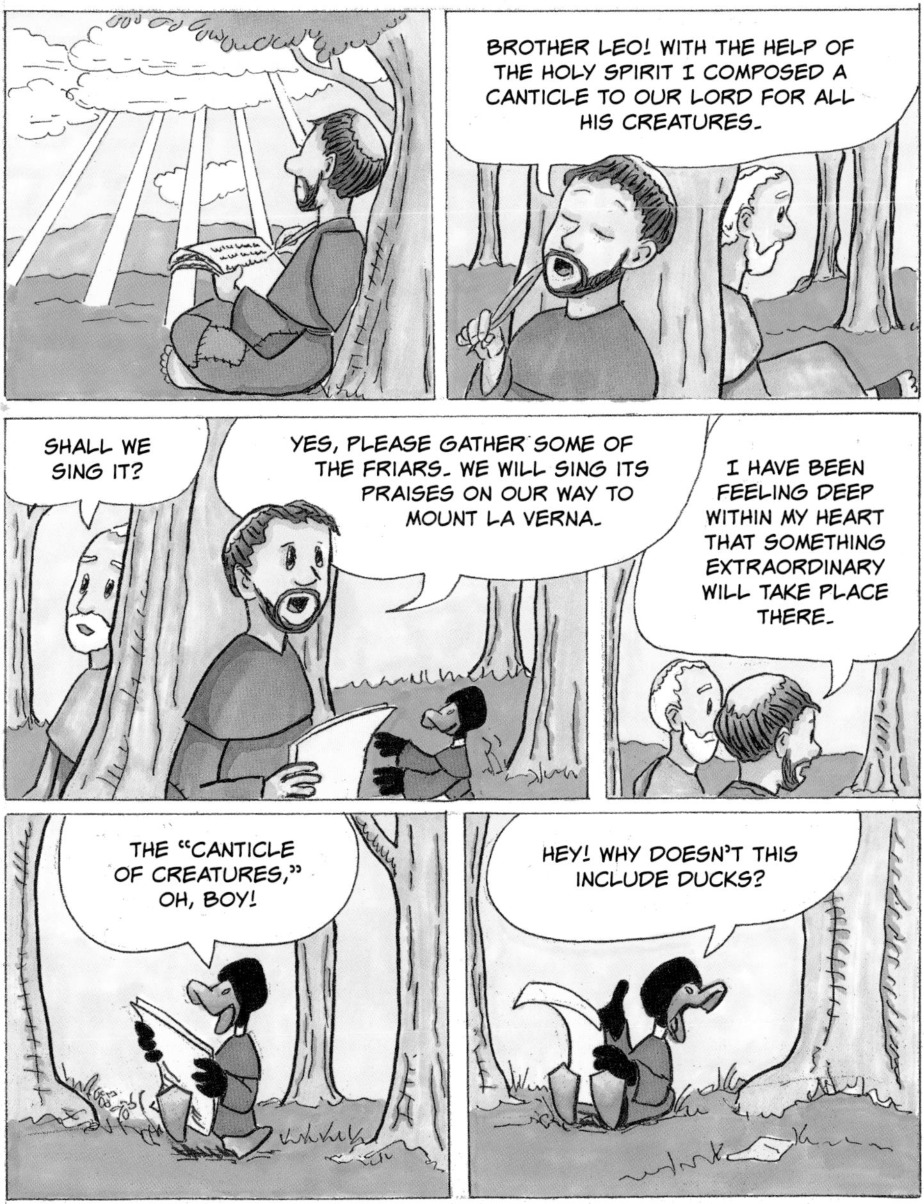
BROTHER LEO! WITH THE HELP OF THE HOLY SPIRIT I COMPOSED A CANTICLE TO OUR LORD FOR ALL HIS CREATURES.
SHALL WE SING IT?
YES, PLEASE GATHER SOME OF THE FRIARS. WE WILL SING ITS PRAISES ON OUR WAY TO MOUNT LA VERNA.
I HAVE BEEN FEELING DEEP WITHIN MY HEART THAT SOMETHING EXTRAORDINARY WILL TAKE PLACE THERE.
THE "CANTICLE OF CREATURES," OH, BOY!
HEY! WHY DOESN'T THIS INCLUDE DUCKS?

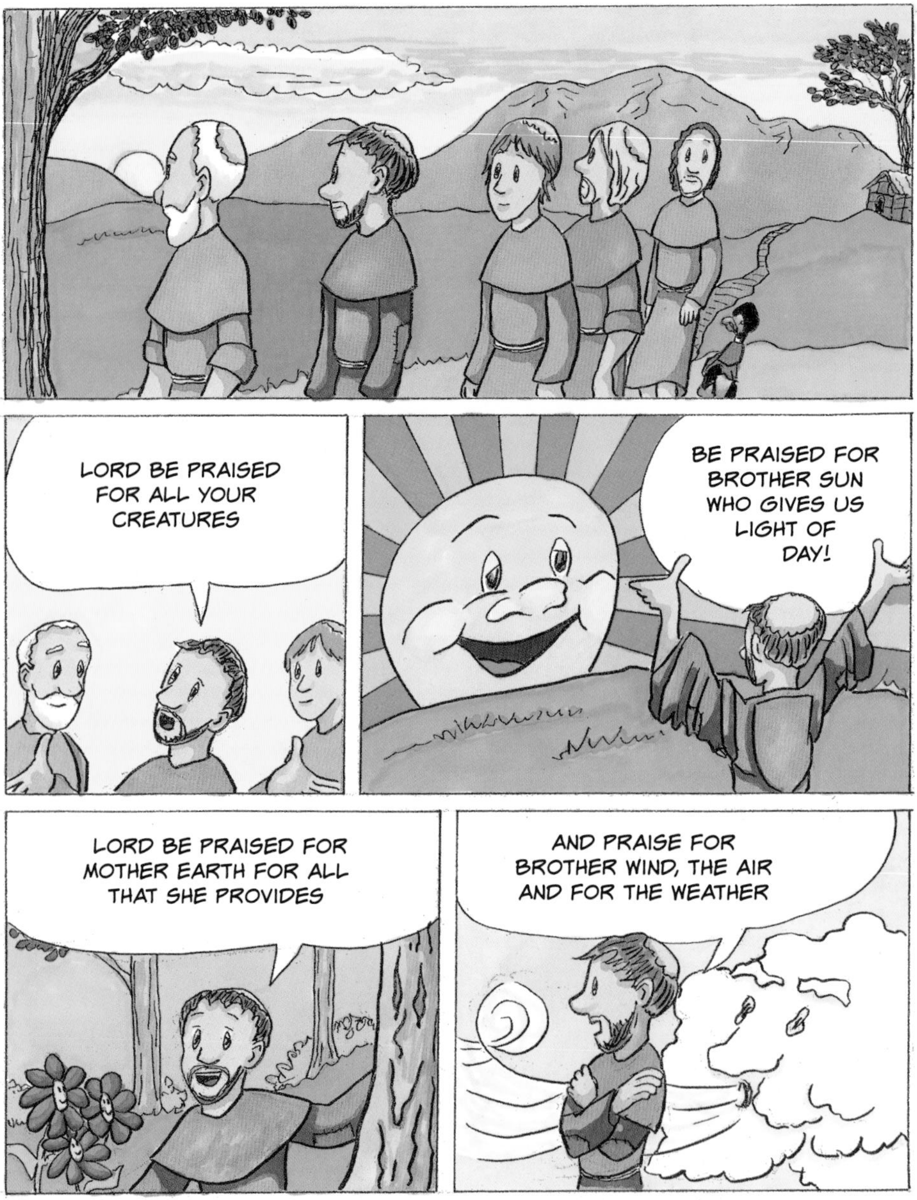
LORD BE PRAISED FOR ALL YOUR CREATURES
BE PRAISED FOR BROTHER SUN WHO GIVES US LIGHT OF DAY!
LORD BE PRAISED FOR MOTHER EARTH FOR ALL THAT SHE PROVIDES
AND PRAISE FOR BROTHER WIND, THE AIR AND FOR THE WEATHER

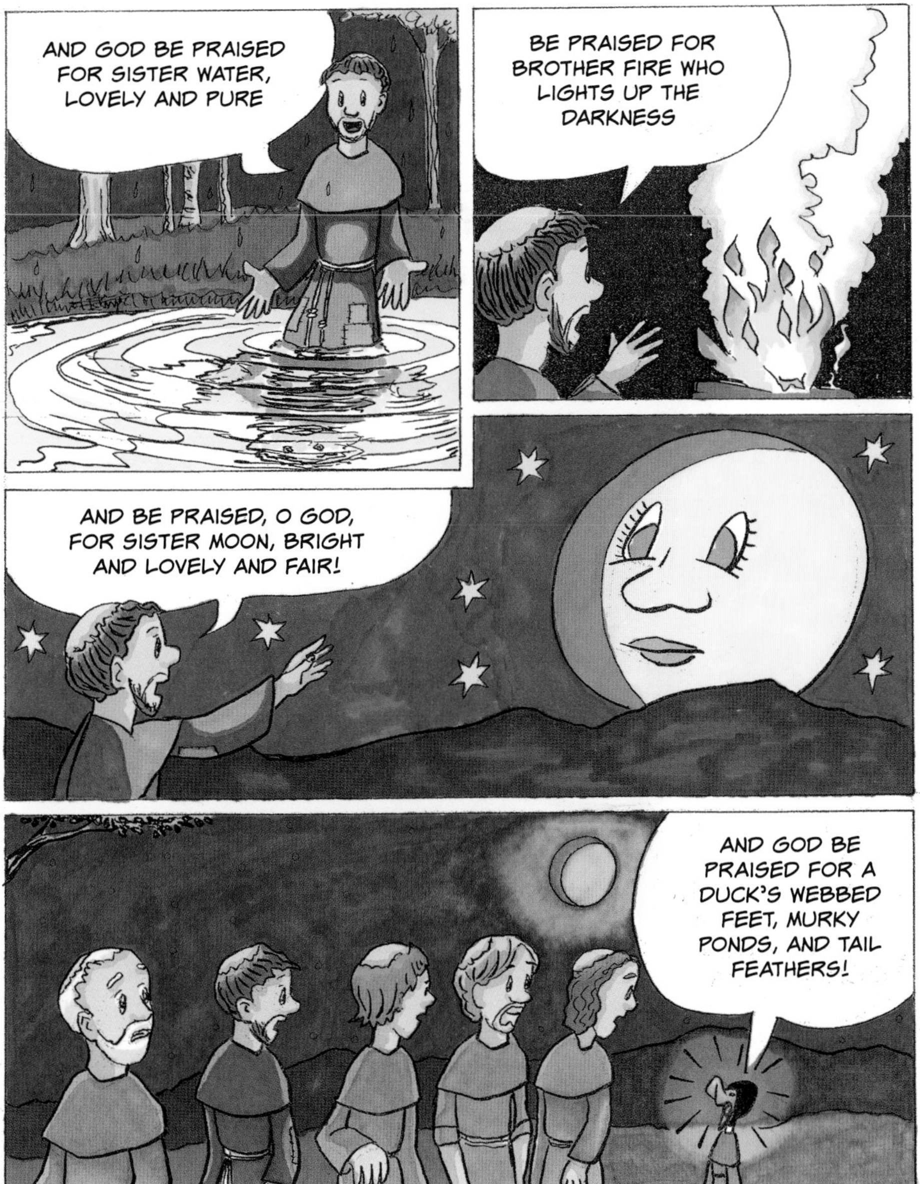
AND GOD BE PRAISED FOR SISTER WATER, LOVELY AND PURE
BE PRAISED FOR BROTHER FIRE WHO LIGHTS UP THE DARKNESS
AND BE PRAISED, O GOD, FOR SISTER MOON, BRIGHT AND LOVELY AND FAIR!
AND GOD BE PRAISED FOR A DUCK'S WEBBED FEET, MURKY PONDS, AND TAIL FEATHERS!

UPON MOUNT LA VERNA, ITALY, SEPTEMBER 1224

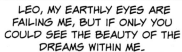

LEO, MY EARTHLY EYES ARE FAILING ME, BUT IF ONLY YOU COULD SEE THE BEAUTY OF THE DREAMS WITHIN ME.

YET THROUGH THESE DREAMS OUR LORD BECKONS ME TO THAT SPACE ACROSS THE BRIDGE. I DO NOT KNOW WHAT AWAITS ME THERE, BUT I ANTICIPATE THE COMING DAYS WITH BOTH JOY AND TREPIDATION.

TAKE ME THERE! WE MUSTN'T KEEP OUR SAVIOR WAITING! AND IN HOLY OBEDIENCE, LET NO ONE COME TO ME EXCEPT FOR YOU WHENEVER I SHOULD CALL.

WHAT WILL YOU DO THERE, MY OLD FRIEND?

FAST AND PRAY -- FOR MY SINS ARE MANY.

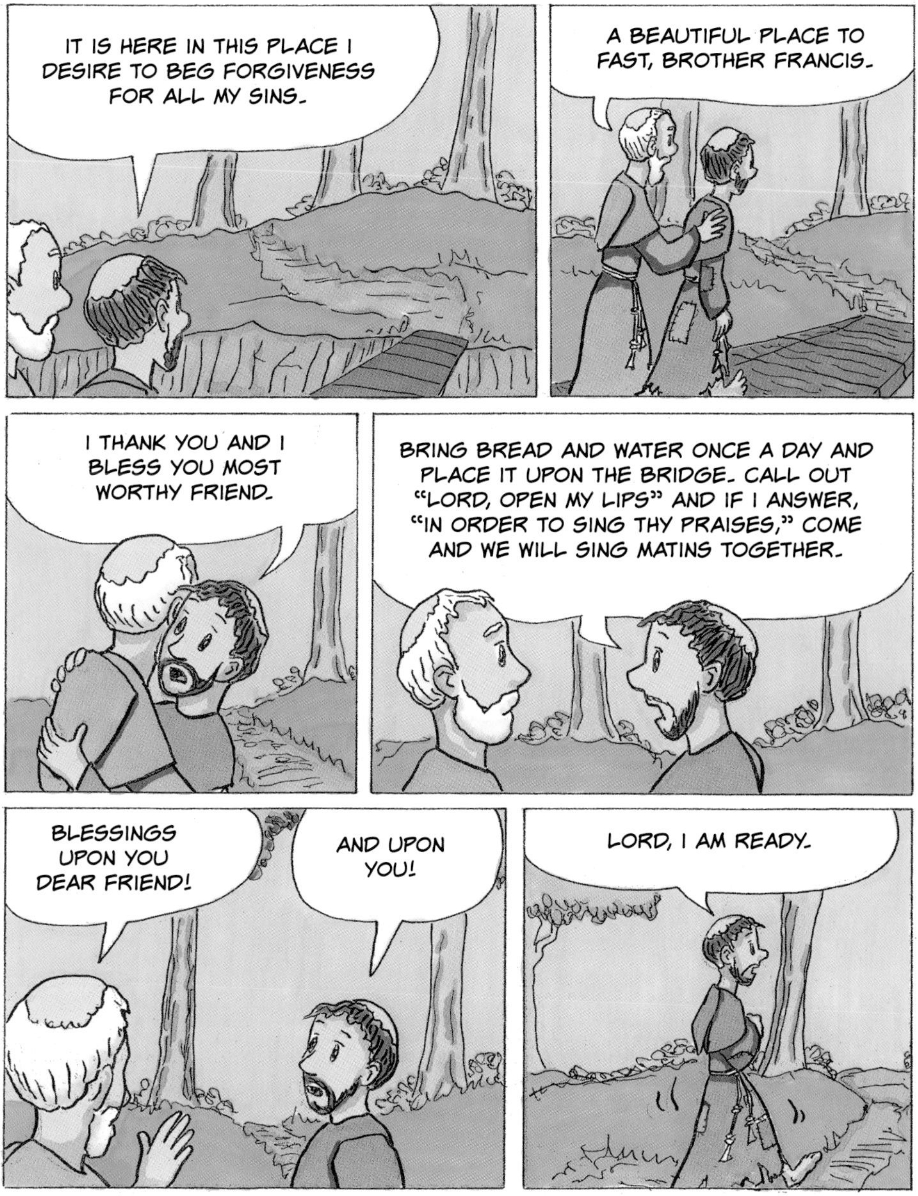
IT IS HERE IN THIS PLACE I DESIRE TO BEG FORGIVENESS FOR ALL MY SINS.
A BEAUTIFUL PLACE TO FAST, BROTHER FRANCIS.
I THANK YOU AND I BLESS YOU MOST WORTHY FRIEND.
BRING BREAD AND WATER ONCE A DAY AND PLACE IT UPON THE BRIDGE. CALL OUT "LORD, OPEN MY LIPS" AND IF I ANSWER, "IN ORDER TO SING THY PRAISES," COME AND WE WILL SING MATINS TOGETHER.
BLESSINGS UPON YOU DEAR FRIEND!
AND UPON YOU!
LORD, I AM READY.

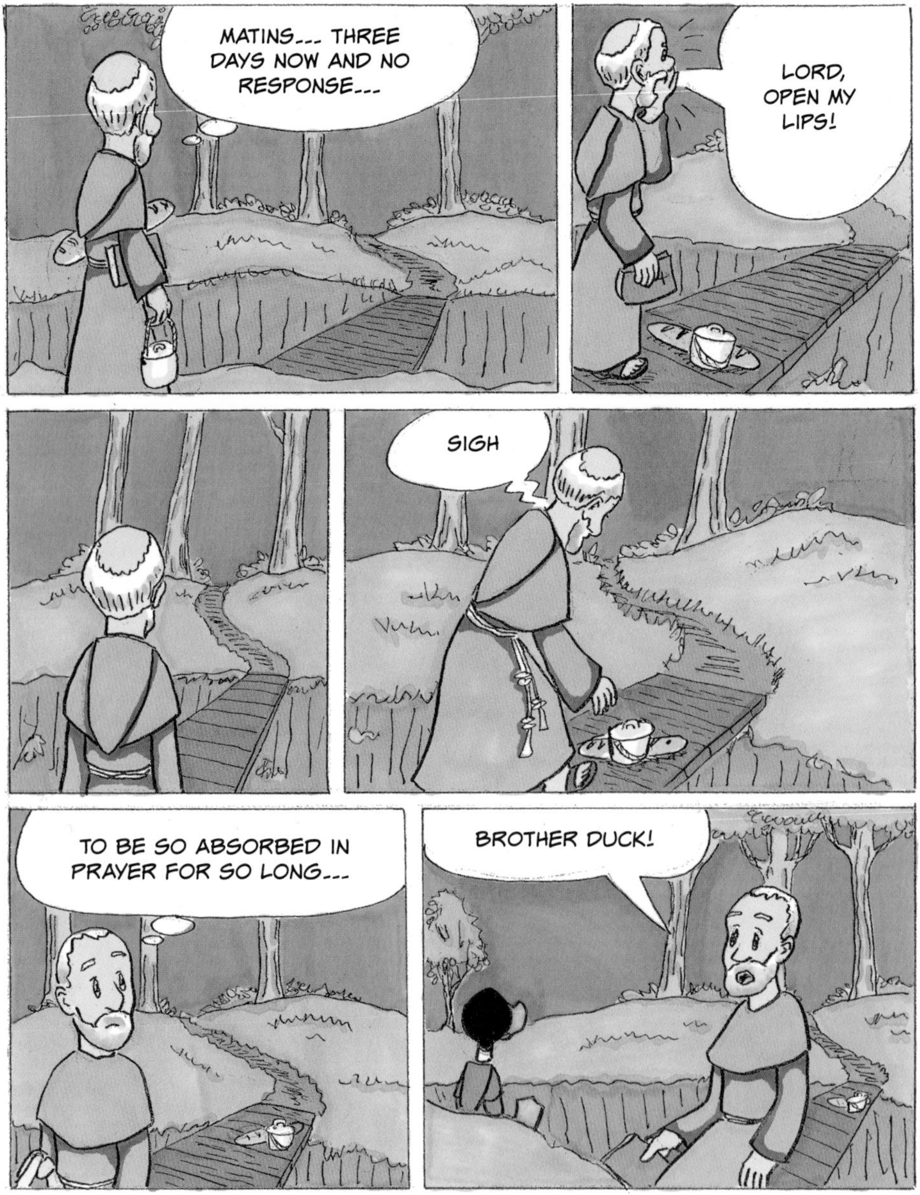
MATINS... THREE DAYS NOW AND NO RESPONSE...
LORD, OPEN MY LIPS!
SIGH
TO BE SO ABSORBED IN PRAYER FOR SO LONG...
BROTHER DUCK!

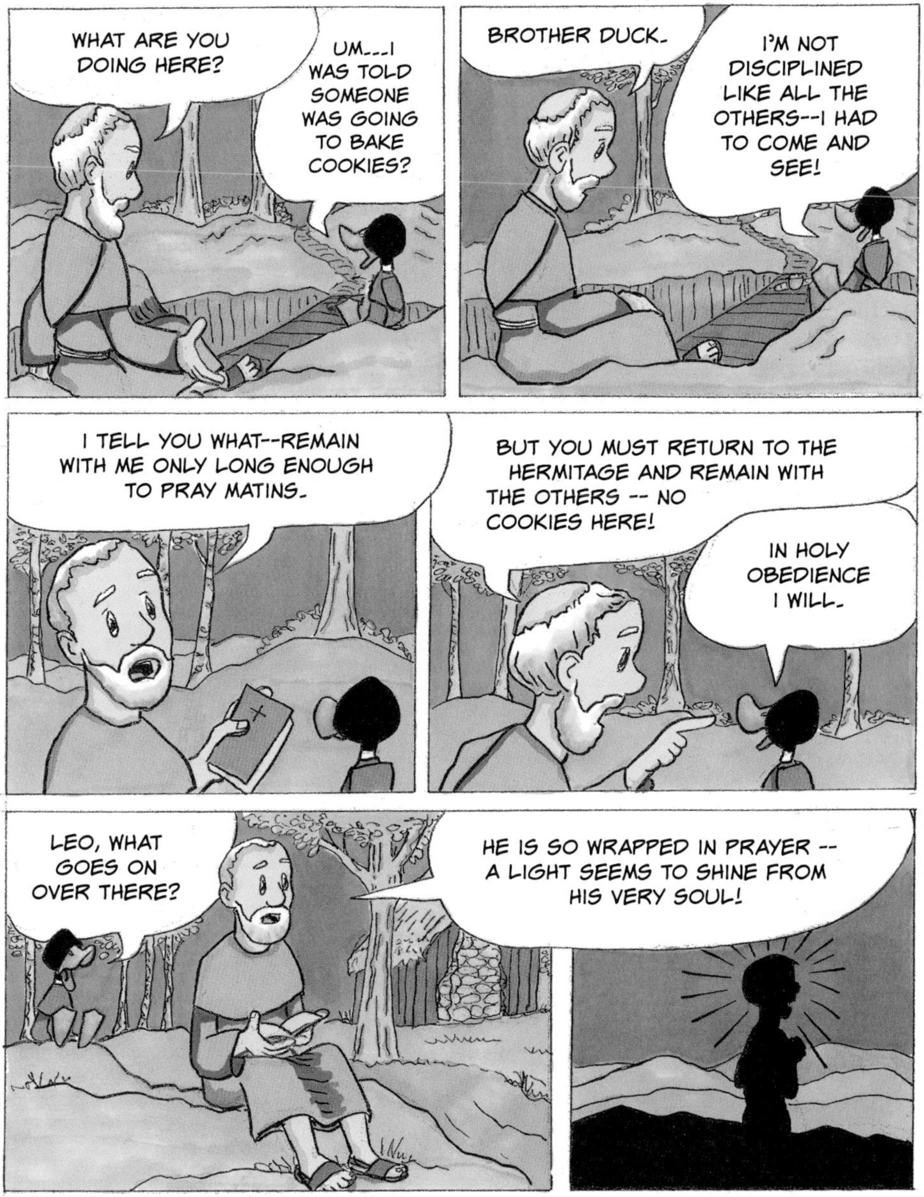
WHAT ARE YOU DOING HERE?
UM...I WAS TOLD SOMEONE WAS GOING TO BAKE COOKIES?
BROTHER DUCK.
I'M NOT DISCIPLINED LIKE ALL THE OTHERS--I HAD TO COME AND SEE!
I TELL YOU WHAT--REMAIN WITH ME ONLY LONG ENOUGH TO PRAY MATINS.
BUT YOU MUST RETURN TO THE HERMITAGE AND REMAIN WITH THE OTHERS -- NO COOKIES HERE!
IN HOLY OBEDIENCE I WILL.
LEO, WHAT GOES ON OVER THERE?
HE IS SO WRAPPED IN PRAYER -- A LIGHT SEEMS TO SHINE FROM HIS VERY SOUL!

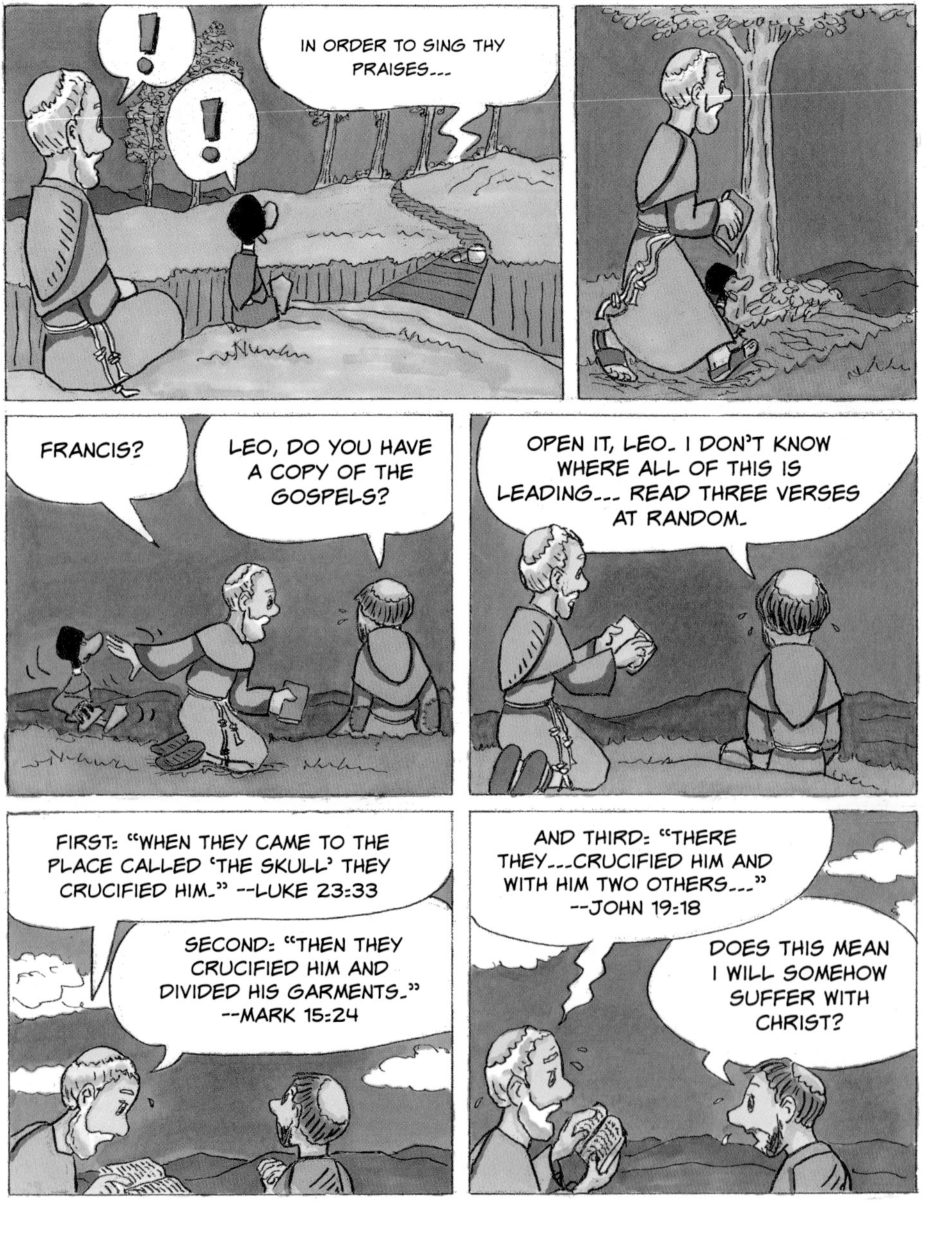
!
!
IN ORDER TO SING THY PRAISES...
FRANCIS?
LEO, DO YOU HAVE A COPY OF THE GOSPELS?
OPEN IT, LEO. I DON'T KNOW WHERE ALL OF THIS IS LEADING... READ THREE VERSES AT RANDOM.
FIRST: "WHEN THEY CAME TO THE PLACE CALLED 'THE SKULL' THEY CRUCIFIED HIM." --LUKE 23:33
SECOND: "THEN THEY CRUCIFIED HIM AND DIVIDED HIS GARMENTS." --MARK 15:24
AND THIRD: "THERE THEY...CRUCIFIED HIM AND WITH HIM TWO OTHERS..." --JOHN 19:18
DOES THIS MEAN I WILL SOMEHOW SUFFER WITH CHRIST?

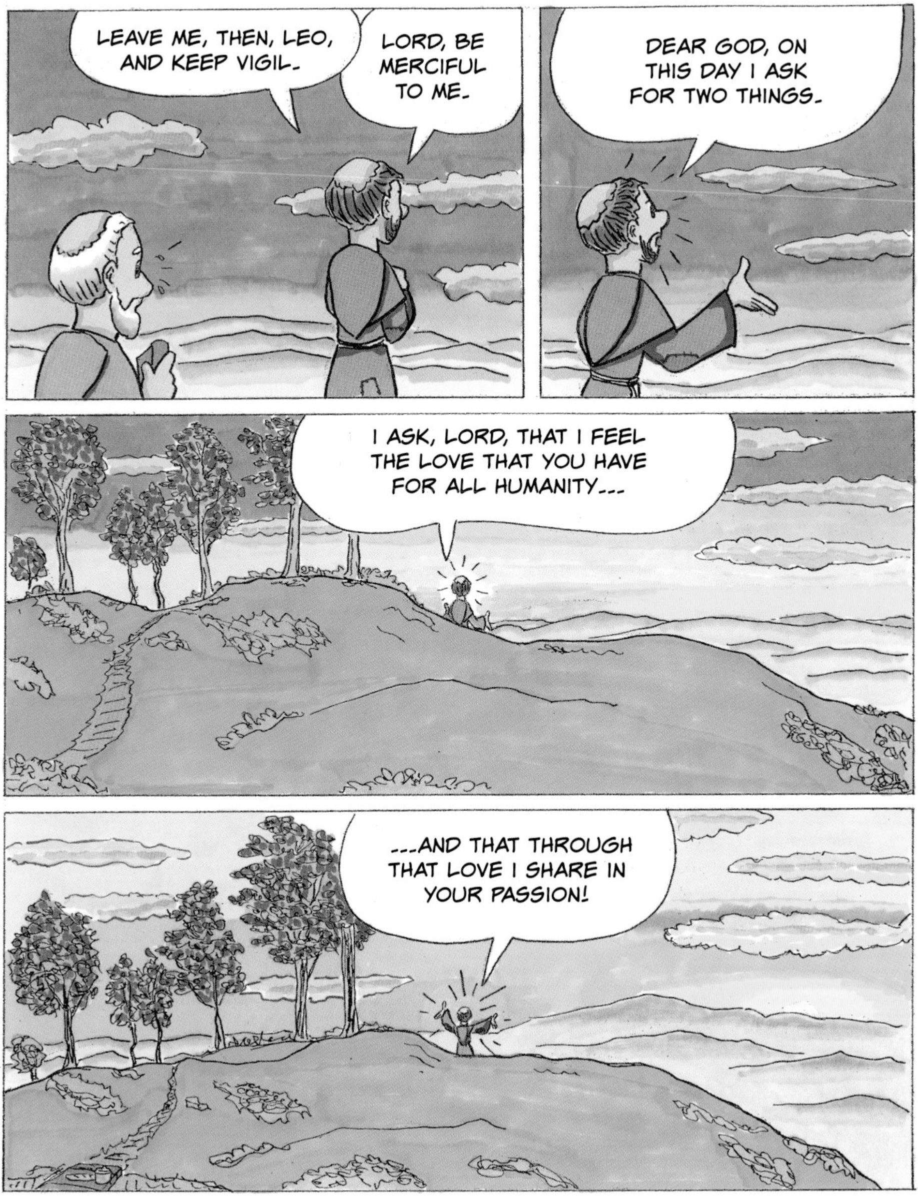
LEAVE ME, THEN, LEO, AND KEEP VIGIL.
LORD, BE MERCIFUL TO ME.
DEAR GOD, ON THIS DAY I ASK FOR TWO THINGS.
I ASK, LORD, THAT I FEEL THE LOVE THAT YOU HAVE FOR ALL HUMANITY...
...AND THAT THROUGH THAT LOVE I SHARE IN YOUR PASSION!

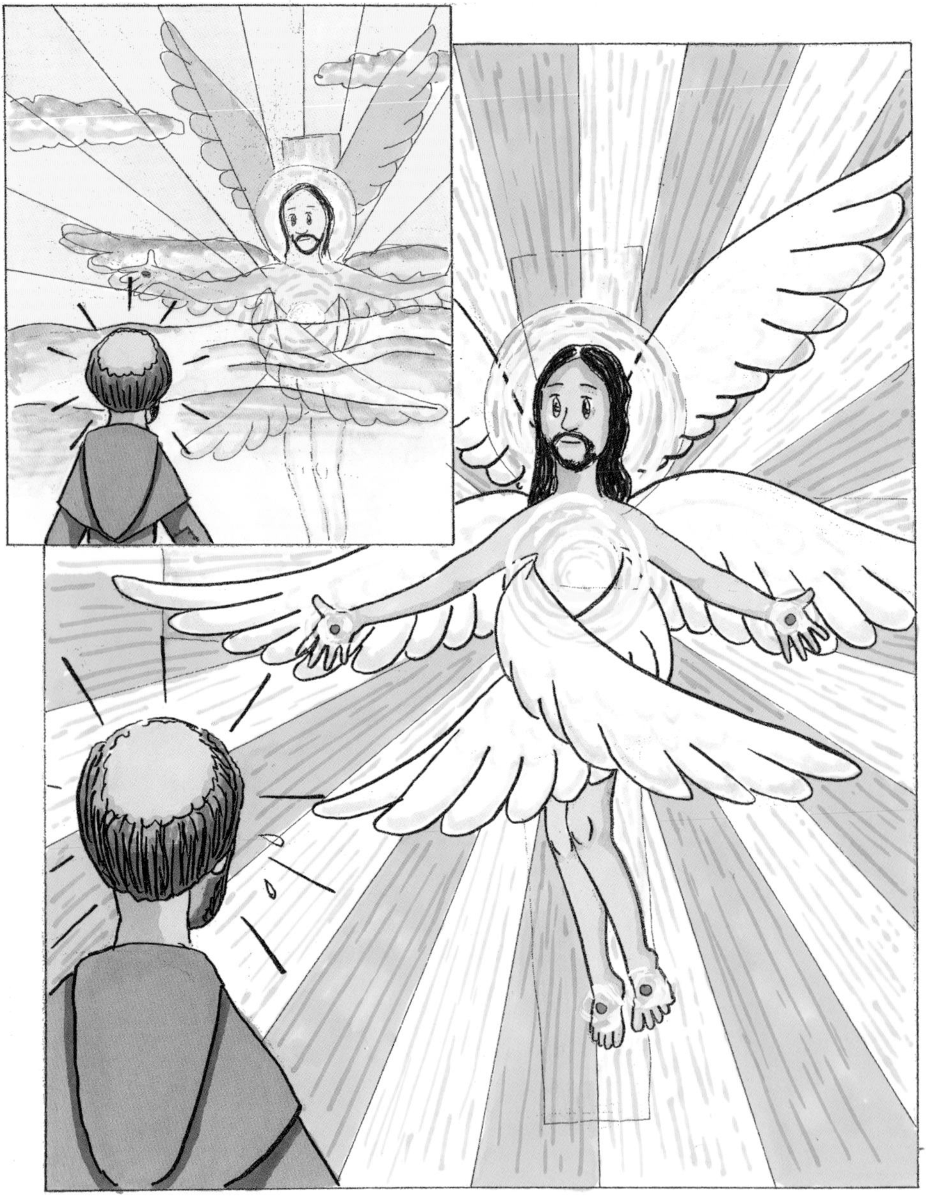

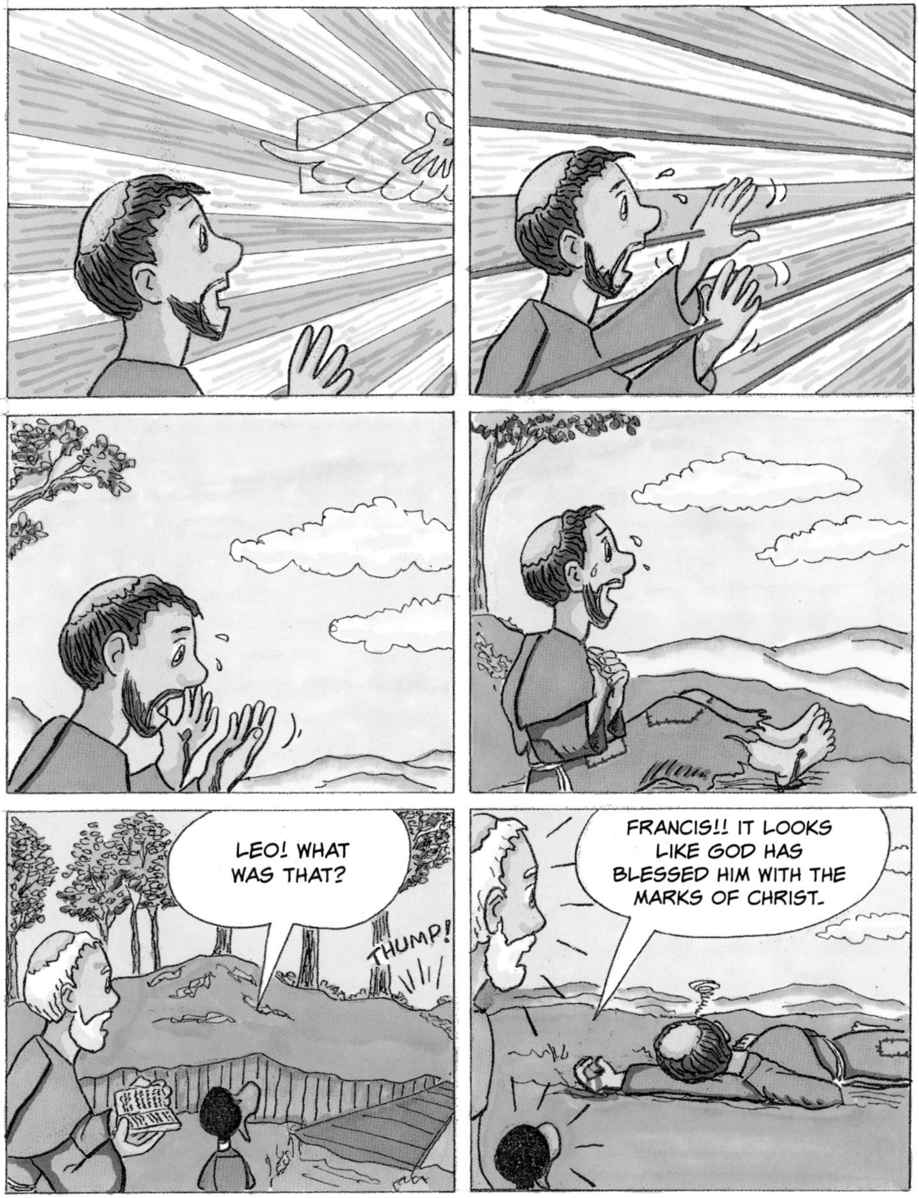
LEO! WHAT WAS THAT?
THUMP!
FRANCIS!! IT LOOKS LIKE GOD HAS BLESSED HIM WITH THE MARKS OF CHRIST.

CHAPTER 9

AN IMITATION OF CHRIST

His glorious life reveals in even brighter light
The perfection of earlier saints;
The passion of Jesus proves this,
And his cross shows it clearly.
For Francis was in fact marked in five parts of his body
With the marks of the passion and the cross,
As if he had hung on the cross with the Son of God.
—THOMAS OF CELANO

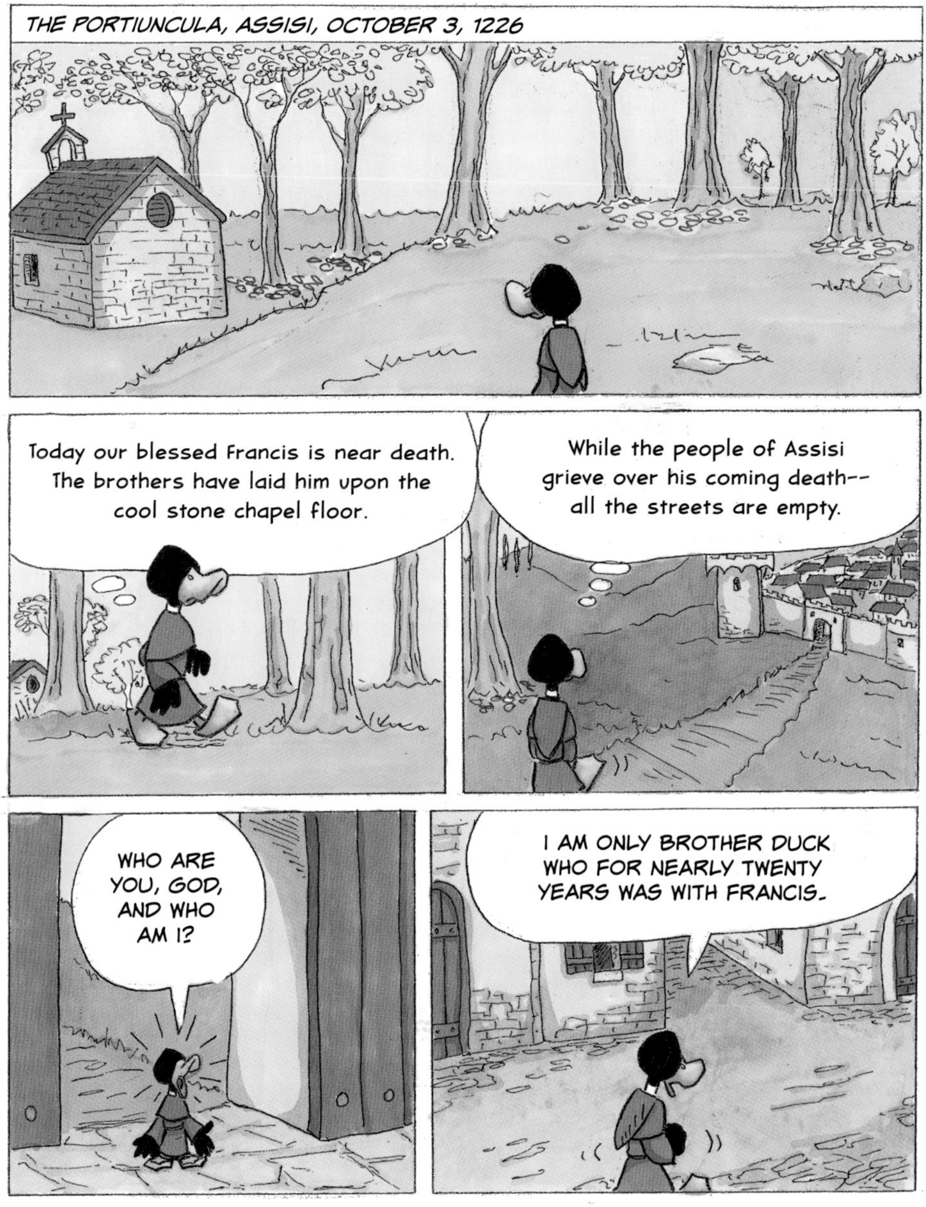
THE PORTIUNCULA, ASSISI, OCTOBER 3, 1226
Today our blessed Francis is near death. The brothers have laid him upon the cool stone chapel floor.
While the people of Assisi grieve over his coming death--all the streets are empty.
WHO ARE YOU, GOD, AND WHO AM I?
I AM ONLY BROTHER DUCK WHO FOR NEARLY TWENTY YEARS WAS WITH FRANCIS.

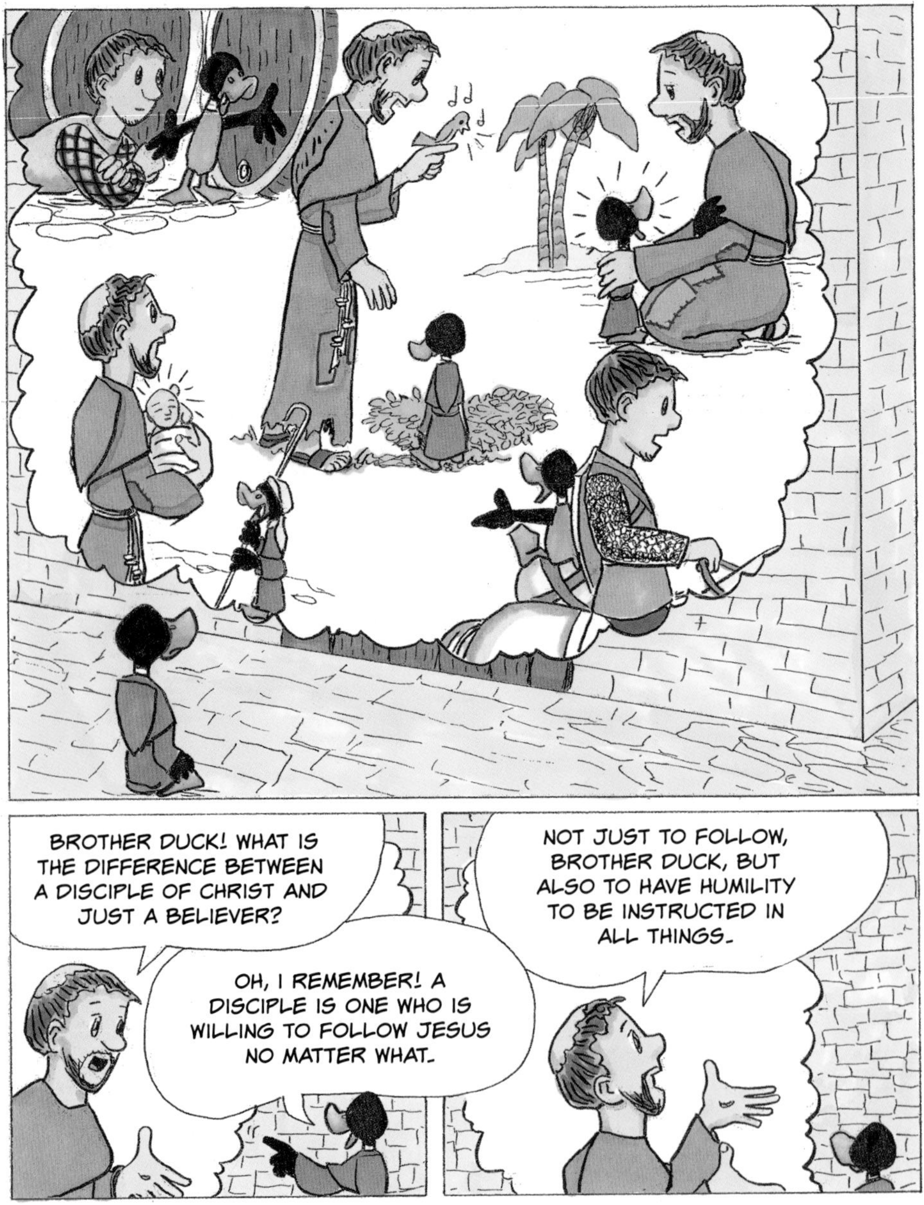
BROTHER DUCK! WHAT IS THE DIFFERENCE BETWEEN A DISCIPLE OF CHRIST AND JUST A BELIEVER?
OH, I REMEMBER! A DISCIPLE IS ONE WHO IS WILLING TO FOLLOW JESUS NO MATTER WHAT.
NOT JUST TO FOLLOW, BROTHER DUCK, BUT ALSO TO HAVE HUMILITY TO BE INSTRUCTED IN ALL THINGS.

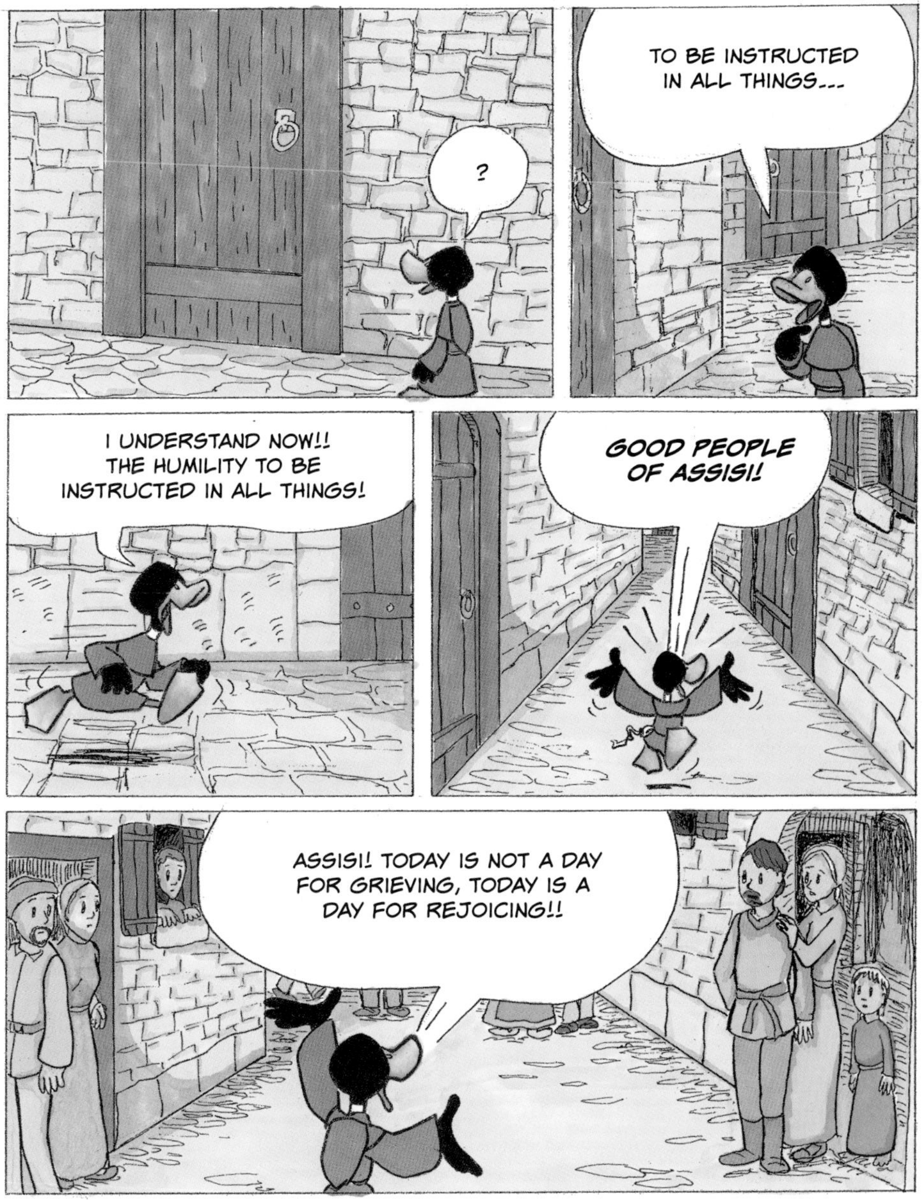
?
TO BE INSTRUCTED IN ALL THINGS...
I UNDERSTAND NOW!! THE HUMILITY TO BE INSTRUCTED IN ALL THINGS!
GOOD PEOPLE OF ASSISI!
ASSISI! TODAY IS NOT A DAY FOR GRIEVING, TODAY IS A DAY FOR REJOICING!!

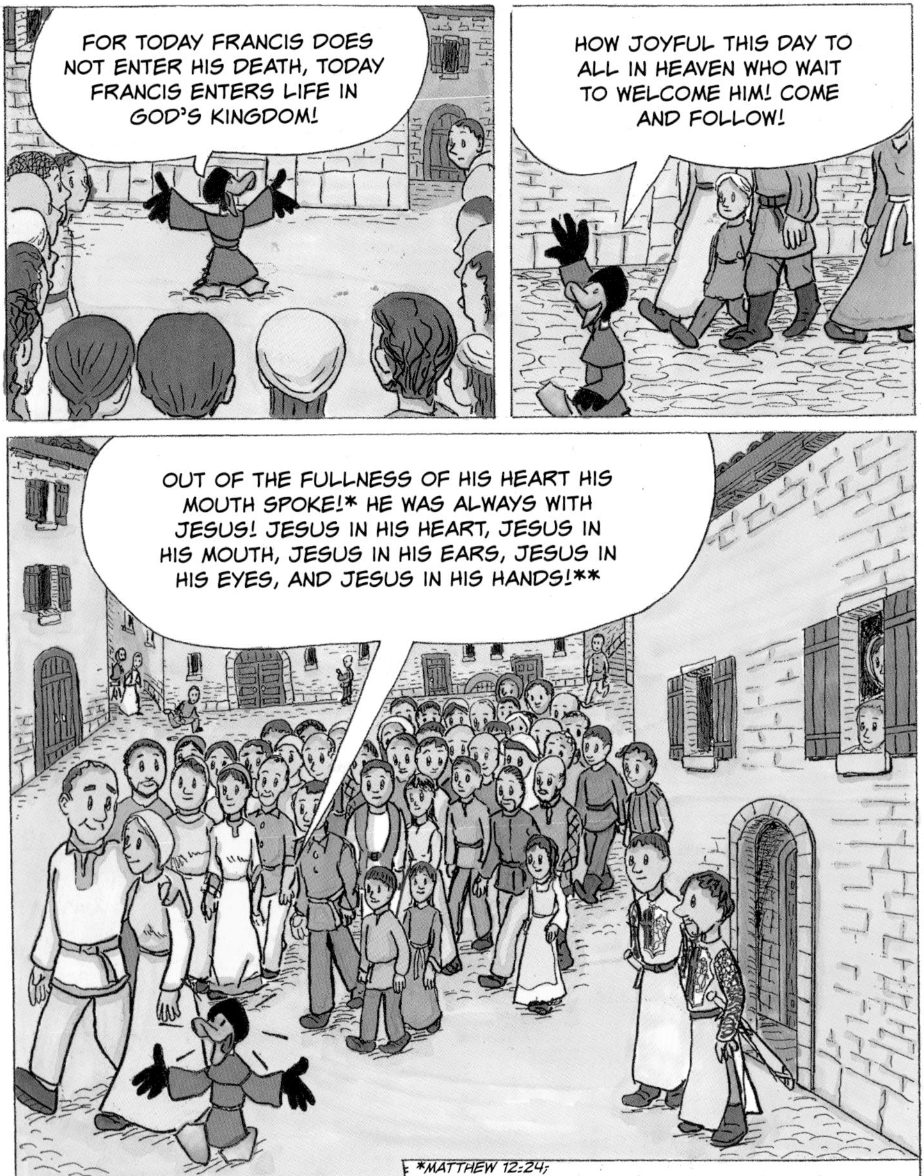
FOR TODAY FRANCIS DOES NOT ENTER HIS DEATH, TODAY FRANCIS ENTERS LIFE IN GOD'S KINGDOM!
HOW JOYFUL THIS DAY TO ALL IN HEAVEN WHO WAIT TO WELCOME HIM! COME AND FOLLOW!
OUT OF THE FULLNESS OF HIS HEART HIS MOUTH SPOKE!* HE WAS ALWAYS WITH JESUS! JESUS IN HIS HEART, JESUS IN HIS MOUTH, JESUS IN HIS EARS, JESUS IN HIS EYES, AND JESUS IN HIS HANDS!**
*MATTHEW 12:24;
**FROM THOMAS OF CELANO'S LIFE OF ST. FRANCIS.

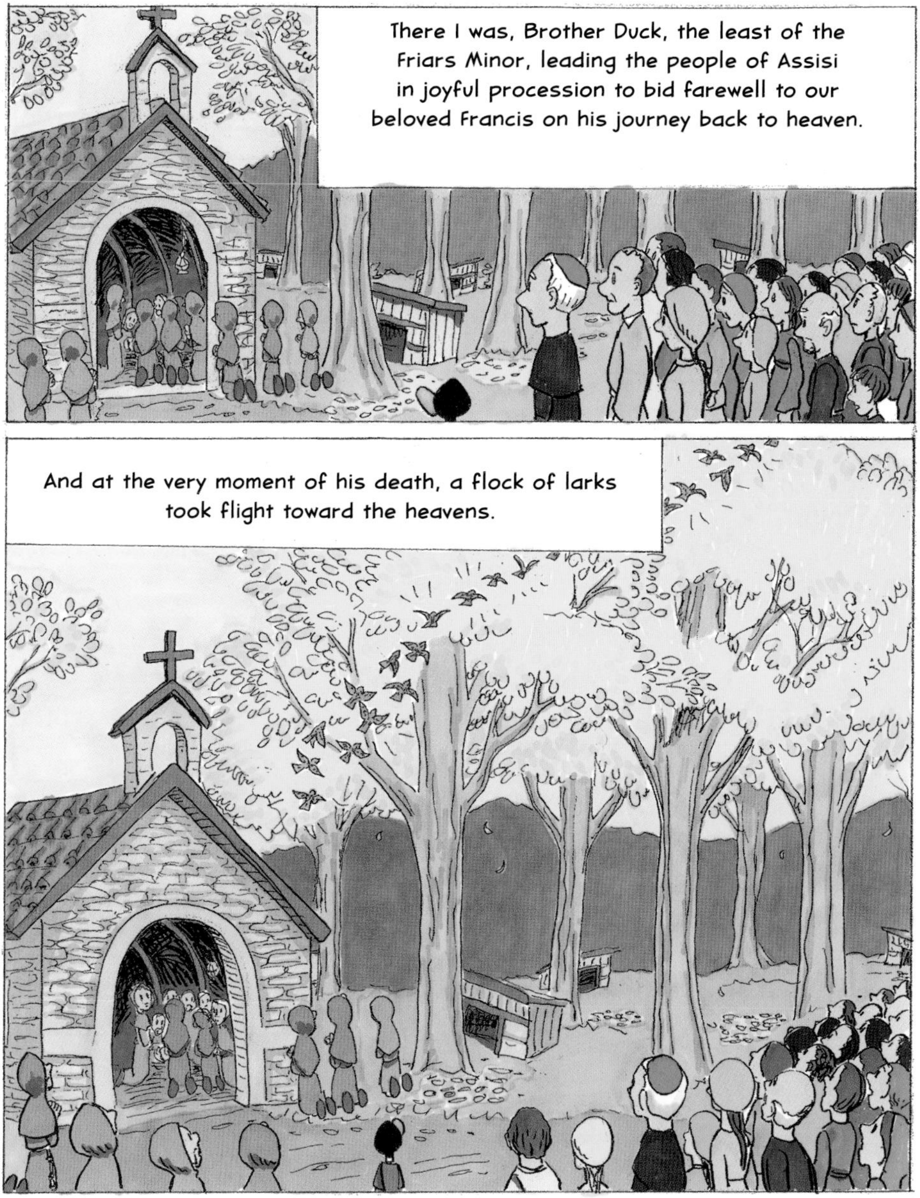
There I was, Brother Duck, the least of the Friars Minor, leading the people of Assisi in joyful procession to bid farewell to our beloved Francis on his journey back to heaven.
And at the very moment of his death, a flock of larks took flight toward the heavens.

ASSISI, ITALY, AD 1200

WHERE FRANCIS LIVED

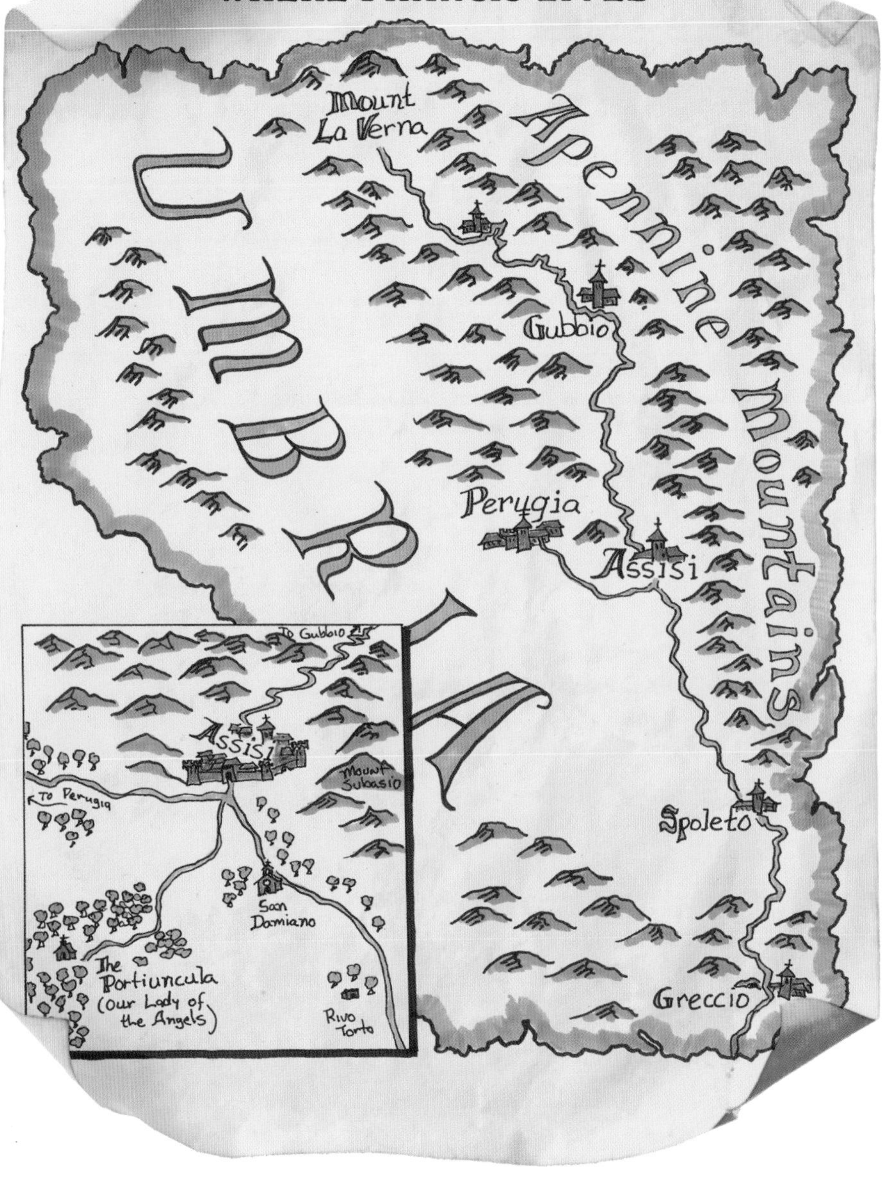
Mount La Verna
Apennine Mountains
UMBRIA
Gubbio
Perugia
Assisi
Spoleto
Greccio
To Gubbio
Assisi
Mount Subasio
To Perugia
San Damiano
The Portiuncula (our Lady of the Angels)
Rivo Torto

ABOUT PARACLETE PRESS

Who We Are

Paraclete Press is a publisher of books, recordings, and DVDs on Christian spirituality. Our publishing represents a full expression of Christian belief and practice—from Catholic to Evangelical, from Protestant to Orthodox.

We are the publishing arm of the Community of Jesus, an ecumenical monastic community in the Benedictine tradition. As such, we are uniquely positioned in the marketplace without connection to a large corporation and with informal relationships to many branches and denominations of faith.

What We Are Doing

Books Paraclete publishes books that show the richness and depth of what it means to be Christian. Although Benedictine spirituality is at the heart of all that we do, we publish books that reflect the Christian experience across many cultures, time periods, and houses of worship. We publish books that nourish the vibrant life of the church and its people—books about spiritual practice, formation, history, ideas, and customs.

We have several different series, including the best-selling Paraclete Essentials and Paraclete Giants series of classic texts in contemporary English; A Voice from the Monastery—men and women monastics writing about living a spiritual life today; award-winning poetry; best-selling gift books for children on the occasions of baptism and first communion; and the Active Prayer Series that brings creativity and liveliness to any life of prayer.

Recordings From Gregorian chant to contemporary American choral works, our music recordings celebrate sacred choral music through the centuries. Paraclete distributes the recordings of the internationally acclaimed choir Gloriæ Dei Cantores, praised for their "rapt and fathomless spiritual intensity" by *American Record Guide*, and the Gloriæ Dei Cantores Schola, which specializes in the study and performance of Gregorian chant. Paraclete is also the exclusive North American distributor of the recordings of the Monastic Choir of St. Peter's Abbey in Solesmes, France, long considered to be a leading authority on Gregorian chant.

Videos Our videos offer spiritual help, healing, and biblical guidance for life issues: grief and loss, marriage, forgiveness, anger management, facing death, and spiritual formation.

Learn more about us at our website:
www.paracletepress.com, or call us toll-free at 1-800-451-5006.

SCAN TO READ MORE

READING FRANCIS'S WRITINGS
IS LIKE BEING "ON THE ROAD" WITH HIM IN THOSE FIRST DAYS.

FRANCIS OF ASSISI *In His Own Words*
Francis of Assisi
Translated and annotated by Jon M. Sweeney

Biographies of the saint will only take you so far. It's impossible to truly understand Francis of Assisi without reading his writings. Jon M. Sweeney has compiled all of the ones that we are most certain come from Francis himself, including his first Rule of life, the Rule he wrote for the Third Order, letters to friends, letters to people in power, messages to all Franciscans, songs, praises, canticles, and his final spiritual Testament. An introduction and explanatory notes throughout the book help to put the writings into historical and theological context.

ISBN: 1-978-1-61261-069-6 • $16.99 • French flaps

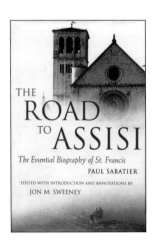

THE ROAD TO ASSISI
Paul Sabatier
Edited by Jon M. Sweeney

He conversed with both the Pope and the sultan. He transformed a taste for fine things and troubadour poetry into greater loves for poverty and joyful devotion to God. He never intended to found a traditional religious "movement," but nevertheless, he did. This foundational biography explores who Francis of Assisi was, and what we can learn from his life.
ISBN: 1-978-55725-401-6 • $15.99 • Paperback

Available from most booksellers or through Paraclete Press
www.paracletepress.com   1-800-451-5006